C000183296

AUSTRALIA
IN THE
GREAT WAR

Also available from Robert Hale

Fields of Death – Peter Slowe and Richard Woods
Gallipoli: A Soldier's Story – Arthur Edward Beecroft

AUSTRALIA
IN THE
GREAT WAR

PHILIP PAYTON

ROBERT HALE • LONDON

© Philip Payton 2015
First published in Great Britain 2015

ISBN 978-0-7198-0875-3

Robert Hale Limited
Clerkenwell House
Clerkenwell Green
London EC1R 0HT

www.halebooks.com

The right of Philip Payton to be identified as author of
this work has been asserted by him in accordance with the
Copyright, Designs and Patents Act 1988

A catalogue record for this book is available from the British Library

2 4 6 8 10 9 7 5 3 1

Printed in Great Britain by TJ International

For Dee

Contents

Preface

FEW SUBJECTS IN Australian history have attracted more attention than the Great War and, with the arrival of the centenary of that conflict, interest has intensified. 'Why another book on Australia and the First World War?', the reader is entitled to ask. Part of the answer is simply that the enduring fascination of the war is bound to draw in any writer with an interest in twentieth-century Australia. A more considered response is that, despite the millions of words that have been devoted to the subject already, there is still a need for a general narrative history of the conflict, one which will appeal to the informed reader as well as the specialist, but also engage with the many debates and controversies that have attended the study of the Great War.

This book attempts to do just that, and in so doing takes care to illuminate both the battlefront and the home front, and the relation-ship between the two, as well as examining the experience of the Australians in 'Blighty', the mother country. Understanding the nature of the battlefield – what it was like to be at Gallipoli or Fromelles or Bullecourt – is critical to grasping the essence of Australia and the First World War. But so too is an appreciation of what it was like in Australia itself during those war years, for those who did not go to war and for the women and children who stayed at home. Behind the veneer of homo-geneity and solidarity, so apparent at the outbreak of war, was a medley of religious, ethnic, regional, political and class differences which became more pronounced over time, contributing among other things to the intensity and bitterness of the conscription debate. When it was all over, and the troops came home, deep divisions were still apparent in Australian society, and many returned servicemen found difficulty in settling. Australia had changed. But within that experience lay the roots – or some of them, at least – of the modern Australian nation.

I have been fortunate enough to draw on the works of those who have tackled the subject before me, not only those former soldiers who penned their memoirs in the immediate aftermath of war, but those recent historians who came to it much later. Volumes by Jean Beaumont, Les Carlyon, Susanna de Vries, Jillian Durance, Bill Gammage, Katrina Hedditch, Robert Kimber, Michael McKernan, John McQuilton, Lyn Macdonald, Peter Pedersen, Richard Travers, and many others, have been constantly at my elbow, and to each and every historian who has written about Australia and the First World War I owe a profound debt of gratitude. Especial thanks are due to Alexander Stilwell at Robert Hale, whose idea this book was, and who has tactfully steered it towards completion and publication. Thanks too to Nikki Edwards and Lavinia Porter, my editors at Robert Hale, whose close attention to detail has saved me from many errors. I also thank my colleagues at the University of Exeter in the UK and at Flinders University in Australia, including the ever-helpful staff of the university libraries at Exeter and Flinders, together with those at the University of Tasmania (where I was fortunate enough to spend almost three weeks as Visiting Scholar in 2014). In Adelaide, the delightful hospitality of the Naval, Military & Air Force Club of South Australia, not least its ever-attentive staff, has also smoothed this book on its way, and I have been fortunate to use the Club's extensive library. Finally, I am indebted to my wife Deidre ('Dee'), who has accompanied me on my numerous research visits, and who shares my passion for Australia. To her this book is dedicated.

Philip Payton
School of International Studies,
Flinders University,
Adelaide, Australia.

Chapter One

To 'our last man and our last shilling':
Australia Goes to War

WHEN THE COUNTDOWN to war began in the summer of 1914, Australia was in the midst of a general election. Campaigning in the country town of Colac, in Victoria, Andrew Fisher – leader of the Labor Opposition – was unequivocal in his insistence that a Labor government would stick by Britain through thick and thin. 'Australians will stand beside our own and help defend her' he emphasized, 'to our last man and our last shilling'.[1] It was a phrase that would go down in Australian history, a ringing cry of defiance and of loyalty that would contribute to Fisher's electoral victory only a few weeks later. On the very same day, 31 July, the current Prime Minister, Joseph Cook, had been speaking at Horsham, in western Victoria. Not to be outdone, he too declared his determination to support Britain, should war break out. 'All our resources in Australia are in the [British] Empire and for the Empire', he explained, 'and for the preservation and security of the Empire'.[2] At a stroke, the two competing leaders had expressed a remarkable political unity, a consensus all the more surprising in the middle of an election campaign when parties were normally at pains to emphasize their policy and ideological differences. Together, they had spoken for Australia.

The slide into war

A few days later, on 4 August 1914, Britain declared war on Germany, and so Australia was drawn inexorably and inevitably into the emerging conflict. For many Australians, the slide into war appeared a bewildering chain of events, acted out at great distance half a world away. On 28 June Archduke Franz Ferdinand, heir to the Austro-Hungarian Empire, was shot dead (along with his wife) in Sarajevo by a Bosnian Serb separatist. Austria was outraged and demanded satisfaction from Serbia, which it had long regarded as a hostile and subversive neighbouring state. When insufficient reparation was forthcoming, Austria declared war on Serbia on 28 July, a month after Franz Ferdinand's assassination. In the intervening period, Vienna had been careful to sound out the mood in Berlin, and had been gratified to receive the Kaiser's 'blank cheque', as historians have called it. Emboldened by Germany's enthusiastic and unqualified support, the Austrians determined to crush Serbia for all time. However, the Serbs had an important ally in Russia, which saw itself as the natural 'protector' of Slav peoples everywhere, and was bound to come to Serbia's aid in a crisis – as Berlin and Vienna were well aware. They also knew that Russia was aligned to Britain and France in a 'Triple Entente', and that there was now a real danger of precipitating a pan-European – and ultimately global – conflict of terrifying proportions.

Today, in debating the causes of the Great War, and in apportioning blame, there is often a tendency towards 'moral equivalence', a belief that it was the flawed international system itself – the great-power rivalry that pitted one empire against the next – that brought about the catastrophe that was shortly to engulf Europe and the world. In such a view, Britain was as culpable as Germany; France as much as Austro-Hungary.[3] However, many historians – now as in the past – still point an accusatory finger at Germany, arguing that the *Kaiserreich* – the German Empire – flirted dangerously and irresponsibly with the prospect of war as part of its drive for self-aggrandisement and Continental domination. As Max Hastings has noted, there is real evidence of reckless behaviour in Berlin in the summer of 1914, fuelled by the German military establishment in its opportunist desire to exploit the volatile situation to the full. Germany had prevailed in and profited from three hugely successful military adventures in the previous fifty years

– against Denmark, Austria and France – and there was widespread belief that the country could (and perhaps should) do it again. For example, Helmuth von Moltke, Chief of Staff of the German army, had made no secret of his view that a European war was inevitable, indeed desirable. When the Kaiser approved Germany's mobilization against Russia on 1 August, there was a celebratory atmosphere in the war ministry in Berlin. According to one eyewitness: 'Everywhere [were] beaming faces, people shaking hands in the corridors, congratulating one another on having cleared the ditch'.[4]

Germany demanded the surrender of French frontier fortresses as its price for recognizing France's neutrality in the emerging crisis. It was, of course, an impossible request. In Britain, where many looked askance at the manoeuvrings of the Continental powers, there was a feeling that even now the country might escape embroilment in the unfolding drama. But the mood changed irrevocably when Germany, in accordance with its pre-ordained Schlieffen plan, struck at France through Belgium, violating the neutrality of Belgium that Britain was, by treaty and moral obligation, bound to defend. Accordingly, on 4 August Britain entered the war. In the ensuing propaganda offensive, 'Prussian militarism' was roundly condemned in the British press, and the *Kaiserreich*'s autocratic system of government denounced as an unacceptable threat to democracy, at home and abroad. Extravagant claims were made as to the likely extent of German war aims. Chillingly, many of these were confirmed when Germany, anticipating an early victory, listed the spoils it expected shortly to enjoy. These would range, the Germans imagined, from the annexation of Dunkirk, Boulogne and Luxembourg, along with the reduction of Belgium and the Netherlands to satellite states, to vast territorial acquisitions in Russia and Africa.[5]

For many in Australia, the pattern of European alliances and the complex series of occurrences that had led somehow to war may indeed have seemed unfathomable. For the poet C.J. Dennis, whose collections *Songs of a Sentimental Bloke* (1915) and *The Moods of Ginger Mick* (1916) struck a chord with the Australian public, it was all:

Becos a crook done in a prince, an' narked an Emperor,
An' stuck a light that set the world aflame;
Becos the bugles East an' West sooled on the dawgs o' war . . .[6]

Becos ole Europe lost 'er block and started 'eavin bricks,
Becos the bugles wailed a song uv war . . .[7]

But if the good horse-sense of C.J. Dennis and others like him detected something absurd in the chain of events, there was nonetheless a solid core of opinion in favour of supporting Britain in the war. Andrew Fisher and Joseph Cook had very publicly nailed Australia's colours to the Empire's mast, the Australian government having already been informed by London – as had the other Dominions (Canada, Newfoundland, New Zealand, South Africa) – that hostilities were now considered inevitable. On the eve of war, the Royal Australian Navy was placed at the disposal of the British Admiralty, while the government pledged to raise 20,000 troops to support the war effort. At Federation in 1901, the six Australian colonies had come together to form the new self-governing Commonwealth of Australia. But, despite the veneer of independence, the fledgling nation was still in many ways reliant on the mother country, not least for defence and in foreign affairs, and when Britain declared war the general assumption – in Australia as much as in Britain – was that Australia would automatically follow suit. From that perspective, Andrew Fisher and Joseph Cook had actually very little choice in pledging Australia's compliance. As Cook had put it, speaking in Horsham: 'Remember that when the Empire is at war, so is Australia at war'.[8]

'Independent Australian Britons'

Support for the war among Australians reflected ties of kinship and affection as well as obligation. They thought of themselves as 'independent Australian Britons', as Alfred Deakin, the former Prime Minister, had explained, proud to be members of the newly federated and self-governing Commonwealth of Australia but still tied by sentiment to the mother country.[9] A common monarchy and a parliamentary democracy modelled on Westminster underscored this profound sense of cultural and political affinity, even unity. Yet there was also an emergent Australian nationalism, apparent before Federation but gathering apace thereafter, which asserted a subtly different set of values. There was a greater egalitarianism – a legacy, perhaps, of gold rush days and

Australia's own divergent historical experience – and a celebration of the country's distinctive landscape, flora and fauna, which were seen as deeply emblematic of the new nation. Although the majority of Australians, then as now, lived in towns and cities along the littoral line, the 'bush' and 'outback' were celebrated in art and literature as quintessentially Australian. In the stories and poetry of Henry Lawson, for instance, or in Banjo Paterson and his 'Waltzing Matilda' and 'The Man from Snowy River', Australians saw and admired their own country.[10] It was a partial view – it glossed over the great metropolises, and ignored Aboriginal Australians, or at least reduced them to minor roles among the flora and fauna – but it was a nationalist imagining to which many subscribed.

Not all were convinced, however. Rudyard Kipling, for instance, the ardent imperialist who longed to build an ever-closer fraternity of the 'Five Free Nations'[11] – Australia, Canada, New Zealand and South Africa, along with Britain – was yet to be persuaded. He complained to Banjo Paterson: 'You people in Australia haven't grown up yet'. Impatient for the emergence of a more self-conscious and self-confident Australian national identity, Kipling quipped petulantly that 'You think the Melbourne Cup is the most important thing in the world'.[12] In a sense he was right. This prestigious horse race, held on the first Tuesday of November, was the one event – the one institution, perhaps – to create a genuinely Australia-wide sense of national enthusiasm and cohesion. But Kipling's criticism, cutting as it was, was designed to foster not independence but rather an enhanced sense of place for Australia within the Empire, an equality with the other Dominions and in time with Britain herself. It was a vision to which many Australians responded. For most, Australian nationalism and the enhancement of Australia's role in the British Empire amounted to the same thing, and they saw no contradiction or confusion. W.H. 'Billy' Hughes, destined to succeed Fisher as Prime Minister of Australia, expressed it thus: 'A man may be a very loyal and devoted adherent to, and worshipper of, the Empire, and still he may be a very loyal and patriotic Australian all the time'.[13]

Increasingly, Australia was encouraged to see itself as an integral part of a unified 'British world'. Indeed, as Neville Meaney has remarked, by 1914 this sense of 'Britishness was probably stronger in Australia than in Britain itself'.[14] The outbreak of the Boer War, on the eve of Federation,

had been a timely opportunity for Australia to demonstrate its importance and status within the Empire, lending the mother country a
helping hand in its hour of need. Australian light horsemen, operating
in landscapes often reminiscent of home, showed they could match the
bush skills of the elusive Boers, succeeding where British troops – unused
and unsuited to South African terrain – often failed. As well as pride
in bringing Australian attributes to bear on the imperial battlefield, it
was an experience that suggested soldierly superiority, anticipating the
Anzac myth at Gallipoli in 1915. Australia had entered the Boer War as
six self-governing colonies. It emerged from the peace as a fully-fledged
Dominion, an elevation within the Empire that seemed somehow to
reflect and reward this superior performance. When, in the summer of
1914, a yet greater call went out to defend the Empire's cause, it appeared
only natural that Australians should respond with alacrity. 'All over
Australia there is manifested a spirit of Imperial enthusiasm', detected
the *Sydney Morning Herald*. 'Thousands are offering for service in the
expeditionary forces', it noted with undisguised approval: 'From various
parts of the country come reports of light horsemen, infantry, ex-South
African soldiers and bushmen anxious to join'.[15] It was an enthusiasm
soon to be expressed on the lips of thousands in the words of the popular
patriotic song, with its insistent refrain – 'Australia will be there!':

> Rally round the banner of your country,
> Take the field with brothers o'er the foam.
> On land or sea, wherever you be,
> Keep your eye on Liberty!
> England, home and beauty have no cause to fear,
> Should Auld acquaintance be forgot?
> No! No! No! No!
> Australia will be there – Australia will be there![16]

In Kipling's view, the war would be Australia's chance to 'grow up',
to define herself fully as a nation. 'It is our baptism of fire', agreed
the *Sydney Morning Herald*, and here, the newspaper explained, was
Australia's opportunity to add to the 'moral strength and prestige of
the British race'. Australia was now 'engaged with the mother country
in fighting for peace and liberty'. It went on: 'It is no war of aggression
. . . but one in defence of small nations threatened with humiliation and

absorption'. Here the *Sydney Morning Herald* was thinking principally of Belgium, of course, but it may have spared a thought for Serbia. It was also shrewd enough to recognize an Irish dimension, so important to Australia with its large Irish-Catholic population, and argued that Britain's concern for the rights of small nations extended to its commitment to implement Home Rule for Ireland once the war was won. It was a solemn undertaking that had 'satisfied Ireland', the newspaper claimed, the inference being that Irish-Australian opinion would be likewise reassured. Moreover, Australians generally should be in no doubt about German culpability, the paper added: 'Germany is now shown to be responsible . . . She stands before the world discredited, a breaker of treaties, and as an assailant of small nations'. But in its earnest affirmation of the Empire's cause, the *Sydney Morning Herald* added a sober note of warning: 'Australia knows something of the flames of war, but its realities have never been brought so close as they will be in the future'.[17]

The German threat in the Pacific

This call for steadfastness, solidarity and resolve added a strong moral tone to Australia's embrace of war. In supporting Britain and the Empire, it was argued, Australia was also standing up for the rights of beleaguered small nations and defending democracy and freedom against tyranny. The Methodist *Australian Christian Commonwealth* magazine, published in Adelaide, thought so too. 'Every soldier we send', it explained, 'goes out in defence of great moral principles, and to check a braggart power that is prepared to trample every principle of . . . righteousness under foot'.[18] It was an opinion shared by the *Western Mail* in Perth, Western Australia, which quoted enthusiastically and at length from the parliamentary speech of Senator Edward Millen, the Minister of Defence, delivered on the outbreak of war. Millen had spoken of 'the passionate desire of the Dominions to rally to the support of the mother land in her hour of trial, and to unite with her in the preservation of her common traditions and a joint inheritance'. But, significantly, he had also been careful to explain that:

> Australia is proceeding with the development of a strong and vigorous nationhood within the Empire, and [therefore] she appreciates the more

the noble stand taken by Britain on behalf of those smaller nationalities struggling to remain free which have appealed not in vain for the
protection of the might and power of the great liberty-loving Empire of
which the Commonwealth [of Australia] forms a part.[19]

The implied connection between Australia's fledgling nationhood
and 'those smaller nationalities struggling to remain free' was telling.
Here Millen was articulating a strategic as well as moral concern.
Although the principal events leading to war had been performed on
the European stage, seemingly a world away, there was a strategic threat
much closer to home of which Millen, as Minister of Defence, was
keenly aware. Australians had appeared obsessed by the 'yellow peril',
the teeming Asiatic hordes that lay to the north, of which the rising
star of the Japanese Imperial Navy was the latest variant, but they were
also increasingly aware of other great-power interest and activity in
the Pacific region. The visit to Australia in August 1908 of America's
'Great White Fleet' – so-named after the white hulls and buff super-
structures of its warships – had aroused enormous enthusiasm among
Australians (and some irritation in British government circles), and the
United States was generally considered a reassuring, benign influence
in the Pacific. But Germany was another matter.

German expansionist designs in the region had been a cause of
anxiety for some time. New Guinea was annexed as a German protectorate in 1884, and when Australia inherited the neighbouring
territory of Papua from Britain in 1906, it thus acquired a land border
of its own with the German colony. The German navy had also established an unwelcome presence in the wider Pacific; its East Asiatic
Cruiser Squadron was based strategically at Tsingtao in China, and
German radio communication stations such as that at Rabaul added
to the sense of threatening regional penetration. On the outbreak of
war, therefore, there was a not unreasonable fear that, if things went
badly, Australia might easily share the fate of poor little Belgium. 'If
Germany were to win', opined one observer, 'Australia would probably suffer most'.[20] Indeed, when evidence emerged that Australian
missionaries had been 'shockingly treated' by the Germans in New
Ireland (in the south-west Pacific), Australia's worst fears appeared to
be confirmed.[21] Although lurid tales amplified by Allied propaganda
exaggerated the extent of German 'barbarity', some 6,000 civilians

had been systematically killed by the German army during its advance through Belgium and France in 1914, many executed as trumped-up reprisals for non-existent guerrilla outrages. News of such happenings, filtering through to Australia, caused alarm among those who feared a German attack in the Pacific. 'The world stands horrified as it beholds how completely thorough-going the German can be in connection with oppression', exclaimed one Australian newspaper in October 1914, 'how utterly and callously abandoned he can become to barbarism in his murder of the innocent . . . With little provocation he tears the Belgian babe from its mother's breast and shoots it before her eyes'.[22]

Whose war?

Such reports were calculated to enrage Australian opinion. As well as redoubling conviction that the war was just, they were also a powerful stimulus to recruitment to the armed forces. Australia had promised the Empire 20,000 men. By December 1914, nearly 53,000 had joined the colours, while the queues to enlist grew ever longer. Publicly, such recruits joined in response to exhortations – in the press and by political, civic, religious and other leaders – to do their patriotic duty. But privately, there were any number of reasons why men came forward. Some, of course, did rally to the flag in defence of Australia, Britain and the Empire, adopting the mantle of 'King and Country'. Others, however, were enticed by the prospect of a secure and well-paid job (at six shillings a day for a private, Australians were the best-paid soldiers of any army in the war), and some were attracted by the promise of adventure in far-away lands and the opportunity to escape a humdrum existence at home. For those born in Britain, or with close family there, there was also the attraction of what they imagined to be a free ticket 'home', although many were to be sorely disappointed when they found themselves in Egypt instead. Peer pressure was another factor, the desire not to be left out or to be seen as hesitant, especially by the opposite sex. The uniform itself had a certain allure, and sometimes that was enough to persuade men who were otherwise unsure why they were joining up. It was an uncertainty caught by C.J. Dennis in his *The Moods of Ginger Mick*:

Wot price ole Ginger Mick? E's done a break –
Gone to the flamin' war to stoush the foe.
Wus it for glory, or a women's sake?
Ar, arst me somethin' easy! I dunno.
'Is Kharki clobber set 'im off a treat,
That's all I know; 'is motive's got me beat.[23]

Significantly, C.J. Dennis had also detected a wider uncertainty.
Despite the robust patriotic rhetoric on the surface, there was an unset-
tling feeling underneath, in some quarters at least, that a European
conflict had really little to do with Australia, and that surely Britain
had enough resources of her own to manage the crisis:

'E sez to me, 'Wot's all this flamin' war?
The papers torks uv nothin' else but scraps.
An' wot's old England got snake-headed for?
An' wot's the strength uv calling out our chaps?'
'E sez to me, 'Struth! Don't she rule the sea?
Wot does she want wiv us?' 'e sez to me.[24]

It was a view shared by the left-wing *Australian Worker*, which warned
that ordinary people would suffer – on the battlefield and on the home
front – while, as usual, the capitalists made huge profits from the war.[25]
As C.J. Dennis had it, 'The 'eads is makin' piles'.[26] It was an opinion
given some credibility by the sharp rise in prices attendant upon the
outbreak of hostilities, when shortages of staple goods were anticipated. In New South Wales, for example, imported groceries rose in
price by as much as twenty per cent during the first month of the war.
Unemployment also increased alarmingly, as export markets closed,
and in New South Wales it rose from 13,500 to 29,313 between 10 and
31 August 1914. Ironically, this surge in unemployment was a boost to
recruitment, as many of those thrown out of work sought the king's shilling instead. At the same time as companies shed workers or put them
on half-time, so many firms made large and ostentatious donations
to the myriad patriotic funds that had sprung up across the country,
a further irony not lost on the *Australian Worker* which contrasted
this largesse with the fact that such donors 'have sacked thousands of
breadwinners'.[27]

Enemies within?

However, despite such undercurrents of resentment, there was little organized opposition to the war in 1914, and the settled mood across Australia appeared to be one of unequivocal support for the war. Regional as well as metropolitan newspapers were unanimous in their pronouncements. The *Corryong Courier*, for instance, published in north-eastern Victoria, reported solemnly that the 'call of Empire has brought all into line. Class, creed and faction are swept aside by the common wave of enthusiasm with which the Empire swings to the common cause'.[28] The *Western Australian* agreed, deciding that in a 'moment political factions have become obliterated, the tumult of partisans' voices stilled, and a united nation stands prepared to do its duty'.[29] In Hobart, the left-leaning *Daily Post* emphasized that: 'Our people love the Empire and would come down to their shirt-sleeves to save it'.[30] The paper's editor was Edmund Dwyer-Gray, an Irishman, and in expressing support for the war he reflected the attitude of Irish-Australians more generally. The Melbourne Celtic Club announced that it would suspend agitation for Irish Home Rule for the duration of the war, and John Gavan Duffy – a prominent Irish Nationalist politician in Victoria – explained that Irish-Catholics in Australia were 'ready, eager and willing to stand shoulder to shoulder, knee to knee, fighting the battle of the great Empire to which they belonged'.[31]

The Irish, deeply ingrained in Australian society, were embraced unhesitatingly in the rush to war. But other groups aroused suspicion, especially the sizable pockets of German settlers scattered across Australia. The *Australian Christian Commonwealth* saw its religious duty to be charitable. It spoke fondly of 'our fellow German colonists' – of which there were a great many in South Australia, where the magazine was produced – explaining that they 'have laboured with us to develop these fair lands, they have proven themselves loyal and noble citizens of our Commonwealth, their blood is mingled with ours'. Indeed, it warned readers to 'guard well our feelings, our patriotism must not be mingled with bitterness and weakened by revenge . . . Let us beware lest the sword of justice should be forged in the fires of hate into a dagger of malice'.[32] Later, in December 1914, the magazine added that it was incumbent upon all Methodists – indeed, all Christians – to 'ever treat the Germans who are amongst us, not as we think they would treat us if we were in Germany, but as we should wish them to treat us if we were in Berlin'.[33]

Others, however, were less high-minded. At Wongarbon, near Dubbo in New South Wales, one correspondent in the local newspaper roundly condemned what he saw as unwarranted leniency towards the German communities. 'The very name [German] should be obnoxious to any fair-minded man', he exclaimed, 'yes, to any man, woman or child . . . Any true Britisher should scorn them and hate them with a hatred too deep, too firmly rooted in the precincts of their heart ever to be removed'. As he concluded, rhetorically, 'is it just to allow any German, whether he be naturalised or Australian born, to roam this fair land of ours and taint its shores by his very presence?' The answer, in his opinion, was that 'every German should be interned, without respect to person'.[34] In fact, 'enemy aliens' had been interned or placed on parole at the outbreak of war but this did not extend automatically to those 'Germans' who had been naturalized as 'British subjects' or were born in Australia. However, the boundary became hazy when those in the latter categories fell under suspicion and were deemed a threat to security, and it soon became clear that naturalization particularly did not bring immunity from arrest. By March 1915, almost 2,000 Germans had been interned, and the numbers continued to rise throughout the war.

Across Australia, police forces were meticulous in weeding out 'enemy aliens'. At Corryong in north-eastern Victoria, for example, two men who were technically German Army reservists were promptly arrested on the outbreak of war, and at Chiltern in the same district one Alphonso Gaupp, who had been in Australia for just seven months, was swiftly packed off to an internment camp near Sydney. Communities where those of German descent had lived harmoniously alongside their neighbours suddenly became hotbeds of suspicion. At Wodonga, on the Victoria–New South Wales border, for example, there was a fight between August Schliebs and John Fulford, who had called Schliebs a 'half-breed German bastard' and accused him of stealing his job. The matter went to court where, interestingly, the bench found in favour of Schliebs.[35] In Adelaide, in South Australia, a man reported to have murmured '*Glück für Deutschland*' ('Good luck, Germany') in a cinema during newsreel of German troops marching into Brussels, was taken outside and beaten up by the crowd. For their part, most German-Lutheran communities were punctilious in their declarations of loyalty to the Crown, and their sincerity was demonstrated by those young men of German descent who made a point of volunteering for the Australian Imperial Force. But the animosity took its toll. At Tanunda, for instance, in South Australia's predominantly German Barossa Valley, Adolph Schulz, chairman of the local District Council, committed suicide. Greatly disturbed by the turn of recent events, it was explained, he left a widow and small son to mourn his passing. Likewise, at Mount Barker, in the Adelaide Hills, Franz Ernst Jahn killed himself when he was summarily ejected from his job as a railway worker on account of his 'nationality'.[36]

Railways were considered of prime strategic importance, and, therefore, could not be left exposed to the presence of 'enemy aliens' who might be spies or saboteurs. Rheinhold Rau, for example, who had arrived in Australia in 1911, had been placed on parole at Hay in New South Wales when the war started. However, he soon drifted to Wodonga, where he failed to report to the local police station, a condition of his parole. He was discovered asleep on the footplate of a steam locomotive in the engine shed at Wodonga railway yard. Despite his protestations that he was only 'having a bit of a warm', he was fined twenty shillings for breaking his parole and was subsequently interned.[37] At Murray Bridge, where the railway made its strategic crossing of the mighty River Murray, linking South Australia to Victoria and the other eastern states, such was the level of concern that calls were made for armed guards to be placed on the bridge itself. Faced with official indifference, members of the Murray Bridge rifle club took it upon themselves to protect the bridge, confident in the knowledge that they were playing a key role in the defence of Australia's vital infrastructure. A local larrikin decided to test the club's resolve. 'The gun's not loaded', he teased as he approached one of the guards, 'you wouldn't shoot, would you?' The irresponsible young man was forcibly removed from the bridge by its protectors, and left in no doubt as to the importance of Murray Bridge in Australia's war effort.[38]

The Battle of Broken Hill

Even more absurd than the Murray Bridge situation, perhaps, was the fear that Germans from the Lutheran Finke River Mission in central

Australia might, with the acquisition of a few machine guns, pose a threat to the strategic railway link between South Australia and the interior of the continent. Yet, despite this absurdity, something very similar did happen near Broken Hill, in outback New South Wales, a few months into the war on New Year's Day 1915. The occasion was the annual miners' picnic excursion train from Broken Hill to nearby Silverton. For many it was the highlight of the year, eagerly looked forward to and drawing large crowds. In 1915 there were more passengers than ever, over a thousand holidaymakers, including women and children, packed into forty open mineral wagons. It was said at the time that it was one of the longest picnic trains ever to leave from Broken Hill. The passengers were in carnival mood until, about two miles into the journey, they were fired upon suddenly by two 'Turks' flying the Ottoman flag. Two of the travellers were killed, and several others wounded. The Turks, having created mayhem, then fled to a quartz outcrop to the north of Broken Hill, where they were promptly hunted down by the local police and militia and shot dead – but not before a stray bullet had killed another onlooker. One eyewitness described the ambush. 'I was sitting in one of the open trucks watching the two men shooting', he wrote in a letter to his parents, 'not realising, of course, that they were firing bullets'. What had appeared at first an ebullient salute, proved to be an altogether more deadly affair. 'When our truck was directly opposite them (only about thirty yards away)', continued the observer, 'I saw one of the Turks fire in the air. The other fired point blank at our carriage. I then thought it was time to duck'. Bullets were soon flying 'all ways', he said, and the 'sight was dreadful in the truck behind. One woman . . . tried to shield her baby and was shot in the mouth. The baby was covered in blood'.[39]

A man following the train on a bicycle was also shot down. In Broken Hill itself everyone 'seemed to be running to and fro carrying guns, and the whole town had the appearance of a military camp'. Enraged inhabitants intent on revenge made their way to Camel Camp, home of the 'Afghan' cameleers who plied the outback routes, but found their way barred by police and militia. They turned their fury instead upon the town's German Club, deserted since the outbreak of war, burning it to the ground. The two 'Turks', it transpired, were Mullah Abdullah – a local camel driver turned Muslim mullah, originally from Baluchistan, whose ritual slaughter of sheep had run foul of the local health authorities – and Gool Mahomet, an Afghan who had served in the Ottoman army. Local Muslims were quick to dissociate themselves from the two assassins, and, in an effort to diffuse the situation, community leaders in Broken Hill were swift to point out that the Afghan cameleers were a familiar and loyal element of local society, while large numbers of Muslims were even now serving in the armed forces of the British Empire. Nonetheless, such placatory efforts did not prevent a renewed round of arrests of enemy aliens, including six Austrians, four Germans and one Turk. At the large Central mine, the management required all aliens 'to stand down for the time being'.[40]

Securing the mining economy

Like the base metal industry across Australia, the Broken Hill mines had suffered severe dislocation on the outbreak of war, and the community remained fraught and anxious, culminating in a bitter strike in 1919. By 1914, in a deliberate policy of 'peaceful penetration' (a phrase that the Australians would turn ironically against the Germans on the battlefields of France and Belgium), several large German companies more or less controlled Australia's entire base metal industry.[41] At Broken Hill, the North Broken Hill Mine, the Broken Hill South, and the Zinc Corporation – three of the largest mines in the locality – sold almost all their lead concentrate to German smelters. Now they were abruptly cut off from their main market, throwing them into crisis. The lead smelters in Australia – Port Pirie (South Australia), Zeehan (Tasmania) and Cockle Creek (New South Wales) – had the capacity to deal with only half of this additional volume. The solution was for the big three – the North, South, and Zinc Corporation – to acquire a controlling interest in the Port Pirie smelters (the closest geographically to Broken Hill), investing heavily to greatly increase their capacity. The target market would now, of course, be the Allied nations.

Zinc, also produced in large quantities at the Broken Hill mines, was likewise disrupted by the outbreak of hostilities. Before 1914, zinc concentrate was sent by rail to Port Pirie, and from there by sea to the smelters of Belgium and Germany. The Port Pirie smelters were capable of treating only a tiny fraction of Broken Hill's zinc output, and huge dumps of unsold concentrate grew up around the mines. But zinc, with its corrosion-resistant qualities, was essential for the manufacture of munitions. Eventually, W.M. Hughes, as Prime Minister, persuaded Britain to purchase the existing Broken Hill concentrate, while Australia's principal zinc producers moved to adopt the new and more efficient electrolytic process for producing metallic zinc developed by the Anaconda Copper Mining Company in America in 1914.[42]

Copper was also hit by the outbreak of war in 1914, causing considerable alarm across the country, evidence of the significance of mining to the Australian economy as well as its critical importance to many of the communities of regional Australia, beyond the great metropolises. At Mount Lyell, in Tasmania, the great copper mine had only just recovered from a terrible underground fire, which had claimed the lives of forty-two miners, when its very survival was put in jeopardy by the First World War. As elsewhere, Germany had been the main buyer of Tasmanian copper and, when the market dried up suddenly, it was feared that the mine would have to close.[43] In late 1914, W.H. Hughes, not yet Prime Minister but Attorney General in Fisher's Labor government, intervened to ensure permanent national control over what was obviously a vital strategic metal. This included the formation of an association of principal copper producers, designed to sell all copper surplus to Australia's needs to Britain for the manufacture of munitions. At Port Kembla, in New South Wales, the German-owned copper smelter was acquired by the government. At Mount Lyell, Hughes' timely intervention had ensured the survival of the mine, and indeed its buoyancy throughout the war years.

At Moonta and Wallaroo in South Australia, the story was the same. In August 1914, H. Lipson Hancock, general manager of the Wallaroo and Moonta Mining and Smelting Company, had warned gravely that 'in consequence of the outbreak of war in Europe, and the inability of the contractors to take delivery of our copper, it has become imperative to at once curtail operations'.[44] Some 2,000 workers lost their jobs, and thousands more in the regional economy of northern Yorke Peninsula were put at risk. But, as at Mount Lyell, Hughes' speedy action had saved the day. The locality's skilled mineworkers were swiftly re-engaged, ushering in a period of hectic production that would bring prosperity to the region's mining towns during the First World War. By the end of November 1914, the *Yorke's Peninsula Advertiser* could note with satisfaction that although the district had been 'seriously affected on the outbreak of war by the closing of Mines', the 'successful financial negotiations' conducted by the government had 'permitted and enabled our mining industry to resume'. The newspaper reserved particular praise for both employers and workers. The mine company had evidenced its 'patriotic feelings in so actively dealing with the serious situation and restarting work', it reported, while the 'employees too assisted in the situation by willing co-operation'.[45]

'Although politically a "red hot Labour centre"', the *Register* had noted in August 1914, 'the Yorke's Peninsula mines have been remarkably free of labour troubles'.[46] The Amalgamated Miners' Association had used its strength to negotiate a series of advantageous agreements in return for co-operation with the company's wide-ranging modernization plans in the years before 1914, and this provided the basis for the mutual understanding and goodwill between company and workers after the outbreak of war. However, there were those – on Yorke Peninsula, and in the Labor movement across Australia – who had looked askance at the especially generous treatment afforded corporate interests by Hughes, warning that these were a recipe for huge wartime profits, ultimately at the expense of the workers. Eventually, such suspicions would erupt in a series of complex disputes at Moonta and Wallaroo after the war, but for the moment there appeared to be only industrial harmony as the two sides pulled together in the interests of the war effort and the regional economy.

The destruction of the *Emden*

The Australian government had moved decisively to safeguard and take control of vital strategic metals. In the same way, it acted against the perceived German threat in the Pacific and the coasts around Australia. In 1911 the Royal Australian Navy had come into being. Inspired by the visit of the American fleet, and reacting against the growing maritime power of Japan, Australia ordered a series of modern, highly expensive warships from British yards. When the brand new battlecruiser HMAS *Australia*, accompanied by the equally new light cruiser HMAS *Sydney*, arrived with her escorts in Australian waters in 1913, she was met by eager crowds anxious to celebrate Australia's elevation as a

regional naval power to be reckoned with. As one observer, who had
witnessed HMAS *Australia's* stately entry into Sydney harbour, remarked,
the 'sight of her revealed the nation's dreadnought in all her beauty and
majesty . . . a living sentient thing whose mission is to guard our shores
and protect our commerce and trade routes'. As he put it, the country
did 'not look upon her as standing for war but for peace which comes
from being prepared for war'.[47]

In fact, Australia's first shot in the war was fired not by these mighty
warships of the Royal Australian Navy but by the gunners of Fort
Nepean, which guarded the entrance to Port Philip Bay and Melbourne
harbour. The German steamer *Pfalz*, with an Australian pilot on board,
discreetly made its bid for freedom on 5 August 1914, in the immediate aftermath of the declaration of war. However, it had not reckoned
with the Fort Nepean battery, which launched a well-aimed shell
across its bows. The pilot remonstrated with the ship's master, convincing him that the next shot would hit the vessel. Reluctantly, the ship
turned around and was arrested by the Australian authorities. In all,
more than forty enemy merchant ships were captured or detained in
Australian waters in the first weeks of the war. Meanwhile, the decision
had been made to seize German territories in the Pacific and to destroy
the German wireless stations that were allegedly relaying important
intelligence to the German East Asiatic Cruiser Squadron, thought
now to be in the vicinity. A hastily constructed Australian Naval and
Military Expeditionary Force (AN&MEF), consisting of an infantry
battalion and a naval landing party some 500-strong (mainly reservists), set sail from Sydney under the protection of the Royal Australian
Navy. The AN&MEF reached Rabaul, the capital of German New
Guinea and site of one of the offending transmitters, on 11 September
and its surprisingly ill-equipped garrison was swiftly overwhelmed.
Nauru wireless station was destroyed on 9 September, while the New
Zealanders captured Samoa. Ominously, Japan, which had entered the
war on the Allied side on 23 August, occupied the Caroline Islands –
earlier an Australian objective – and other German territories north of
the equator. Australia had secured its northern border but Japan, its
putative ally, had moved a threatening step closer.[48]

The mysterious loss of the Australian submarine *AE1* off Rabaul
on 20 September took the lustre off some of these early Australian
and New Zealand successes. The Royal Australian Navy was also

disappointed that its support for the AN&MEF landings had allowed the German East Asiatic Squadron to escape its clutches. The German warships sped across the Pacific, encountering and sinking two British cruisers in the Battle of Coronel, off the Chilean coast. The squadron then rounded Cape Horn but was intercepted and sunk near the Falklands by another British naval force on 8 December 1914. However, Von Spee, the German commander, had left behind the light cruiser *Emden* to operate as a raider in the Indian Ocean. In its short but spectacular career, the *Emden* caused havoc. It set the oil tanks of Madras ablaze, and sank two allied warships – one Russian, the other French – in a daring attack on Penang harbour. In an astonishing performance, it also destroyed twenty-one merchant vessels. But the *Emden's* run of good luck came abruptly to an end when it decided to cut the submarine telegraph cable between Britain and Australia at the Cocos Islands. Unaware that Australian warships were already in the vicinity, escorting Australian and New Zealand troops into theatre, the *Emden* appeared off Cocos at 6.30 a.m. on 8 November 1914. HMAS *Sydney* was immediately detached from the convoy, and established visual contact with the *Emden* at 9.15 a.m. It was an unequal contest between two ships of contrasting capabilities but the *Emden* fought bravely with great skill and determination. No fewer than fifteen of its shells struck the *Sydney* in the opening minutes of the battle. Fortunately for the Australians, ten of these proved to be duds, and when the *Sydney* found the range of its opponent it unleashed a terrible bombardment from its superior six-inch guns. By 11 a.m. the *Emden* was on fire, with only one gun left in operation. It too was silenced, as the ship was pulverized into an almost unrecognizable heap. Intent on saving the lives of his remaining crew members, Von Muller, the *Emden's* captain, made for North Keeling Island, where he beached his ship.[49]

The *Sydney*, meanwhile, considering the destruction of the *Emden* complete, made off in pursuit of the German auxiliary collier *Buresk*, capturing it before it could be scuttled. When the warship returned to the wreck of the *Emden*, it was surprised to find it still flying its German battle ensign. Reluctantly, Captain Glossop, the *Sydney's* commanding officer, gave the order to open fire. Immediately, the offending ensign was struck, and a large white sheet was placed across the quarterdeck as a formal mark of surrender. When Glossop eventually went on board the remains of the *Emden*, he was appalled by what he found:

AUSTRALIAN WAR MEMORIAL A03399

'Well done Australia!' HMAS *Sydney,* pride of the Royal Australian Navy and victor in its famous encounter with the German raider *Emden* on 8 November 1914.

> My God, what a sight! . . . everybody on board was demented by shock, and fumes, and the roar of shells bursting among them. She was a shambles. Blood, guts, flesh, and uniforms were all scattered about. One of our shells had landed behind a gun shield, and blown the whole gun crew into one pulp. You couldn't even tell how many men there had been.[50]

In all the Germans had lost 134 dead, with sixty-five wounded, from a total ship's company of 315, as against four deaths and a dozen or so injuries in HMAS *Sydney.* Glossop treated Von Muller with great courtesy, acknowledging his considerable courage and skill, and allowed him to keep his sword. News of the victory soon sped to the Australian Imperial Force (AIF), embarked in the nearby convoy, where there was great celebration and rejoicing, a welcome boost to morale as they headed towards 'the front', wherever that might prove to be. Accompanying the AIF as a war correspondent was Banjo Paterson, who duly reported the mood on-board. Remembering, perhaps, Kipling's upbraid, he saw the destruction of the *Emden* as evidence of the worth and new-found self-confidence of the embryonic Australian nation:

everybody in a wild state of excitement over the sinking ... We can hardly believe that Australia's first naval engagement could have been such a sensational win, for our people are not seagoing people and our navy – which some of us used to call a pannikin navy – was never taken very seriously. And now we have actually sunk a German ship![51]

Indeed, within only a few months, the Royal Australian Navy had supported the successful invasion of German territory in the Pacific, destroying enemy communications infrastructure in the process, and by its very presence – the 'fleet in being' – it had driven the East Asiatic Squadron from local waters and ultimately to destruction. Now it had sunk the elusive *Emden*, removing the immediate threat to Australia's security and opening sea-lanes for the safe convoy of troops abroad and the uninterrupted passage of allied merchant vessels. For Australia it was an auspicious start to the war, and appeared to confirm the coun-try's growing stature within the Empire and among the nations of the world. It seemed to auger well for whatever the future might hold.

Chapter Two

Making a Nation? The Gallipoli Landing

'W[HAT SORT OF] team will we have?' worried the sports editor of the *Independent* newspaper, published in Footscray, a western suburb of Melbourne, on Saturday 17 April 1915. It was the eve of the Australian Rules football season, and Footscray, winner of the prestigious Victorian Football Association premiership on several occasions in the past, seemed in disappointing disarray at this eleventh hour, ill-prepared for its imminent string of challenging fixtures. It was a difficult question to confront, acknowledged the sports editor, 'and it is a fairly hard thing to answer with meaning'. And yet, he added, tongue-in-cheek, it was not nearly so problematic as the continual cry 'When will the Dardenelles be forced?'[1]

'When will the Dardenelles be forced?'

The subject of the Dardenelles had dominated the press in Australia in recent weeks and, as the Footscray *Independent* intimated, public opinion was now becoming a little weary about the whole operation. On 29 October 1914, Turkey had entered the First World War on the side of the Central Powers – Germany and Austro-Hungary – and immediately posed a threat to the Suez Canal, the British Empire's lifeline to the East (Australasia as much as India), and to British interests in the Middle East itself. Indeed, the Turks made a badly prepared attack on the canal in early February 1915, which was easily repulsed but had demonstrated Turkish intent in the region. The British response, already in the making and enthusiastically embraced by Winston Churchill, First Lord of the Admiralty, was to try to knock Turkey out of the war altogether with a decisive hammer blow, threatening the Ottoman Empire at its heart in Constantinople. The plan was that warships of the Royal Navy, supported by vessels from Britain's French allies, would force the Dardenelles, sailing into the Sea of Marmara where they would confront Constantinople, intimidating or battering the Turks into submission. The route to India and Australasia would be safeguarded, with the added bonus that Russian ports on the Black Sea would now be open to Allied shipping.

There had been preliminary raids in November and December 1914, which may have whetted Allied appetites, and certainly alerted Turkey to the possibilities of hostile acts in the Dardenelles. First of all, in the December, British and French warships searching for the German battlecruiser *Goeben* had opened fire in a brief attack on Turkish forts guarding the entrance to the Dardenelles. In the following month, a British submarine had penetrated the Dardenelles, dodging minefields and sinking the Turkish battleship *Messudieh* before making good its escape. The boat's captain, Lieutenant Norman Holbrook, was awarded the Victoria Cross for his daring exploit. Neither initiative was followed up until, in January 1915, a plan to force the Dardenelles was first put forward. The Turks, meanwhile, had turned to German assistance to improve their defence of the straits, acquiring mobile howitzer batteries and new searchlights, as well as laying further minefields. In London, the assumption was that forcing the Dardenelles would be an operation especially suited to the Royal Navy's sizeable collection of obsolete battleships, those not equipped to engage in actions with modern 'dreadnought' vessels but nonetheless able to bring formidable fire-power to bear as floating batteries. To the ageing fleet thus assembled was added the modern battleship *Queen Elizabeth*, which was to act as flagship, together with an elderly French squadron.

Forty miles long, the Dardenelles were just 4,000 yards wide at Cape Helles, the Mediterranean entrance. Thereafter, the two banks – one European, the other Asiatic – opened out gradually to a distance of about four and half miles before closing at the Narrows (fourteen miles upstream) to a mere 1,600 yards. Thereafter, they opened once more to about four miles apart at the entrance of the Sea of Marmara. The assault on the Dardenelles began on the morning of 19 February 1915. The Turks hardly replied to the sustained bombardment their forts were receiving until late in the afternoon, when some of the Allied ships moved closer in and began to draw enemy fire. Frustratingly, despite this apparently promising beginning, bad weather prevented further action until 25 February. Then, in what looked like a decisive move, the warships closed on the forts guarding the mouth of the Dardenelles, laying down a fearsome barrage that drove the Turkish and German gunners from their positions. Over the next few days, parties of marines and sailors were put ashore, where they destroyed guns, emplacements and searchlights. Meanwhile, minesweepers had penetrated six miles upstream without encountering minefields. The Allies agreed that they would be in Constantinople in a fortnight.

It was news that sent waves of excitement through the Allied countries, and Australia shared in the widespread anticipation of the great victory that was at hand. The *Bunbury Herald* newspaper, in Western Australia, speculated that the Turks were even now making 'frantic haste to save Constantinople', desperately trying to reinforce their capital before it was overrun by the Allies, while the *Globe and Sunday Times War Pictorial* in Sydney, New South Wales, described the 'pathway to Turkey's downfall', the 'famous Dardenelles through which the Allied Fleets are now battering their way'.[2] The Melbourne *Argus* offered a more careful analysis, recognizing the might of the Allied naval assault but adding that the Turkish army had been completely reorganized and professionalized by the Germans, with 100,000 troops ready to be committed to the Gallipoli peninsula. However, it too was optimistic about the outcome of the operation, reporting that preparations were being made by the Allies to land an expeditionary force in Turkey, once the straits had been forced. Indeed, the *Argus* had heard it rumoured that a large contingent of Canadian and Senegalese troops was already poised off the Dardenelles.[3]

'Touching the Dardenelles disaster'

As the days and weeks passed, the prospect of swift victory seemed to evaporate. By 8 March, when poor weather again hampered operations, it was clear that the initial momentum had been lost. Gun emplacements that had apparently been destroyed suddenly sprang to life again, and the mobile howitzers caused confusion by their constant movement. Under heavy fire, the minesweepers continued to sweep ahead of the fleet, and finally it was decided to make an all-out assault on the Narrows on 18 March. The great battle commenced at about 10.30 a.m., a fierce contest between the Turkish guns ashore and the Allied ships at sea. By early afternoon, the Turkish fire had become desultory, and Allied commanders suspected a collapse of Turkish morale. But, just as the French squadron manoeuvred out of the firing line, so the battleship *Bouvet* was suddenly stricken by a huge explosion, keeling over and sinking almost immediately. Later that afternoon, the *Inflexible* hit a mine, to be followed by the *Irresistible*, which was thought to have been torpedoed. Soon the *Ocean* too was hit, its steering-gear damaged, the ship steaming helplessly in circles. The *Inflexible* was taken in tow and salvaged, but both the *Irresistible* and *Ocean* were lost to enemy action that day. In all, more than a third of the British and French naval force was sunk or damaged on 18 March, and the military planners were forced to think again.

In Australia, as elsewhere, the public waited anxiously for further news from the Dardenelles. Early enthusiasm turned to impatience, and eventually to a wry cynicism of the type expressed by the laconic sports editor of the Footscray *Independent*. When, at last, news began to seep through it was not good. In Britain, the Dardenelles disaster – for that is what it was – had rocked Asquith's Liberal government. It attempted to conceal the scale and significance of the defeat from the British – and thus Australian – public, and it was not for some weeks that the full picture began to emerge. It had reached rural New South Wales by mid-April. The *Cessnock Eagle and South Maitland Recorder* carried a searching article 'Touching the Dardenelles Disaster', and likewise at Tamworth the *Daily Observer* reported an alarming 'Crisis in the Dardenelles Operations'.[4] 'All the operations are of course attended by certain risks', the newspaper conceded, but it wondered if 'they are justified' in attempting to force the Dardenelles. Moreover, the paper warned presciently that the real 'strength of the Turks is ashore and not afloat', suggesting that any attempt to land a military force would be hotly contested by the enemy. Plainly, the Dardenelles was no longer the easy option that observers had imagined only a month or so before. The *Sydney Morning Herald* offered its own explanation for the recent reverse, speculating that the 'science of the German gunners is greatly helping the Turks otherwise the Allied Fleet would already be before Constantinople'.[5]

Back in Britain, the fallout from the crisis included the resignation of 'Jacky' Fisher, the First Sea Lord, who was exasperated and embarrassed by the defeat, 'when we have a fleet in the Dardenelles which is bigger than the German Navy'.[6] Fisher's resignation precipitated the creation of a new Coalition government, which Lloyd George was shortly to lead. Churchill's task, as First Lord of the Admiralty, was to reassure opinion at home and across the Empire that all was well in the Dardenelles. Although bombardment had continued since 18 March, he explained, there had been no further Allied losses. It was an announcement, thought the insightful *Goulburn Evening Penny Post*, crafted with 'a view to dispelling rumours of a disaster in the Dardanelles', a statement designed to reduce the debacle of 18 March to a temporary tactical setback in an otherwise developing campaign.[7] But what the newspaper and its readers could not have known, when the article appeared on 20 April 1915, was that within a few days the Dardenelles adventure would take a dramatic new turn, in which the Australians and their New Zealand cousins would play a key role.

Initially, the Dardenelles operation had envisaged that, once the Turkish guns were knocked out and the Allied warships had forced the Narrows, troops would be put ashore to secure the Gallipoli peninsula, guarding against any enemy attempt to retake the forts and supporting the capture of Constantinople. Now, however, the plan was reversed. This time, Allied troops would land on the Aegean coast of the peninsula, overrunning the Turkish fortifications and thus allowing the British and French fleets to sail unmolested into the Sea of Marmara. The Melbourne *Argus* had imagined that Canadian and Senegalese troops had already been earmarked for such a task, but in fact a rather different and much larger force had been amassing in and around the Aegean islands of Imbros and Lemnos. This was the grandly named Mediterranean Expeditionary Force, some 70,000 strong, which included 20,000 Australians in the two Divisions of the Australian and New Zealand Army Corps (or simply ANZAC, as it would soon be known) under the command of Lieutenant-General Sir William Birdwood.

In fact, the Australians and New Zealanders had already been organizing and training in Egypt for several months. After various delays, caused by anxieties about the possible presence of German raiders around the Australian coastline, a convoy of thirty-six troop ships, mustered from across Australia and New Zealand, had sailed from the south-western port of Albany on 1 November 1914. They left in the early evening, steaming three abreast in a column three miles wide and seven miles long, accompanied by the Australian warships *Sydney* and *Melbourne*, together with the British cruiser *Minotaur* and the Japanese *Ibuki* – the latter a strange maritime bedfellow for many Australians, brought up to fear the Asiatic 'yellow peril' and suspicious of Japan's growing naval presence in the Pacific region. On the long sea-journey via Ceylon, Aden and the Suez Canal, the troops speculated about their final destination. Rumours ('furphies' in Australian parlance) that they might be bound for Egypt were scotched by news that they were heading instead for the training camps of Salisbury Plain in England. But as it entered the Red Sea, the convoy was instructed to make for Egypt after all. To an accommodation crisis in the burgeoning English training camps, made worse by the spectre of the approaching winter, was added the new strategic threat posed by Turkey's recent entry into the war – sending the Australians and New Zealanders to Egypt made military as well as practical sense. They arrived in Alexandria in early December and made their way swiftly to Cairo. The Australians of the 1st Division went straight to Mena, near the pyramids, where they pitched camp. The New Zealanders found a home at Zeitoun, on the outskirts of Cairo, and the Australian Light Horse was posted to Maadi, on the Nile. Training began almost immediately.

Training and tourism in Egypt

The proximity of pyramids, mosques and antiquities had a great effect on many Australians, who began to imagine themselves involved in some bizarre military tourism adventure: the 'six bob a day tourists' of popular fancy. Private Edward Cairns, from Ardrossan in South Australia, found time to visit 'three native mosques', as he put it, the first called El-Rifai, 'where I was thunderstruck at the marvellous work inside'. In deference to the Muslim religion, he covered his boots with 'large slippers' before entering the mosques – 'wonderful buildings', as he described them – and was fascinated by the 'beautiful mosaic designs' he encountered in their interiors, each inlaid with marble, granite, ebony, gold, silver, ivory, mother of pearl, bronze 'and other stones or metals I cannot think of'. Cairns also visited the Rasr-el-Nil Museum, with its 'carved stones and old Egyptian relics', noting in his diary that the 'mummies are well worth seeing', and went to the Zoological Gardens to view 'all manner of African animals and birds'. He took a camel ride, was greatly impressed by the Sphinx, and ventured inside the 'Pyramid of Cheop (largest)' where, by candlelight, he gazed upon the 'Queen's Chamber' and the 'King's Chamber'. For Eddie Cairns it was an enchanting experience, unexpected in its intensity, not least when he climbed the minaret of the Blue Mosque, obtaining breathtaking views across Cairo, the Nile and the pyramids.[8]

Private Cliff Green, also from South Australia, wrote home to explain that he too 'had visited some of the fine historic buildings' in Egypt which were, he said, 'equal to anything seen in Adelaide'. He had been especially 'privileged to see a tomb 700 years old', along with other 'ancient sights'.[9] Another Australian soldier thought Cairo Museum 'a wonderful place' full of 'marvellous things', and yet another was entranced by 'the Mosque of a thousand lights' in Cairo, 'a beautiful sight'.[10] Edgar Rule, then an NCO in the 14th Battalion, originally from Cobar in outback New South Wales, was likewise impressed. 'I could not believe that four walls could contain so much beauty and interest', he wrote later in his memoirs, musing on the treasures of the Cairo Museum; 'it was overwhelming'. He was especially fascinated, he said, 'by a bas relief representing a march of soldiers thousands of years before Christ. They carried their spears as we carried our rifles, they were all in step, and were marching in fours'. Moreover, he added, 'it seemed incredible that we should stand beside a large case and gaze at the body of a Pharaoh'. He (Rameses II) 'looked like a man who had died in the prime of life and been dried out by the sun'.[11]

However, as Edgar Rule also observed, for the Australians the 'attractions of Cairo were many and varied', and despite their respect for the antiquity of Egyptian culture, they had little time for the Egyptians themselves. Rule complained that food 'purchased from dirty Gyppos', as he termed them, 'had the effect of putting the battalion out of action for a few days'. Similarly, 'the fleshpots of Egypt led some astray', many seduced by 'the delights of the Wozzer', the red-light district in Cairo, which encouraged men to outstay their leave and was the inevitable source of debilitating venereal disease. Indeed, of all the attractions in Cairo, reckoned Edgar Rule, 'the famous Wozzer was the most notorious and generally came first'. He recalled an amusing incident he had witnessed first-hand in the district, 'when two military policemen darted out of one house and into another', to the accompaniment of loud female screams 'as the police chased the male lovers upstairs and down, knocking the furniture all ways'. But he was also genuinely moved by the presence on 'the edge of the Wozzer' of 'two old British ladies' who 'ran an imitation Y.M.C.A.' and 'sought to entertain men who were at a loose end. Their motherly ways must have served to remind men of mothers and sweethearts, and acted as a brake on many wild spirits'.[12]

Albert Facey, a naïve young soldier from Western Australia, was one of those wary of the Wozzer. 'I was shy where women were concerned', he explained, 'and we had been lectured several times about the bad women who had come to Cairo when it was known that the A.I.F. [Australian Imperial Force] was there'. One lecturer had estimated that there were 30,000 prostitutes 'doing a roaring trade' in Egypt, and Facey added that the 'lecturers didn't pull their punches when describing what could happen if you got a dose of venereal disease. So I completely refused to have anything to do with these women'.[13] Others, as Albert Facey acknowledged, were less fastidious. Private Bert Bishop, for example, was spellbound by a visit to the Wozzer. He had never seen a naked woman before, he confessed, and here he was confronted by 'a perfectly nude brownish-black woman' who 'smiled at us' and 'turned herself slowly around as if to show off her attractiveness from all angles'. He signed up there and then for an erotic show: 'Two girls and two donkey-boys, all nude, took up station . . . and the show commenced'. Modesty prevented Bert Bishop from describing their antics – the act 'did not lend itself to respectable reporting' – but just as the performance 'reached its climax', some wag in the audience set light to a screwed-up newspaper and hurled it into the middle of the stage. Chaos ensued; 'nude girls were everywhere, screaming their heads off', and Bishop and his mates decided that it was prudent to make a speedy retreat.[14]

Edgar Rule's sceptical assessment of the Egyptians was not discouraged by his contact with the guides who clamoured to show Australians the sites and sights of Cairo. On one occasion he was accosted 'by a Gyppo in flowing robes' down by the Nile, who insisted that he could point out the very spot where Moses had been found in the bulrushes.

Much to Rule's mirth, the would-be guide showed him a book of testimonials. Some of the observations were serious 'but most were written by Aussies and were literary gems'. Among such wry commentaries was that by a certain T. Brown: 'He is the biggest damned liar I've met. Give him a good kick on the backside from me'.[15] Likewise, a 'very old Egyptian' told Albert Facey a tall story about the origins of the pyramids, explaining that they were built as protection against marauding tribesmen, 'for storing food and as places for women, girls and children to go'. Moreover, he said, the pyramids had been constructed by dinosaurs, who carted the stones on their backs until wiped out by a mystery disease. Another guide took Facey and his mates into one of the pyramids. He showed the Australians a flame that had been burning near the entrance of the tomb 'for over one thousand years'. As one candle burned low, it was explained, so the flame was transferred to another, and so on again and again over the generations. One of the Aussies decided it was high time the flame was extinguished, and promptly blew on it. 'There, it's out now', he beamed. This time it was Albert Facey's turn to beat a hasty retreat!

Facey also noted that the Australians 'had to keep a close watch on our clothes and equipment or it would be stolen'. Once, he said, his tunic went missing, a loss he duly reported to the military police. The very next day, an Egyptian turned up wearing the outfit. It was obviously several sizes too big but this did not prevent the thief from insisting that he was an Australian soldier: 'It didn't seem to occur to him that he would be arrested for stealing'.[16]

The 'Wozzer' riots

For every Australian, like Albert Facey, who found the Egyptians merely amusing, there were others who could not disguise their utter contempt. Donald Dowling, serving with the 4th Field Ambulance, thought them 'yelling . . . disease-ridden niggers . . . the dirtiest people I have seen'. They were 'absolutely filthy and disgusting', he added: 'They don't worry about going to sanitary convenience . . . the gutter or the side of the road is good enough for them, and such a thing as modesty does not enter into their reckoning at all'. Dowling was also convinced that the 'Egyptians have many dread diseases', and speculated that between eighty and ninety per cent of them suffered from venereal disease: it 'shows up in some appalling forms. I saw a poor beggar with no nose at all, just a hole above his mouth'.[17] Sister Anne Donnell, an Australian nurse serving with the army in Egypt, was less condemnatory, deciding that the 'natives make excellent servants; you can't help admiring their keen perception'. But she too was horrified by 'the poor, the blind, the maimed, the horrible deformed creatures of humanity, freaks of nature, the starving . . . what I think is so appalling about the place is its filth'.[18]

Such opinions revealed a deeply ingrained racism, an almost unconscious assumption of 'British race' superiority to which the overwhelming majority of Australians subscribed. The Egyptians had limited value as servants, guides and (sometimes) casual sexual partners, it was conceded, but generally were to be avoided as unwholesome and unclean. Even Albert Facey, with his more gentle estimation of the 'Gyppos' (as he too called them), was unquestioning in his belief that Egypt benefited from its status as a British Protectorate. He was pleased when a local guide readily agreed with his imperial sentiments: 'Before British protection his people were in constant danger from raiders who would come from the many surrounding Arab tribes . . . killing and stealing was their way of life'.[19] But if the British had brought peace, law and order to a troubled land, then the Australians were about to disturb it. On Good Friday, 2 April 1915, several Australian and New Zealand units received orders to pack for imminent deployment to the front.

That night, they went wild in the Wozzer, letting off weeks of pent-up steam and wreaking vengeance on those who had sold them bad beer, rotten food or archaeological trinkets of dubious provenance. Misogynist contempt for the district's prostitutes (especially among those soldiers who had contracted venereal disease from their encounters with these women) also fuelled the riot – as it soon became – and several buildings were set ablaze as properties were wrecked and individuals assaulted. British military police, firing revolvers to disperse the crowd, made matters worse and were met by a hail of beer bottles and ripe abuse. The Australians had already acquired a reputation for indiscipline – their reluctance to salute officers was common knowledge – and Albert Facey had detected the superior attitudes of the British officers, with 'their high-faluting way of speaking . . . We got into a lot of strife laughing at their commands'.[20] The British had also resented demonstrations of Australian sporting prowess in organized contests in the training camps – athletics, boxing, wrestling – and now the rivalry had taken on an altogether uglier dimension. Eventually, the Lancashire Territorials, with bayonets fixed, persuaded the Australians and New Zealanders to calm down, and slowly the mob melted away.[21]

The Wozzer riot had done little to improve estimations of the Australians, and Lord Kitchener complained that in twenty-four hours they had undermined all the goodwill the British had carefully nurtured over many years. 'I rather doubt that', snorted one Australian soldier, Corporal John Edey from Melbourne, 'many people were pleased to see this street of iniquity destroyed', an evil spot where 'every conceivable or inconceivable form of depravity was practiced'.[22]

Nevertheless, news of the disturbance filtered back to Australia, where it caused considerable disquiet. Donald Dowling, with his low opinion of the Egyptians, thought that 'the Gyppos' had brought the trouble on themselves. He wrote to the *Kadina and Wallaroo Times*, published in his hometown of Kadina in South Australia, admitting that its readers had probably 'heard awful tales about the behaviour of our troops here'. But these stories were 'mostly baseless', he reported reassuringly. He criticized the Egyptians for their shortcomings but also claimed in self-defence that 'the New Zealanders have been the rowdiest' of the rioters.[23] Fred Carthew, a soldier from Western Australia, agreed. The 'New Zealanders took a very important part' in the riot, he insisted: 'in fact they started most of the trouble, but it is the poor old Aussie that has to take all the blame'.[24]

Perhaps; but the Australians were very clearly responsible for a second outbreak of 'high spirits' in the Wozzer in July 1915, when newly arrived reinforcements took to the streets in another orgy of destruction. Harold Williams, from New South Wales, part of the 5th Reinforcements for the 20th Battalion, came ashore from the troopship *Argyllshire* at the end of October, several months later, and was posted to Zeitoun camp. Like those before him, he made for the Wozzer and 'saw the ruins of several houses which had been burned by the members of the New South Wales Brigade in a great riot some time before'. Yet despite the destruction, welcomed by the likes of John Edey as a just and purifying retribution, the Wozzer went on much as before, attracting 'a great muster of soldiers', as Harold Williams put it, 'Australians, New Zealanders, Jocks and Tommies'. The women continued to ply their trade – 'coal-black Nubians, slim copper-coloured Arabs, a few

Frenchwomen, fair-headed Russians … black-headed Greeks' – and Williams made his way through 'Moorish buildings' and 'evil-smelling lanes' to witness 'a cancan dance performed for our amazed education'.[25] Indeed, very little had changed!

Meanwhile, back home, the *Barrier Miner*, published in the outback mining town of Broken Hill in New South Wales, vigorously defended the reputation of the Australians in Egypt, indignantly dismissing negative reports of continuing bad behaviour. The Australians were excellent soldiers and fine ambassadors for their country, it reported. Their 'physique and smart military appearance have been universally admired', it explained, and 'they have been befriended by all sorts and conditions of people'. In fact, the paper added, with 'the exception of a few isolated cases of insubordination, quite unavoidable where large bodies of troops have been dealt with, their conduct has … been exceptionally good'.[26] The months in Egypt had moulded many of the stereotypes that would become enduring components of the 'Anzac myth' – the Australians as boisterous larrikins with a healthy disrespect for authority and a wry and irreverent sense of humour, resourceful and physically fit individualists who would stick with their mates through thick and thin.[27] But the experience in Egypt had also nurtured a fierce protective pride of the sort voiced by the *Barrier Miner*, an incipient Australian nationalism that was to become all the more apparent in the weeks and months ahead as the Aussies saw action for the first time.

The 'Dawn Landing'

The first batch of Australian troops had left Cairo for Alexandria by train in late February 1915, where they joined transport ships bound for the Aegean islands, to be followed by further contingents over the next few weeks. Albert Facey was one of the last to leave, receiving his order to move late on the evening of 18 April and joining the transport *Sussex* for the short journey – a few days – to Lemnos. Arriving in Mudros harbour, he was astonished by the build-up of Allied shipping – battleships, cruisers, transports and an array of smaller vessels, perhaps as many as sixty in all, he estimated – with many of the Australians and New Zealanders already embarked for the Dardenelles. There was no time for him to go ashore, and instead he was transferred to another transport to join troops bound for the Gallipoli peninsula. Many were from Western Australia, Facey's home state, some from the coastal town of Bunbury, south of the capital Perth, and he was glad to be attached to them for the ordeal that lay ahead.[28] The plan was for the Australians and New Zealanders to land at Gallipoli at what became known as Anzac Cove, north of the Turkish guns at Gaba Tepe, while British and Indian troops would go ashore at Cape Helles, along with the French who would attack both at Cape Helles and on the opposite Asiatic side of the Dardenelles.

Some of the Australians had been on Lemnos for up to nine weeks, practising the infant art of amphibious warfare and learning the discipline of landing in complete silence. Among them was Corporal Roy Pickering, from South Australia, a member of the 'famous' or 'fighting tenth', as the 10th Battalion would soon be known, who shortly wrote home to describe his experiences. He explained how, with their training at last complete, he and his colleagues had joined the battleship HMS *Prince of Wales*. They went on board at 11 a.m. on 24 April, and sailed the next day in company (he estimated) with a dozen or more major warships, some twenty torpedo boats, and over one hundred transports. Pickering appears to have been one of a specially selected group of advanced scouts embarked in the *Prince of Wales*, their task once ashore at Gallipoli to move quickly to secure key tactical positions. 'When you get out of the boat, go like hell for Third Ridge' was the simple order given to these men on the eve of the attack.[29] Pickering did exactly as he was told, and was among the first waves on the beach at Anzac Cove, as the landing place was known thereafter. As he explained it:

> At about midnight, Saturday [24 April 1915], we were given a good
> hot meal, marched up on deck (no lights), and then put into lifeboats
> – each man knowing where to go. We then had a little steam pinnace
> to tow three or four boats each . . . everything was nice and quiet and
> you could hardly hear the throb of the engine of the pinnace. We were
> about 50 yards from the shore, when there was a rifle shot . . . and in
> about five minutes a thousand rifles and machine guns were pouring
> lead at us as fast as they could.[30]

'The sailor in our boat was hit', Pickering continued, 'but you can't frighten the English navy men, and our boat load got out of the water

with bullets spitting all around us and waded ashore up to our necks'.
He fell over twice during the stumble through the shallows, his heavy
pack weighing him down, but once on the beach he dumped his kit,
fixed his bayonet, and charged for all he was worth. The Turks were
entrenched halfway up the steep hill that rose immediately from the
shoreline: 'We went like wild men at those Turks yelling at the tops of
our voices . . . There were two Turks left in a trench I passed but our
chaps soon finished them with bayonets.' In all, he said, the Australians
drove the Turks back over three hills before they were ordered to pause
and dig in. This was perhaps the 'Third Ridge' that the scouts had
been told to attack and hold – 'Gun Ridge' as it was later known in
accounts of the Gallipoli campaign. At first, the handful of Australians
to have reached Third – or Gun – Ridge met little resistance. But soon
the Turks began to outflank them, enfilading them with heavy fire and
forcing them to retreat. As Pickering described it: 'We had not long
been there before they put a few big guns around us on our left flank
and infiladed [sic] us with shrapnel and what with rifle fire, machine
guns and artillery it was terrible, they were knocking our chaps out
in dozens yet we would not give in'. Pickering estimated that they had
hung on until about 5 p.m., with 'comrades falling one by one and
laying about all over the battlefield', when they retired to less exposed
positions nearer the shore. As Pickering retreated, he was hit, first in his
hand and then in the shoulder and head, putting him out of action for
the time being and sending him to a hospital in Cairo. 'Our men have
got a footing now and the Turks will never shift them', he wrote later
from his hospital bed, adding optimistically: 'before long our troops will
be marching into Constantinople'.[31]

Roy Pickering, together with the few who ventured briefly beyond
Gun Ridge to gaze at the blue waters of the straits beyond, the ultimate objective of the assault at Gallipoli, had reached the farthest
points penetrated by the Australians during the whole campaign.
Their achievement, against impossibly difficult terrain and a determined enemy, was remarkable. But the Australians had quickly become
scattered, isolated in small groups, and in such confused conditions
communication and command had broken down. Gains were not con-
solidated, and the tactical picture was difficult to read, let alone control.
Pickering himself recovered from the wounds received that evening
on 25 April but, like many of the Anzacs who fought at Gallipoli and

survived, he was later killed in action at Pozières on the Somme in the northern summer of 1916.[32]

When Albert Facey landed at Anzac Cove that morning, his orders had been to get ashore and then line up on the beach to await further instructions. But, of course, as they approached the landing ground 'all hell broke loose' and, having successfully waded through water 'in some places up to my shoulders', he and his mates were met by murderous fire. He recalled years later how he had run for his life, stumbling blindly over the bodies of fallen comrades, and making for the relative cover of the scrub and bush. The cries of the wounded and dying were unnerving and pitiful, but he dare not stop to lend a hand – something that would always trouble him when he looked back on that awful morning – and instead joined others in using their entrenching tools to throw up rudimentary defences against the continuous machine-gun fire that swept their positions. As he reflected, 'I am sure that there wouldn't have been one of us left if we had obeyed that damn fool order to line up on the beach'.[33]

Private Harry Banfield, from Moonta in South Australia, was another who went ashore that fateful morning. Nearly forty-four years of age when he joined up in 1914, Banfield was a comparatively old man (his hair was already grey) among the youthful throng of new recruits in the 10th Battalion. Yet he acquitted himself well at Gallipoli. He too remembered the absolute silence that 'reigned supreme' as the ships approached the peninsula. But before he and his colleagues had had an opportunity to clamber 'into the small boats to effect the landing the enemy discovered [our] presence and commenced a heavy fire . . . Many men were killed or wounded'. One boat was capsized by a shell, he said, but the others continued into the shallows and on 'nearing the shore the men jumped out into the water to their armpits in depth, and dashed on to the beach . . . One man undid another's pack, dropped it onto the beach, and, with a yell, they charged up a steep hill with bayonets fixed'. Banfield described how the Australians drove the Turks from their trenches, the latter 'crying "Allah" as they went'. The 10th had been told to capture and hold the First Ridge 'at all costs'. For good measure, said Banfield, they pressed on to the next 'and subsequently dug themselves in on the second hill'.[34] It was during this battle for Second Ridge that Harry Banfield was seriously wounded. He reckoned he had been fighting for all of fifteen hours before he was struck

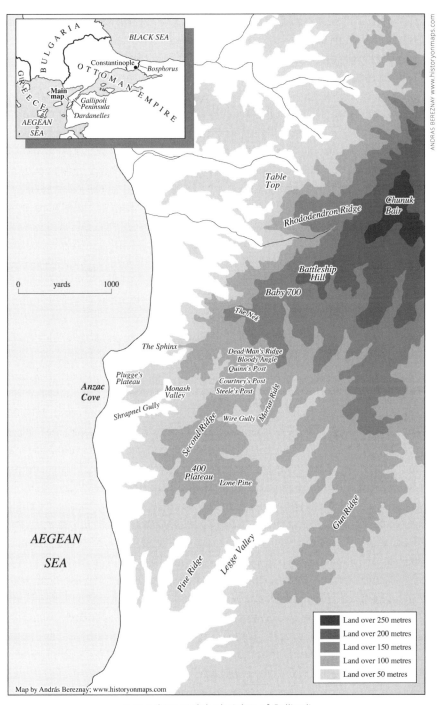

Anzac Cove and the heights of Gallipoli

down, hit in the back, buttocks and thigh. Fortunately, stretcher-bearers were on hand to carry him to the beach, whence he was evacuated to Alexandria and eventually returned to Australia where he was discharged as unfit for further military service.

Morale was high among the Australians that morning, and they were anxious to put months of training into practice. They called out to each other as they ran, exhorting their mates to go forward and urging them to flush out the Turks from their positions. 'This is no good to us', Private Frank Brent heard someone cry in frustration: 'Come on. Heads down, arse up and get stuck into it!' Brent needed no second bidding. 'We went into it', he recalled. 'We cleared them. Bayoneted them, shot them and the others ran'. Then 'a bloke from the 8th Battalion' shouted a warning: 'Here, look at that bloody bush', he yelled: 'It's moving!' Brent decided that 'it was obviously a sniper and he was done up like a Christmas tree. But he didn't look like a bush when we'd finished with him!' There was a strange sense of exhilaration: 'One bloke shouted: "Share that amongst you, you bastards"'. But even as they exalted in their moment of triumph, the fortunes of war turned against Frank Brent and his pals. 'The bloke next to me was Robbie Robinson', he said, 'a corporal in my battalion. He was laughing at the remark and . . . the next thing his head fell on my shoulder and a sniper had got him through the jugular vein. I really think that was my baptism of fire', Brent added, 'because Robbie's blood spent all over my tunic'.[35]

There were countless other displays of gallantry and tenacity on that first day, from the 'dawn landing' at Anzac Cove until about 10 p.m. when night closed in at last. Observing the action from a Royal Navy warship, the British journalist Ellis Ashmead-Bartlett had watched the progress of the Australians and New Zealanders. His dramatic account of the assault was the first to reach Australia, where it caused a sensation. It appeared in the Melbourne *Argus* on 8 May, galvanizing the paper's readership, and was reprinted time and again across Australia, holding the country enthralled. 'The Australians rose to the occasion', Ashmead-Bartlett reported: 'Not waiting for orders, or for the boats to reach the beach, they sprang into the sea, and, forming a sort of rough line, rushed the enemy's trenches'. The Australians, he added, 'were happy because they knew they had been tried for the first time and had not been found wanting . . . There has been no finer feat in this war than this sudden landing in the dark and the storming of the heights'.[36]

If, like the Footscray sports commentator, who had wondered in a different context 'What sort of team will we have?', Australians had been nervous about how their troops might perform, here was evidence to put their minds at rest. The *Sydney Morning Herald* mingled relief with pride, observing that 'even while we mourn the loss of our men who have gone, we cannot but rejoice that they showed the same brave spirit, the same devotion to duty, as the Canadians'.[37]

Anzacs

The comparison was significant. On 22 April 1915, just a few days before the Gallipoli landings, the Germans had launched an attack north of Ypres, in Belgium, wreaking serious damage on its French defenders. It was checked by the resolute stand of the 1st Canadian Division. This was to be the first of a series of distinguished contributions by the Canadians to the Allied effort on the Western Front. But in April 1915 its importance, in Australian as well as Canadian estimation, was the evidence it afforded of the steadfast qualities of the Canadian soldiery and of Canada's unwavering contribution to the Empire. In time, the Australians and Canadians would be considered the 'shock troops of the British Empire' but for now it was enough to note that the Canadians' heroic performance near Ypres had been matched by the Anzacs at Gallipoli. As the king, George V, put it: 'The Australians and New Zealand troops have indeed proved themselves worthy sons of Empire'.[38] It was a welcome accolade, enhanced status within the British Empire bolstering Australia's emerging sense of nationhood as well as encouraging common feeling and solidarity among the Dominions. It also invited favourable comparison with the mother country itself, as the *Traralgon Record* (published in the Gippsland region of Victoria) recognized: 'Australia's sons have shown in their initial conflict with the Turks that they are possessed of the same courage and determination which characterise the British soldier'.[39] It was no surprise when the *Colac Herald,* another Victoria paper, reported on 24 May – almost a month after the first landings – that 'Empire Day was celebrated in Colac on Saturday with remarkable success'.[40]

Estimations of the Australian achievement at Gallipoli continued to grow. General Birdwood confided his glowing appreciation to Ashmead-Bartlett, and his comments were reproduced faithfully in newspapers across the country such as the *Barrier Miner* and the Perth *Daily News*. 'I cannot sufficiently praise the courage, endurance, and soldierly qualities of the colonials', Birdwood was reported as saying: 'The manner in which they hung on to their position day and night was magnificent, considering their heavy losses, the shortage of water, and the incessant shrapnel fire to which they were exposed without cover'.[41] The *Bendigo Advertiser* decided that the Australians were now simply the 'Bravest Soldiers in the World', while the *Casterton News* explained with gushing enthusiasm that a new word had found an honoured and cherished place in the lexicon of the English language: Anzac, to be applied variously to the place where the Australians had landed and to the soldiers themselves, along with the army corps of which they were a part. 'Anzac looks like a foreign word', admitted the newspaper's editor. But instead, he revealed, it 'is a pure Australasian word, brand-new, just coined at the Dardenelles . . . to commemorate the gallant manner in which the foreshore of the little Gallipoli bay, now named Anzac Cove, was taken by the Australians and the New Zealanders'.[42]

However, despite their tremendous energy and gallantry, their cool-ness and initiative under fire, and their newly acquired reputation, the uncomfortable truth was that the Australians had not dislodged the Turks from the heights of Gallipoli. In the subsequent days, weeks and months the enemy would be able to machine-gun, bombard, and snipe at the Anzacs in their tenuously held positions – Quinn's Post, Bloody Angle, Steele's Post, The Nek, and so on – and on the beach itself, where Ashmead-Bartlett observed with astonishment that one 'of the strangest sights was to see men bathing in the sea with shrapnel bursting all around them'.[43] For all his congratulatory remarks about the Australians and New Zealanders, Birdwood perhaps knew in his heart that strategically the enterprise had failed already, and he won-dered whether an immediate evacuation might be the best option. His superior officer, General Sir Ian Hamilton, at sea with his staff aboard HMS *Queen Elizabeth* would have none of it. 'You have got through the difficult business', he insisted, 'now you only have to dig, dig, dig, until you are safe'.[44]

But if Birdwood had doubts, he appeared resolute in the days ahead as he toured the front lines, cajoling, reassuring, and praising the men under his command. Even Hamilton recognized Birdwood's qualities, deciding he was 'the soul of Anzac'. He was 'Cheery and full of human sympathy', said Hamilton, and 'he has spent many hours of each twenty-four inspiring the defenders of the front trenches, and if he does not know every soldier in his force, at least every soldier in the force believes he is known to his chief'.[45] It was an opinion shared by John Monash, then a major at Gallipoli but soon to rise to command the Australian forces on the Western Front. Despite Birdwood's stammer and unsoldierly 'nervy' manner, Monash conceded that he understood 'the whole business of soldiering', and that, at Gallipoli, 'I have been around with him for hours talking to privates, buglers, drivers, gunners, colonels, signallers and generals and every time he has left the man with a better knowledge of his business than he had before'.[46] The democratic and egalitarian streak of the Australian soldiers appealed to Birdwood, and his amused regard for their informality was reflected in the various yarns the Anzacs told about 'Birdie', as they called him affectionately. On one occasion, it was said, Birdwood on his rounds had approached a dangerously exposed part of a trench. An alarmed sentry called out: 'Duck, Birdie; you'd better ✱✱✱✱✱✱✱ well duck!' Birdwood later recounted the tale to a gathering of generals, who were aghast at this example of colonial insolence. 'What did you do?', they asked in amazed disbelief. 'Do?', replied Birdwood, 'Why, I ✱✱✱✱✱✱✱ well ducked!'[47] As it was, he had had his scalp grazed by a sniper's bullet during a recent visit to Quinn's Post, and was appreciative of timely warnings, however expressed. But, as the Australians knew, behind his friendly façade, Birdwood was just doing his job, instilling confidence and urging them on to yet greater things. To the hymn tune 'Jesus Loves Me, This I Know', the Anzacs would sing:

> Birdie loves us, this we know,
> For he often tells us so.
> He can kid you and me,
> He could kid us up a tree.[48]

Birdwood was not the only one in mortal danger from Turkish positions on the heights. Australian reinforcements arriving after the initial landings were also subjected to withering Turkish fire. John Edey, for example, sailed from Lemnos with other members of the 5th Battalion on 24 May, almost a month after the first assault, in the destroyer *Harpy*. The ship arrived off Gallipoli in broad daylight, Edey recalled, its decks protected from the fierce sunlight by white canvas awnings – 'a perfect target for the Turkish guns', in his estimation.[49] Several shells hit the destroyer, as he had feared, with the inevitable casualties (forty killed and a similar number wounded, according to Edey). The ship hastened out of range before making a second attempt to come inshore to unload the troops into the waiting whaleboats and pinnaces. Edey marvelled that the whaleboats were in the charge of 'fifteen year old midshipmen who did not dare show concern for any untoward experience. They trained them well in the Royal Navy'.[50] Once ashore, Edey was hurried to Steele's Post, almost a mile from the beach and some 395 feet up the steep hills, reinforcing the troops who held the exposed position.

'No one had expected so many casualties'

As many as 27,000 Australian troops had come ashore by 1 May, with further substantial reinforcements on their way. Yet they lacked the military resources to enable them to break out of their tactically disadvantageous positions – especially heavy artillery – and continual attrition sapped their numbers. To the constant fire from the Turks, and the resultant stream of casualties, was added the spread of disease, especially gastroenteritis and dysentery, which swiftly reduced men to emaciated wrecks incapable of performing the simplest soldierly tasks. Along with the wounded, the sick were evacuated in large numbers, first to Lemnos and then on to either Malta or Alexandria, with long-term cases that required extended treatment and convalescence being sent to Britain. From the start, medical support was inadequate. Early assumptions that arrangements for dealing with the sick and wounded would be administered by the British War Office, as part of the common effort, were upset when the formation of the Australian and New Zealand Army Corps created a separate organizational identity. As a result, 'negotiations over medical arrangements were left hanging' (as Katrina Hedditch has put it) until too late, unresolved by the eve of the Gallipoli landings.[51] To organizational uncertainty was added ill fortune, when the transport *Hindoo*, sailing from Alexandria with medical stores and orderlies earmarked for Anzac Cove, was delayed

Private Thomas Makin, from Korumburra in Victoria, was among the reinforcements landed at Gallipoli in the weeks following 25 April 1915. In trouble in Egypt for being absent without leave, Makin was killed in action at Kaiajik Dere, Gallipoli, on 8 August 1915. He has no known grave.

AUSTRALIAN WAR MEMORIAL DA08393

by bad weather. Arriving late at Mudros, she was inadvertently sent to Cape Helles on the southern tip of Gallipoli, where the British and Indian forces had gone ashore. The result was the presence of just one fully equipped hospital ship at Anzac Cove, the *Gascon*, together with the transport *City of Benares*, which was to cater for the more lightly wounded. Other transports stood by to assist, expecting medical supplies and personnel from the *Hindoo* that never arrived.

On the first day of the landing, the wounded lay on stretchers in ever-growing numbers on the beach, waiting for small craft and barges – then fully occupied ferrying men and equipment ashore – to become available to evacuate them. When, at last, the wounded were taken off the beach, they found that many of the transports refused to accept them because the medical stores and staff had failed to arrive. The master of the *Itonus* relented, allowing wounded Australians on board at 11 p.m. that night, even though he had not yet finished disembarking the New Zealanders he was putting ashore. The injured found 'mules on the foredeck . . . the latrines choked, the food bad, ventilation very imperfect'.[52] Likewise, the *Lutzow* (a 'filthy horse-transport vessel'), accepted its quota of wounded Anzacs, despite having no medical kit whatsoever.[53] Eventually, on 27 April, 2,500 wounded men set sail for

Alexandria in the transports *Itonus, Lutzow, Ionian, Clan Macgillivray* and *Seeang Choon*. The lucky ones, however, had found their way on board the *Gascon*, the hospital ship, which had arrived off Gaba Tepe two hours before the dawn landing on 25 April.

A former Union Castle cruise liner, the *Gascon* had been acquired by the British government, which refitted it as a floating hospital, painting its hull white with a distinctive green stripe and red crosses to signify its status. Among its staff was Nursing Sister Muriel Wakeford. From her vantage point on the foredeck, she could look out across Anzac Cove and see through her binoculars 'wounded men lying in gullies'. She 'hoped stretcher bearers could reach them before they bled to death'. She noted impatiently that not 'until nine a.m. that morning did the first lot of wounded arrive on board as there were few small craft to bring them to us'. Most of the wounds were in the left arm, shoulder or face, but, she said, there was 'a number of spinal injuries and skulls fractured by shrapnel'. By 3 p.m., she continued, 'we had 500 wounded men on our wards, 100 men more than had been allowed for', while more lightly injured soldiers were allowed to congregate on the foredeck. 'No one had expected so many casualties', she confessed with alarm, 'or that some of them would be so horrific. We prayed the morphine would not run out'. At 6.30 p.m., Sister Wakeford recorded, 'we left for Lemnos with almost 600 wounded men in the wards or lying on the decks, far more patients than it was intended we should take'.[54] Arriving at Mudros harbour, they disembarked the 'walking wounded' before making fast passage to Alexandria with the more serious cases. Then it was back to Anzac Cove to pick up yet further casualties, a routine the *Gascon* followed repeatedly in the days ahead.

Inevitably, some of the wounded succumbed to their injuries on-board the *Gascon*. Lance-Corporal Arthur Elphick, for example, from Wallaroo in South Australia, had been shot in the buttocks. Evacuated to the *Gascon*, he died of his wounds on 6 May, and was subsequently buried at sea. Eventually, his pitifully few personal belongings were returned to his widowed mother, Sarah Jane Elphick, in Australia: 'Disc; Wristwatch and strap, 2 knives, Military book, Notebook, fountain pen'. Sarah Jane was required to sign for the safe arrival of the items, returning her receipt to the Base Records Office (the military authorities) in Melbourne. As she did so, she appended a short note. 'Enclosed pleas [*sic*] find receipt for 1 package, which I received with thanks'. But she also explained that: 'Their [sic] is a gold ring, set with sapphires, which my son had, before leaving home, and which I prize very much. If you hear or see anything of the same ring will you please communicate with me. Thanking you for the trouble you have taken'.[55] Poor Mrs Elphick. Her trust was implicit, but, whatever had happened to the ring, it was unlikely to have been committed to the deep with her son. Yet James Blackie, a chemist at Euroa in north-eastern Victoria, was gratified when the ring belonging to his late and only son Norman was duly returned with his other personal items – a jack-knife, pipe, purse, and pocket-book. Norman Blackie had also expired on the *Gascon*, on 31 May, suffering from gunshot wounds to the stomach, and had been buried at sea three miles off Gaba Tepe. Someone had ensured that his ring, certain to have sentimental value for his grieving family, had been saved and sent home.[56]

By 15 May, according to Muriel Wakeford, there were up to six deaths every twenty-four hours on the *Gascon*, a result of appalling injuries but also the long delays in getting many of the wounded on-board. Ten days later she was on night duty in the ship, which she found particularly harrowing. Every night, she wrote, 'there are two or three deaths, sometimes five or six. It's just awful flying from one ward to another, dreading to hear what the orderly might have to tell you when you get there, how you wished you could be in all four wards at once'.[57] Penning her diary entry for 15 June, Hilda Samsing, another of the *Gascon* nurses, observed that during the last five trips to and from Anzac Cove, 120 men had been buried at sea. Two days later, off Gaba Tepe, more wounded came on-board. 'Poor boys', wrote Hilda Simsing, 'one of the ones who died in agony was from the 8th Battalion, I think he recognised me, his name was Warren. Another boy who died from abdominal wounds was a fine looking lad with perfect features, dark and tall, only 23 years old but full of pluck. It's all so sad'.[58] A month later, on 14 July 1915, there were no fewer than twenty-three funerals on board the *Gascon* at Anzac Cove, the bodies being taken away by trawler for dumping in deep water.

Like her colleague Muriel Wakeford, Hilda Simsing dreaded the small hours, when the wounded were at their lowest ebb and most likely to slip away. One fellow had lost much blood, the result of a leg injury, and asked Hilda earnestly whether he would die during the night. She answered honestly – that she did not know – adding swiftly that she would do all she could for him. The soldier watched intently as she tended him with quiet determination but gradually, as the night wore on, he became ever weaker, dying at about one o'clock in the morning. 'I stayed with him till the end', she wrote sadly.[59] Sister Alice Kitchen, from western Victoria, was another *Gascon* nurse, and she too felt deeply for the young men in her care. On 17 June, as she recorded in her diary, a minesweeper had brought across the latest batch of wounded. 'Got in one poor boy from the 8th [Battalion]', she wrote, 'with his hand blown off'. The next day 'we got in another man with his R[ight] hand off with a hand grenade: things they make themselves out of jam tins & all sorts of things like that'. As she explained, they 'occasionally go off too soon & then there is tragedy'. Spinal injuries were especially dis-tressing – 'they are so hopeless and tragic' – and abdominal wounds were also often fatal: 'The poor things usually die, in spite of operation'. A 'Benalla boy named Ross' (from Benalla, in Victoria) was one such case, brought on-board on 19 June, 'a bad abdominal that died soon after op'. Five days later there was another 'nice lad from Benalla . . . Poor boy, he said to me just before he died "O Sister, I am sorry I ever went to the front"'.[60]

To the badly injured was added the growing number of the sick at Gallipoli. Often the medical staff felt powerless to deal with them. Wounds could be operated on and injuries treated but, frustratingly, little could be done for the sick, other than cleaning them up and administering medicine. 'The wounded were easy enough to deal with', agreed Sister Mary Fitzgibbon, 'but the sick!' As she explained, they 'were in a terrible state, all suffering from dysentery and enteric. Their insides had simply turned to water, and all they had been able to do with them on shore was to tie their trousers tight round their legs with pieces of string'. She continued: 'We had to rip their trousers off with scissors, and then we washed the boys as best we could. We couldn't do very much for them because we only had them for a few hours . . . to get them back to Mudros.' Suffering from high fevers, the sick called continually for water – although it would not improve their situation; 'all we could do', said Mary Fitzgibbon, 'was to strip them off, clean them up and put them to bed . . . they were mostly stretchers, and the boys were laid out all along the decks. We had to step over them, just lying there, as we tried to attend to them'. Once landed at Mudros, the sick were sent on to hospitals in Alexandria or Malta, while 'we set off back again to Gallipoli to pick up more'. As she reflected years later, 'it's the sick I remember . . . pouring with dysentery – sick, miserable, dehydrated and in terrible pain. It was pitiful to see them, so weak, and blood and water pouring out of them. We had medicine that we gave them, but we could really do very little for them'.[61]

Stalemate

The ferrying of the sick and wounded from Gallipoli had soon become a routine, reflecting a wider sense of routine that had settled upon the Anzacs at Gallipoli. Significant fighting lay ahead, as we shall see, as the Turks and Allies in turn tried desperately to gain the upper hand. But the Australians devoted increasing effort to improving their dugouts and trenches, something Sister Wakeford observed 'quite plainly' (as she put it) with the aid of her field glasses from the deck of the *Gascon*.[62] A veritable shantytown grew up on the steep hillsides and among the gullies, while the beach – still under fire – was a myriad collection of stores dumps, field hospitals and divisional headquarters. 'I would just like you to look up our gully and see some of the dugouts our lads have made for themselves', wrote Private Jake Roach to his mother in South Australia, trying to paint a pen-picture of their extraordinary environment. He had just put the finishing touches to his own dugout, he explained, which he hoped was shrapnel-proof, naming it 'Beaumont House', a sophisticated play on words for a hovel that hugged the hillside. He was also amused by the designations given to other troglodyte huts in the vicinity. 'I will just give you the names of some them', he wrote: '"Savoy House", "St Clair", "Pension Rita", "The Wassa", "The Sphinx Hotel", "The Home for Shrapnel"'.[63] As well as attending to their accommodations and defensive positions, the Anzacs worked to perfect their bomb-making (and throwing) skills, and to develop trench periscopes, soon to be indispensable implements in the art and science of trench warfare.

For those at home in Australia, routine was established by the frequent newspaper reports from Gallipoli, with their encouraging stories of Anzac exploits, but also, more disturbingly, the casualty lists which were published with increasing frequency and at growing length. Initially, there was editorial space sufficient to pen short biographies of the wounded – Private Frank Dunt, from Geelong, who sent the cheery message to his parents 'Hope to see you again in the near future', or Sergeant J.H. Hooke, recently accountant at the head office of the Bank of Australasia in Collins Street, Melbourne, who had married Miss Constance Huon on the eve of his departure – but soon such extensive treatment became difficult.[64] Lists became more perfunctory, although obituaries of the fallen often appeared, especially in the many regional papers across Australia, where letters sent home from the front to friends and relations were also published.[65] When the first casualty lists were announced in the press, football match attendance fell off sharply – crowds in Melbourne 'were the smallest for years' – and the 'theatres also suffered'.[66] As the *Traralgon Record* observed, news of the dead, wounded and missing would 'bring home to Australia the grim reality of the struggle that is taking place'.[67] Individual families lived in dread of the clergyman at the door, of the terse telegram bearing its awful news. Those who heard that their son or husband was 'missing' clung with often forlorn hope to the possibility that he might yet be found, perhaps wounded on the battlefield, maybe in a field hospital or on-board ship, or even as a prisoner of war. Only very occasionally did bad news turn to good, as in the case of Private Harry Brain, from Euroa, whose sister 'has received the joyful news that her brother . . . for whom she had been in mourning for a month, he having been killed at Gallipoli, is not dead but in hospital in England, wounded in the throat and hands'.[68]

Yet the stream of casualty reports did not dent Australian commitment to the war. Pride in Australian achievement, complemented now by a desire to avenge those who had fallen at Gallipoli, continued to drive recruitment to the Australian Imperial Force. Across the country, men were encouraged to follow the example of those who had gone before, and many were keen to share in the new Anzac identity. In July and August of 1915, a further 62,289 men volunteered for service, anxious to join the adventure in the Dardenelles which – although they did not yet know it – had gradually ground into a deadly stalemate.[69]

Chapter Three

Heroic Defeat: Withdrawal from Anzac

'WE HAVE BEEN here a month; it seems to me [as] if I must have been born here, and lived in this wretched country all my life'.[1] So wrote Lieutenant (shortly to be Captain) Richard Casey to his father in Australia, in a letter from Gallipoli dated 24 May 1915. It reflected the frustrations shared by many Anzacs, and their pent-up anger in having failed to eject the Turks from their entrenched positions on the heights. Yet if Casey seemed more vexed than most, this was because his superior, Major-General William Bridges – commander of Australian troops ashore, to whom Casey was aide-de-camp – had died of wounds only a few days before. On the morning of Saturday 15 May, General Bridges, with Richard Casey and other staff officers in attendance, had left his headquarters to call on Colonel Chauvel, commander of the recently arrived 1st Light Horse Brigade, which had been sent to Gallipoli as reinforcements and would shortly fight as infantry.

Bridges and his entourage made their way along Monash Valley, where strong sandbag fortifications had been erected as protection against Turkish surveillance and sniper fire. As they neared Steele's Post, they were warned that some stretches ahead were still exposed to the Turks up on Dead Man's Ridge, and that they would need to be careful. Almost immediately, Bridges collapsed with a gunshot wound to his thigh. A battalion medical officer was on hand to stem the flow of blood, otherwise Bridges would have died on the spot. Painstakingly, he was carried down to the beach, and from there evacuated to the hospital ship *Gascon*. He had lost a great deal of blood, and the doctors on-board considered that amputation would certainly kill him. The only hope was that gangrene would not set in. But gangrene was no respecter of rank, and General Bridges died at sea on 18 May. George V had hastily awarded him a knighthood the day before and, unlike the many who were anonymously committed to the deep, Bridges' body was brought back to Melbourne, where he was afforded a hero's funeral and finally laid to rest at Duntroon military college in Canberra.

Many had found General Bridges a taciturn, even unfriendly, individual. Richard Casey was one of the few to have warmed to him, and he was deeply saddened by the loss of the man he had considered a wise mentor and whose advice he had valued so greatly. Bridges' death 'did not surprise me', Casey confided to his father, 'as the medical officer [near Steele's Post] told me shortly after he was hit that it was a serious matter'. But he could scarcely contain his fury at the manner in which Bridges had been struck down: the 'general was a very brave man', he wrote, 'and for him to have been killed by some brute of a skulking sniper seems very hard'. Casey did not hate the enemy. 'I am rather sorry for the unfortunate Turks', he told his father, 'as they are such ragged, miserable looking creatures; and to see a machine gun mowing down a hundred of them as they make a feeble attempt to charge is not an edifying sight'. Yet he thought them a lesser type of human being: 'they are brave in their way', he admitted, 'but I do not think they can have feelings as possess a white man when under fire'. Their officers were 'fairly smart looking', he conceded, but 'there is a tremendous gap between the officer and the man. They encourage themselves by shouting Allah! Allah Mahomet when they advance, to which our men reply in no uncertain voice "Come on, and we'll give you Allah!"'[2]

Not long after Bridges' death, Richard Casey fell seriously ill with paratyphoid, joining the growing throng of sick soldiers being evacuated from Gallipoli. He found himself in the military hospital in Gibraltar, and from there was sent to England for further treatment and eventual recuperation. He later rejoined his battalion in France, where he served with distinction, winning the Distinguished Service Order and Military Cross, as well as being Mentioned in Despatches. He finished the war as a major. Originally from Brisbane in Queensland, and a mining engineer by training, Casey had graduated with a bachelor's degree from Cambridge in 1913. After the war, he took over his father's business in

Melbourne but in a spectacular career became a successful politician, serving at ministerial level under Joseph Lyons and Robert Menzies. He was eventually appointed Governor-General of Australia, 1965–70.

'The man with the donkey'

Equally famous – probably more so – in the annals of Australian history is Private Jack Simpson Kirkpatrick, the celebrated 'man with the donkey' whose exploits at Gallipoli caught the imagination of successive generations of Australians.[3] Just four days after General Bridges had been fatally wounded near Steele's Post, Private Simpson (as he was known), a stretcher-bearer in the 3rd Field Ambulance, was descending Monash Valley with a casualty astride his donkey, when he approached the same dangerously exposed position. A signaller in a nearby dugout called out the customary warning, adding that a Turkish machine-gunner had been sweeping the area all morning. Simpson acknowledged the caution with a cheery wave but as he did so was hit in the back by a bullet, expiring instantly. In that moment, an Australian legend was made.

Born at South Shields on Tyneside, in the north-east of England, Jack Kirkpatrick (as he was then) spoke with the Geordie accent typical of the region, which most Australians found difficult to place, imagining it to be Scottish or possibly Irish, accounting perhaps for two of his several nicknames – 'Scottie' and 'Murphy'. But 'Simmo', as he was also known, an altogether more Australian appellation, was characterized after his death as the archetypal Anzac – a bit of a larrikin, a humourist, an individualist resistant to authority, and, above all, a cobber who would stand by his mates come what may. As a young lad in South Shields, Simpson had earned pocket money during the school holidays by helping to run donkey rides along the beach for visiting holidaymakers, and later he was employed by a dairy, where caring for the horses was among his duties. He was thought then to have 'a way with animals', an important part of the myth that would grow around him at Gallipoli. Like many Geordies from the maritime north-east, Simpson went to sea as soon as he was able. By all accounts, he enjoyed the life but conditions on one vessel were so dire that he (and thirteen others) jumped ship when it docked at Newcastle in New South Wales. At large in Australia, he made initially for the sugar cane region of northern Queensland, working for a time as a cane-cutter and later as a jackaroo (a boundary rider on a cattle station). Soon tiring of these occupations, he cut south to the coalfields of New South Wales, finding work in the mines at Corrimal. Among other things, Simpson was involved in a drunken brawl with a pub landlord, breaking a chair over his head, and although acquitted of assault, he decided it was time to move on again.[4]

Simpson joined the steamship *Kooringa*, serving in this and other coastal vessels until he jumped ship for a second time, at Fremantle in Western Australia in August 1914. Learning that war had broken out, he saw his opportunity to return to England to see his family. Deserting a ship was a serious offence under maritime law, so he quietly dropped 'Kirkpatrick' and joined the Australian Imperial Force simply as 'Jack Simpson'. He trained at Blackboy Hill camp, outside Perth, and was selected as a field ambulance stretcher-bearer. He wrote confidently to his widowed mother Sarah in South Shields: 'My address when I get to England will be Private John Simpson, no 202 C Section, 3 Field Ambulance ... I think we are going to Aldershot when we get to England. So I will be able to come and see you pretty often'. It came as a considerable shock, therefore, when the AIF was redirected to Egypt. Dismayed, he wrote to his mother, complaining that it was Christmas Day (1914) and 'I was look[ing] forward to spending today in [South] Shields but I was doomed to be disappointed'. As he admitted, 'I would not have joined this contingent if I had known that they were not going to England. I would have taken a trip home and had a holiday at home then joined the army'. Still, he had his pet possum, acquired at Blackboy Hill, as his prized companion and unit mascot, a cause of much hilarity among his mates, and although he decided that Egypt was a 'hell hole,' he enjoyed himself to the full in Cairo. Further train-ing awaited at Lemnos, and then 3 Field Ambulance was on its way to the dawn landing at Anzac Cove.[5]

Stretchers were soon in short supply, and, so the story goes, Jack Simpson espied the numerous donkeys that had been landed for trans-portation purposes, and was swift to appreciate their value in ferrying the wounded from the battlefield. He commandeered one of these animals – and several others in the weeks ahead, variously dubbed 'Abdul', 'Murphy' and 'Duffy' – and set about his task with alacrity. He soon established a routine, making a dozen or more trips each day up

Private John Simpson Kirkpatrick (enlisted as Simpson), the celebrated 'man with the donkey', 3rd Field Ambulance Brigade, assisting a wounded soldier at Gallipoli.

AUSTRALIAN WAR MUSEUM J06392

and down Monash Valley and Shrapnel Gully, carrying the casualties to the beach. He earned a reputation for courage and coolness under fire. 'I saw some very brave things at Gallipoli', wrote Albert Facey: 'One thing that made a big impression on us was the actions of a man we called "The Man with a Donkey" . . . That man, Simpson was his name, was exposed to enemy fire constantly all the days I was there, and when I left Shrapnel Gully he was still going strong'.[6] The journalist Ernest Buley, writing shortly after Simpson's death, described his method. 'When the enfilading fire down the valley was at its worst and orders were posted that ambulancemen must not go out', he said, 'the Man and the Donkey continued on placidly at their work. At times they held trenches of hundreds of men spellbound'. The donkey would wait patiently under cover while Simpson crawled out to retrieve the wounded soldier. Then, in 'a lightning dash', Buley continued, Simpson had the man on his back and would disappear into the cover, transferring the injured soldier to his donkey and then heading for safety.[7]

Operating on his own, outside his unit, Simpson's relaxed attitude to orders and discipline created tensions and anxieties. At times he may have been technically absent without leave, although this was not recorded in his service documents, and he was increasingly a law unto himself as he worked up and down Monash Valley and Shrapnel Gully. The Perth *Sunday Times*, reporting Simpson's death, agreed that his 'military position was unorthodox' but insisted that he had been given tacit permission to continue acting alone, as he saw fit.[8] As Colonel John Monash informed Divisional Headquarters on 20 May, having investigated the circumstances of Simpson's demise, 'he belonged to none of the A[rmy] M[edical] C[orps] units with this brigade, but became separated from his own unit, and had carried on his perilous work on his own initiative'.[9] It was an independence of action admired by the Anzacs, and which contributed significantly to his myth.

News of Jack Simpson's death spread quickly. 'It was the evening after the Turkish attack on May 19', wrote Charles Bean, the journalist attached to Anzac forces, in an article that would soon be reprinted countless times in newspapers across Australia – in the Hobart *Mercury*, the Adelaide *Daily Herald*, the Perth *West Australian*, and many more. 'Some of us were sitting yarning that evening whilst the sun set over the sea', continued Bean, 'when someone said: "I suppose you've heard that the man with the donkeys is dead"'. As Bean recounted, it 'came as a real shock. Everybody knew the man with the donkeys, and everybody knew that if ever a man deserved honour in this war it was he'. For nearly four weeks the 'fatalistic' Simpson, who had been given a 'roving commission' by his unit, had braved 'the hottest shrapnel' and the 'aimed bullets of snipers', with shell explosions so close that 'others thought it wise to duck for cover' while 'the man with the donkey went his way as if nothing more serious than a summer shower was happening'.[10] Like Ellis Ashmead-Bartlett's earlier descriptions of the dawn landing (see pp.48–9), it was a report that galvanized Australia.

Inventing Private Simpson

The Perth *Sunday Times*, with a hint of proprietorial pride, noted that Simpson had enlisted in Western Australia and trained at Blackboy Hill, where 'this cheery, brawny, presentable young fellow was cordially welcomed'. But, the paper conceded, Simpson was not actually Australian by birth. He was, instead, a 'tall, well-set, finely figured, clean-cut young Englishman'.[11] There were, of course, a great many soldiers from the United Kingdom serving within the ranks of the AIF, and the boundaries of Britishness and Australian identity were in any case blurred and made indistinct by shared imperial sympathies, kinship and connections. Yet a nascent Australian nationalism was now everywhere apparent, and Private Simpson as Anzac hero was easily subsumed within its purview. Little more than a year after Simpson's death, a valedictory poem appeared in the *Globe and Sunday Times War Pictorial*, published in Sydney. Penned by a fellow Anzac, Corporal Leo J. Fitzgerald, it unselfconsciously represented Simpson as quintessentially and irremediably Australian:

> A lean Australian, sunburnt brown,
> Somewhere Outback lies his native town,
> Proud of its boy who has won renown –
> Private Simpson.[12]

To this element of the myth was added the attribution of saintly qualities, something that jarred with the earlier larrikin reputation but now served to elevate Simpson the hero to new heights – as man of peace, not war. As early as October 1915, the *Western Mail* could include a suitably unctuous verse:

> When Australians, home returning, stirring tales of Anzac tell,
> They shall speak of Private Simpson, and how gallantly he fell,
> Not in conflict fierce of battle, in the roar and din of strife,
> But, with calm devoted courage, tending wounded, saving life.[13]

For Sarah Simpson, her son's death and subsequent canonization were bewildering. From eagerly anticipating his imminent return to England only a few months earlier, she had now to accept that she would not see him again, and that his remains were buried somewhere in a foreign land. Moreover, Jack Simpson was now an Australian hero, an almost 'Christ-like' figure (as Les Carlyon has observed) who had given his life to save others.[14] For Mrs Simpson, there was comfort in the emergent myth, and she was unwittingly drawn into the media circus that had grown up around her son's death. Responding to an inquiry from one Frank Keon, from Melbourne, she wrote to say that she had been 'poorly and broken-hearted' on hearing the tragic news but also greatly encouraged to learn of 'the grand work my dear beloved son has done in Gallipoli'. In her earnestness, she asked Keon to tell all Melbourne that her son was 'the donkey-man of Anzac', and to inform the 'Australians from me, his mother, that my heart is bursting with sorrow and with pride to know that my beloved son, and the light of my life, died with the brave Australians'. He was, she added, 'one of the best and most faithful sons that a mother ever had'.[15] Keon was happy to oblige, of course, passing Sarah Simpson's letter to an eager press, and her moving testament duly became an integral part of Jack's legend.

Journalists such as Ernest Bruley and Charles Bean, with their gift for imaginative writing and instinctive understanding of what made a good story, had done much to create the myth of 'the man with the donkey', and the Australian press had swiftly popularized it, ensuring rapt attention across the country. Yet at Gallipoli itself, there were also those who insisted that Simpson had possessed unique qualities worthy of recognition. 'I considered, and so did my mates', wrote Albert Facey, 'that he should be given the Victoria Cross'.[16] Monash himself, the day after Simpson's death, wrote to Divisional Headquarters to recommend him for a decoration. 'I desire to bring under special notice, for favour of transmission to the proper authority, the case of Private Simpson', he began, going on to explain that this 'man has been working in this valley since 26 April, in collecting the wounded, and carrying them to dressing-stations. He had a small donkey which he used to carry all cases unable to walk'. Monash made it clear that 'Private Simpson and his little beast earned the admiration of everyone at the upper end of the valley. They worked all day and night throughout the whole period since the landing, and the help rendered to the wounded was invaluable'. He continued: 'Simpson knew no fear, and moved unconcernedly amid shrapnel and rifle-fire, steadily carrying out his self-imposed task day by day, and he frequently earned the applause of the personnel for his many fearless rescues of wounded men from areas subject to rifle- and shrapnel-fire'.[17] In the end, Private Simpson was posthumously Mentioned in Despatches. The apparent unwillingness to award a higher decoration has been hotly debated over the years – it may be simply that Simpson's reputation was largely anecdotal, lacking the specific-case detail on which such things normally rest.

Nonetheless, when the commemorative Anzac Medallion (featuring Simpson and his donkey), was struck by the Australian government in 1967 and awarded to all veterans of the Gallipoli campaign, or, if deceased, their next of kin, a special presentation was made to Simpson's surviving sister, Anne Simpson Pearson. In a ceremony at Australia House, on the Strand in London, on the afternoon of 16 May 1967, Anne Pearson received the Anzac Medallion on behalf of her late brother. Fittingly, the award was presented to her by the Governor-General of Australia, Lord Casey, the same Richard Casey who had been with General Bridges when he had been fatally wounded in Monash Valley on 15 May 1915, at almost the same spot where Private Simpson was killed just a few days later. Such are the ironies and coin-cidences of war.

The 'great hulking masses shouting "Allah"'

The 'Turkish attack of 19 May', mentioned by Charles Bean in his report of Simpson's death, had been a concerted attempt to break the stalemate at Gallipoli and drive the Australians and New Zealanders back into the sea. As one Turkish officer later explained, Anzac was chosen for the attack instead of the British positions at Cape Helles because the opposing trenches were closer together and the Australian toeholds were so precarious and perilously close to the sea. If the Anzacs could be swept aside, this would release much-needed Turkish divisions to eject the British (and Indians and French) at Cape Helles. As the officer concluded, the Turks had every 'advantage in making a surprise attack'.[18]

Early in the morning of 19 May, thousands of Turks emerged from their trenches, and swarmed along Second Ridge and 400 Plateau. But, unfortunately for them, the Australians were ready. A further Turkish division had arrived recently from Constantinople to reinforce the existing troops, its movement observed by aerial reconnaissance, and the dwindling of enemy fire on 18 May had alerted the Australians to imminent attack. Accordingly, they stood-to in their trenches at 3 a.m. the next morning, twenty minutes before the Turks launched their assault. Private Walter Stagles recalled that they 'came over in two great waves from their trenches, great hulking masses shouting "Allah" and blowing trumpets, whistling and shouting, like schoolboys'. They quickly drew close, he added, and when 'within nice rifle range we had the order to fire and brought them down in hundreds. Hundreds fell'.[19] Albert Facey had also been ready when the attack came. 'The Turks had to come over a small rise', he explained, 'and our trenches were just below this so that when the enemy appeared they showed out clearly to us'. They were shot down as soon as they were visible, he said: 'My section was rushed a couple of times but we stopped them before they reached us – not one Turk got into our trench'. When daylight broke, there were hundreds of dead and dying in No-Man's Land, 'some only a few yards in front of our firing-line'.[20] By 5 a.m. the main assault was already over, although sporadic attacks continued until 11 a.m. The Turks had suffered some 11,000 casualties, for fewer than 200 Australians killed. As the surviving Turks scrambled back to their own trenches, the Anzacs called after them: 'Play yer again next Saturday'.[21]

Private Lee Pomeroy wrote to his father in South Australia to describe the experience. 'We were attacked on 19 May', he reported, 'and being my first time under fire, I was excited. I was blazing away through the loophole as hard as I could with my rifle . . . when I felt a sharp sting on the top of my head'. Stopping to investigate, Pomeroy discovered a new parting in his hair and a painful graze to his scalp. As he reflected, had 'it been slightly lower I should not be writing this'.[22] Private A. 'Wrinkler' Halliday had a similar encounter with the enemy, as he explained in a letter to his mother. Like Lee Pomeroy, 'Wrinkler' Halliday was among recently arrived reinforcements, and had been at Gallipoli for only eight days when the Turks struck. It was 'about an hour before daylight the Turks attacked us', he wrote: 'We could see nothing but a black moving mass, and we were pouring a terrible rifle and machine gun fire into them'. Then 'suddenly', he added, 'I thought a mule must have kicked me on the side of the head, but it was only an ordinary Turkish bullet, which, just missing my temple, cut the flesh in front of the ear . . . taking about a quarter of the ear with it'. Halliday made light of his wound but it was serious enough for him to be evacuated to Egypt, and from there to England where he was treated in hospital in Manchester. Cheerful as ever, he wrote to his mother on 9 July: 'My wound is all healed up now, and all that can be noticed is a scar across the top part of my face and a piece out of my ear'.[23]

Everywhere the Australian line had held firm under Turkish attack, but in a few places it had been a close-run thing. Private Garnet Rundle, an ironmonger from Brighton, Tasmania, described how:

One big Turk had managed to crawl up through the dense undergrowth till he was only yards – in fact, feet – off the trench. He then stood up and lit a grenade. One of our chaps spotted him, and picking up a shovel let fly, knocking the grenade out of the Turk's hand, the latter getting the full benefit of the subsequent explosion. Result: Finish of Turk.[24]

Private Henry Barnes had been at Quinn's Post during the attack, that most precarious of Australian positions, where the opposing trenches were just feet apart and where the two sides had already resorted to tunnelling and counter-tunnelling to try to dislodge each other with explosives. As he explained, the Turks almost broke through: 'There was one he came over bawling some Moslem phrase and he was shot by me and the fellow next to me – two or three shot at the same time – he came through practically on top of my bayonet, right on top of me'. The dead Turk proved too heavy to be lifted from the trench while the Australians remained under fire. 'Literally', said Barnes, 'I sat on that Turk for days, ate my lunch sitting on him!'[25]

At Courtney's Post, another exposed position, the Turks did break through, albeit only momentarily. Seven had bombed their way into a trench-bay where they were now stuck, hemmed in by Australian fire from the adjoining communication trench. Private Albert Jacka, a forestry worker from Wedderburn in Victoria, volunteered with four others to flush them out. Together they rushed headlong into the trench, bayonets fixed, but two of the Australians were immediately wounded. Quickly adopting a better tactic, the remaining Australians distracted the Turks, while Jacka climbed out into No-Man's Land and attacked them from behind. He shot five and bayoneted two, thus securing Courtney's Post for the Australians. It was an act of outstanding courage, and a vital contribution to the holding of the Australian line, for which he was awarded the Victoria Cross – news of which came through when he was on the island of Imbros, recovering from dysentery. Jacka was of Cornish descent, as the *People's Weekly* at Moonta in the Cornish-dominated copper-mining region of South Australia was swift to note. 'The first V.C. to come to Australia', it reported proudly, 'was won by ... [a] Cornishman in the person of Lance-Corporal Jacka', a reminder that within the emerging Australian national identity, regional distinctiveness remained important.[26]

AUSTRALIAN WAR MEMORIAL A02868A

Private Albert Jacka, 14th Battalion, Australian Imperial Force, won Australia's first Victoria Cross, for the defence of Courtney's Post, Gallipoli, on 19 May 1915. He finished the war as a captain (as depicted here), having also won a Military Cross and Bar.

Further decorations and promotions came Jacka's way (he was reckoned to have killed twenty Germans at Pozières in 1916); before the war's end he had risen to the rank of captain and won a Military Cross and Bar. Indeed, after the heroic defence of Courtney's Post, a certain mystique grew up around Albert Jacka. '"Have you seen him yet?" was on all lips', wrote Edgar Rule, 'the man who could point out Jacka seemed to swell with importance. Rule added, in admiration, 'To me, Jacka looked the part; he had medium-sized body, a natty figure, and a determined face and a crooked nose'. For those new reinforcements allotted to D Company, 14th Battalion, there was 'a thrill of self-esteem', for Jacka would become their sergeant-major. His straightforward approach to discipline was much appreciated by his men. Instead of 'criming' them for a misdemeanour, and reporting them to an officer, he would offer his own form of summary punishment. 'I won't crime you', he would say, 'I'll give you a punch on the bloody nose'. High decoration and promotion did not alter Jacka's down-to-earth attitude to soldiering, according to Rule, and 'the whole of the A.I.F. came to look upon him as a rock of strength that never failed. We of the 14th Battalion never ceased to be thrilled when we heard ourselves referred to . . . by passing units on the march as "some of Jacka's mob"'.[27]

'You must not think the Turk an untrained soldier or a coward'

After the slaughter of 19 May, there was the immediate problem of dealing with the swiftly decomposing corpses that littered No-Man's Land. Attempts to clear some of the bodies from the vicinity of the Australian trenches had drawn Turkish fire, resulting in casualties. Likewise, when the Turks came out under their Red Crescent flag to bring in the dead, they too were fired upon for fear that this activity masked a massing of troops in the enemy trenches for another assault. Sensibly, formal talks on 20 May, conducted by Sir Ian Hamilton and Liman von Sanders (the German commanding Turkish forces at Gallipoli), resulted in a temporary armistice. It was to last nine hours. Henry Barnes, who had been in the desperate struggle at Quinn's Post, was glad of the opportunity to see the Turks face-to-face, without trying to kill each other. He offered a tin of bully-beef to one Turk, 'who smiled and seemed very pleased', and was given a string of dates in exchange. All along the line, the Australians were impressed with the quality and humanity of the Turks they met in No-Man's Land that day. 'Jacko, as we called the Turkish soldier, was very highly regarded by me and all the men on our side', Barnes recorded: 'he was always a clean fighter and one of the most courageous men in the world'. As he concluded, when 'we met them at the armistice we came to the conclusion that he was a very good bloke indeed'.[28]

Royce Spinkston, from Adelaide, agreed. 'You must not think the Turk an untrained soldier or a coward', he wrote home. 'Many of them reached within a few feet of our trenches before they were finally dropped. . . .The bulk of those whom we have taken prisoner or buried have been remarkably well supplied with food and ammunition. They are mostly fine-looking chaps'.[29] There were one or two deserters, which amused Garnet Rundle. 'One chap was allowed to come in', he said, 'shouting out in English "Sieda (Good morning); don't shoot; war finish". Didn't he tickle our boys and wasn't the old Turk glad to get on the right side at last'. But Rundle too thought that on 'the whole the Turks are a good stamp of men, well equipped, but very poorly dressed, and all much dirtier looking than we are, which is saying a fair amount'.[30] The armistice itself was punctiliously observed, a report in the *Sydney Morning Herald* noting merely 'one incident'. A Turkish soldier had picked up an Australian grenade on the battlefield and decided to pocket it as a souvenir, running towards his lines to secure his prize. The Australians, observing this breach of protocol, were mightily impressed when a 'Turkish officer took up the chase, and having caught the soldier administered a good kicking and brought the bomb to our staff officer and handed it to him with many bows'. Again, it was agreed that on 'the whole Turkish soldiers are gentlemen', and there was especial regard for the work of the imams, who buried their dead 'in accordance with Mohammedan rites'. As one Australian noted wryly: 'Our enemies expect more from their chaplains (imams) than we do'.[31]

Yet despite this growing respect for 'Johnny Turk' – or 'Jacko' or 'Abdul' as he was variously called – there was now a settled opinion among the Australians that they had 'established individual dominance in bayonet charges'. According to Private W. Brede, in a letter to his relations at Geraldton in Western Australia, written on 11 June, several weeks after the assault of 19 May, the 'Turks are fairly quiet just at present, as they are afraid of the White Gurkhas, as the Australians are called'.[32] It was a new nickname, but one that stuck. Three months later, Eddie Cairns, from Ardrossan in South Australia, recorded in his diary: 'The Turks call us "White Gurkhas" and will not face a bayonet if an Australian is behind it'. Intriguingly, Cairns also noted that: 'Our chaps are great "cobbers" with the Gurkhas here, and they will give anything to an Australian'. They were 'great fighters', he said, 'and make splendid soldiers . . . fearing neither God nor man. They dearly love to be in a charge with the Australian boys'.[33]

In fact, the relative quiet in the Turkish lines after 19 May was not merely a new-found fear of the Anzacs' Gurkha-like qualities. The scale of their losses and their failure everywhere to break through had led to a more nuanced Turkish appreciation of the strengths and weaknesses of the Australian and New Zealand positions. Precarious they might be, but they would not be easily overrun by massed waves in a frontal attack, and the Anzacs could not be simply brushed aside or swept back into the sea. But the Australians too, for all their bravado, had acquired a new admiration for their foe, and a healthy respect for their soldierly abilities and resources, including manpower, provisions, ammunition and weaponry. Many had heard before that the Turks were armed merely with ancient muskets. Royce Spinkston was one of those surprised and impressed to find that the Turkish 'rifles, the [German]

Mauser, are splendid little weapons'.[34] The Australians also realized that, despite the heavy casualties that had been inflicted on the enemy, they were no closer to taking the elusive heights above. Indeed, they had no plan for a counter-attack, and singularly failed to capitalize on the stunning blow they had dealt the Turks.

Turkish morale, after the decimation of 19 May, was considerably improved a few days later when the German submarine *U-21* torpedoed HMS *Triumph* off Anzac Cove just after noon on 25 May 1915. The Turks cheered as the Allies looked on in dismay. Colonel Price Weir, commanding the 10th Battalion, wrote to his father describing the disaster. 'Just after we sat down to dinner [lunch] on May 25', he observed, 'we heard a report and saw smoke issuing from the battleship Triumph. We at once concluded that something was wrong'. Destroyers and launches had gathered round the stricken warship and, with the aid of his binoculars, Price Weir saw 'hundreds of men on the deck of the Triumph'. It was an extraordinary sight, he reported to his father: 'During the 15 minutes, in which I never took my glasses off the Triumph, I watched her gradually list and list until at 12.15 she turned right upside down and remained keel uppermost until 12.50, when she disappeared altogether'. It was, he said, 'an awful calamity to see so magnificent a boat sent to the bottom in less than an hour'.[35] Others blinked in disbelief at the ship 'upside down, with her red hull gleaming in the sun', and one light horseman, guessing that this was the work of a submarine, cried out in anger and frustration: 'They've got her. Blast the German cows [*sic*]'.[36] Price Weir turned resignedly to other matters, as he concluded his letter: 'Glad to hear the drought has completely broken up in South Australia. If we could only break up the war things would be alright, wouldn't they?'[37]

Two days after the loss of the *Triumph*, *U-21* scored its second direct hit, sinking the battleship HMS *Majestic* off Cape Helles. All major warships were now withdrawn from the immediate vicinity, only venturing back when their heavy guns were required for specific tasks. It was a catastrophe that seemed to hark back to the Dardenelles débâcle of 18 March, and caught the same rapt attention in Australia. The Adelaide *Register*, the *Sydney Morning Herald* and all the other big metropolitan dailies carried banner headlines; so too did the provincial press across the country, the *Gundagai Times* (for example) reporting the sombre news on 1 June.[38] Perhaps encouraged by their German ally's success

at sea, the Turks carried out a localized attack at Quinn's Post on
29 May, in the early hours of the morning, setting off a tremendous
underground explosion. It took the rest of the day to clear those Turks
who had been able to penetrate the Australian trenches in the aftermath of the blast, and one of those killed in the attempt was Major
Hugh Quinn himself, the accountant and amateur boxing champion
from northern Queensland after whom the position had been named.
Thereafter, as both sides began to recognize that even small initiatives
could be extremely costly in lives lost, activity settled into the relative
quietude described by Private Brede. It was a respite that many welcomed. Captain Giles, from South Australia, for example, admitted
that 'I long for peace, for I am sick of this killing business; but I must go
on while it lasts'. His 'constant prayer is for peace', he confessed, 'so that
I may return to dear old Australia again and settle down for a quiet life'.
But he recognized that those under his command were more pragmatic
and fatalistic: 'Our boys treat the whole thing as a huge joke, and shoot
Turks with as little compunction as I would a rabbit under ordinary
conditions, and laugh if he happens to yell if they get him'.[39]

Lone Pine

Meanwhile, the action at Gallipoli had switched to the British, Indian
and French sectors at Cape Helles, where battles raged throughout June
and July. Unfortunately, however, this renewed effort at Cape Helles
failed to produce the breakthrough that Sir Ian Hamilton had sought,
and so he was persuaded to turn his attention once more to the stalemate at Anzac. He decided upon a big push. General Birdwood, his
deputy in charge of the Anzac Corps, was painfully aware that a broad
frontal attack – such as the Turks had attempted so disastrously on 19
May – would fail. But he also knew that parts of the Turkish line were
fragmented and weakly held, and advised that they would be vulnerable
to more targeted assaults. Disheartened by the reverses at Cape Helles
but encouraged by news from London that additional divisions were on
their way to Gallipoli, Hamilton came up with a new plan. Operations
would commence on 6 August with a diversionary attack on the enemy
positions at Lone Pine, on the Anzac right flank. The main thrust,
meanwhile, would be to the left, designed to capture the heights of Sari

AUSTRALIAN WAR MEMORIAL H03547

Queenslanders of the 7th Battery, Australian Artillery, rest after action at Lone Pine, Gallipoli.

Bair Ridge – taking Chunuk Bair, Koja Chemen Tepe and other prom-inent positions – before sweeping south to link up with another assault from The Nek against Battleship Hill and Baby 700. While all this was going on, the fresh divisions would be landed at Suvla Bay, their imme-diate task being to secure the beach and its vicinity, establishing it as a bridgehead from which subsequent operations could be launched, once the Anzacs had captured the Sari Bair Ridge.

Lone Pine has survived in popular collective memory as the most savage of all the battles at Gallipoli, a vicious struggle of kill or be killed in the defensive subterranean world the Turks had created for themselves, a labyrinth of galleries, passages and tunnels roofed over with massive timbers. The Australians had also prepared in depth, creating a secret underground trench system which would allow them to approach the Turkish lines unobserved. At 4.30 p.m. on 6 August 1915, the Allied artillery opened fire, designed to distract the attention of the Turks as the Australians massed in their trenches, ready for the attack an hour later. Precisely on time, the Australians emerged from their hidden positions, achieving complete surprise. The Turks had considered their fortifications at Lone Pine impregnable, and were nonplussed at the sudden appearance of the Australians in their midst. Major Carl Jess recalled how at first the Anzacs 'were hopping about on top trying to pull logs off to get into the Turks, poking their rifles into the loopholes and firing'. But once 'they got in the slaughter was tremendous'.[40] Bayoneting and bombing, kicking and biting and gouging and throttling, the two sides were quite literally at each other's throats for the two full days that the battle raged. In some of the most hideous hand-to-hand combat in the Gallipoli campaign, horrific injuries were inflicted in all manner of ways; entrenching tools smashing skulls or severing windpipes, bare hands popping eyes and ripping open cheeks and jaws.

Private John Gammage, from the 1st Battalion, was in the initial assault at Lone Pine. 'The moans of our own men and also Turks as we tramped on their wounded bodies was awful', he wrote, and in places the injured were 'piled up 3 and 4 deep . . . their pleas for mercy were not heeded'.[41] Later, 'I got one most daring Turk from twelve yards off who was throwing bombs . . . We felt like wild beasts but were calm and never fired reckless but deliberate'. James Croker, from Devon, who had emigrated to the Kalgoorlie goldfields in 1910, was also in the thick of it. 'We was like a mob of ferrets in a rabbit-hole', he said, 'I was blood all down the side of me face where the bottom part of me right ear got took off by a bullet . . . And I was blood up to me other wrist from where it splashed out of a Johnny [Turk] when I put the bayonet in. I never reckoned to get out of there'.[42] Sergeant Lawrence, an engineer, one of those who had helped construct the Australian assault tunnels, came forward to work on what would become the new frontline trenches. As he did so, he stumbled across a huddle of Australian wounded in a Turkish passageway. 'These fellows have been crouched up in here all night', he exclaimed. 'some of their wounds are so awful yet they sit there not saying a word, certainly not complaining . . . One had been shot clean through the chest and his singlet and tunic are just saturated with blood, another has his nose and upper lip shot clean away'. Lying nearby, he added, was a man who 'had been wounded somewhere in the head, as he breathed the blood just bubbled and frothed at his nose and mouth'.[43]

Sergeant R.G. Baynes, in a letter to a friend working on the Silverton Tramway, near Broken Hill, wrote with ironic understatement that 'We have had a little bit of fighting . . . It was pretty hot while it lasted, and the Turks suffered a good deal, while we had a lot of wounded, mostly about the head and legs, caused by bombs. The enemy seem to have plenty of bombs'. As he reflected on his own experiences, Baynes tried to convey something of the terror and fever of an infantry charge, although he understood that those at home, those who had not partic-ipated in such an attack, could never really appreciate its intensity and savagery. 'It is impossible to realise what a charge is like', he explained: 'Once you leave your own trenches all you think about is getting to close quarters. Of course, we are under fire as soon as we leave'.[44] He went on:

> When you get to the other [enemy] trench, most of those whom our bombardment have not killed are shifted back to the next trench. From this they start to give us bombs like hailstones. It is useless to stay in the first trench . . so the enemy have to be shifted from the other trench. It is generally only a few yards away so that you are no sooner out of one trench than you are into the next. As soon as you see a man opposite you, your eyes see red and you go mad.[45]

He added:

> All the advantage is with the attackers. Those in the trench can only shoot; they cannot use the bayonet, and the man who hesitates is lost. The worst part is after it is all over and you see your bayonet dripping red. Then you begin to think what you have gone through. It is just like doing a thing when you are drunk and waking up next morning and looking about you – some of them are laughing and some crying.[46]

It took extreme courage to prevail amidst such appalling violence and mayhem, a measure of which was the award of seven Victoria Crosses at Lone Pine. As one Australian officer wrote: 'The sights in the Lone Pine works were too terrible for words, so I won't describe that at all, but the way those chaps took the trenches, and the way they held on, was the equal of any feat of arms ever accomplished'.[47] As Les Carlyon has observed, the background of the Victoria Cross winners at Lone Pine is a valuable insight into the make-up of Australian society at the time. One might add, too, that here were merely ordinary men of ordi-nary origin, who had found themselves in an extraordinary place, and were capable of doing extraordinary things. There was Lance-Corporal Leonard Keysor, a London Jew who had emigrated to Sydney just before the war broke out, and later returned to England. There was Captain Alfred Shout, from Wellington in New Zealand, a Boer War veteran who had settled in Sydney in 1907, and three countrymen from rural Victoria, all 'of Cornish stock'[48] – Lieutenant William Symons, Captain Frederick Tubb and Corporal William Dunstan – together with Private John Hamilton, a butcher's boy before the war, and Corporal Alexander Burton from Euroa, Victoria, who had joined up with Captain Tubb. Tubb had been a farmer (and was killed in Flanders in 1917), Dunstan had worked in a draper's store (and later went on to become a senior newspaperman), and Symons was a grocer's clerk before joining up. Burton died at Lone Pine, killed by a bomb blast in the fight for which he was awarded his Victoria Cross. Alfred Shout expired a few days later, aged thirty-three, having lost both hands and an eye.

For all its ghastly horror, Lone Pine was an Australian victory. When the last of the Turkish counter-attacks had petered out by 10 August, the Anzacs still held the territory they had captured. It had been a well-planned operation, and executed with valour, determination and resolution. In the aftermath of the battle, Captain Ivor Margetts, a schoolmaster from Hobart in Tasmania, surveyed the scene. It looked and smelt 'just like a slaughter house in the cleanest parts', he said, 'in others it is impossible to describe the smell'. There were, he added, 'dead bodies . . . stacked in heaps in places where there was available room and in other parts where there was no room they were left in the floor of the trench and covered with a thin layer of earth and made a soft spongy floor to walk on'.[49]

Among those left for dead with the heaped bodies at Lone Pine was Private Leigh Lennell, from Moonta in South Australia, who was duly reported as 'killed in action'. Only as Margetts and others combed the battlefield was he found to be alive, with a corrective telegram sent at once to his distraught widowed mother in Australia. Thrilled to learn that her son had been discovered among the living, she wired the Base Records Office, the military authorities in Melbourne: 'MOTHER SENDS GREETINGS. ANXIOUS WELFARE. LOVE MRS E. LENNELL MOONTA MINES'. But it was not until she received a letter from the Revd H. Pennerley Dodd, Wesleyan chaplain at Malta, that the full details of her son's injuries became clear. It transpired that Leigh Lennell had been evacuated from Gallipoli in the transport *Dunluce Castle*, undergoing emergency surgery en route in which he lost his shattered right arm. 'It was amputated to save his life', Pennerley Dodd explained, 'and the Drs removed it on the boat whilst he was coming to this island'. The chaplain was pleased to report that Lennell 'is in no great pain' and 'is most cheerful', and he promised to do all he could to 'assist him in any way possible'. Comforted and reassured by the kind words of H. Pennerley Dodd, Mrs Lennell was overjoyed when, after an extended convalescence in Britain, Leigh eventually arrived home – complete with artificial arm – to a hero's welcome in May 1916. In the following November he was married to Violet May Anderson of Broken Hill. As Lennell admitted, with some embarrassment, the loss of his arm had been a blessing in disguise. At 'times I think it was worth losing a limb for', he confessed. 'Nearly all my mates were killed' at Lone Pine, he reflected, and he was amazed to still be alive.[50]

The Nek

Also in military hospital in Malta was one Signaller Cuttris. He too had been in action during Hamilton's big push, attached to the (dismounted) Otago Mounted Rifles, New Zealanders who were part of the main thrust to capture the Sari Bair Ridge. Together with the New Zealand Mounted Rifles Brigade, the Otago Mounted Rifles were tasked with the seizure of Chunuk Bair. To their left, the (dismounted) 3rd Australian Light Horse Brigade, together with Gurkhas and troops from British units, were to capture Koja Chemen Tepe. Having taken their objectives, the combined force would then complete the seizure of the Sari Bair Ridge by moving south to coincide with an attack at The Nek, conducted from existing Anzac positions. As night fell on 6 August, the New Zealanders began their assault. Signaller Cuttris described their progress. 'Well, we had to sweep Turks off . . . two ridges and hold the second', he wrote, and as they did so, the Turks 'started yelling "Allah! Allah!" and some other gibberish. Such a row you never heard'. The New Zealanders responded with 'cheer after cheer from all directions as trench after trench was taken by the colonials'.[51] They were making headway but it was much slower than anticipated, and they were now badly behind schedule. The thrust on their left had made similar progress, slower than expected but securing initial objectives. However, the delays were compounded by further mishaps

– at one point the Canterbury Battalion became hopelessly lost – and missed opportunities, and although the increasingly exhausted troops fought with determination, they were held off by fierce Turkish counter-attacks. As Turkish positions were reinforced, so it was increasingly clear that the ambitious Allied plan had failed.

Part of this failure had been the inability of the main thrust to support the operation at The Nek. By early morning on 7 August, it was clear that if the planned attack from Anzac positions across The Nek to take Baby 700 hill was to go ahead, it would do so without this assistance. Deciding that an assault at The Nek would at least have the advantage of tying down Turkish troops while the main force attempted to take its objectives, Birdwood gave the difficult order to proceed. At 4 a.m. a mighty bombardment was unleashed on the Turkish positions at The Nek, a narrow causeway where No-Man's Land was at best sixty yards wide. It was timed to last for just thirty minutes. The moment the bombardment ceased, the first of four 150-man waves from the 8th and 10th Australian Light Horse would rise from the trenches and charge the Turkish lines. Unaccountably, at 4.23 a.m. (according to Light Horse watches) the artillery suddenly fell silent, a failure, perhaps, of synchronization but also an opportunity for the scattered Turks to return to their trenches and mount their machine guns. Recalling the incident almost a decade later, Lieutenant Wilfred Robinson described the consternation in the Anzac trenches. 'For a few moments no one spoke', he said, the officers wondering if the artillery planned to 'give them a heavy burst to finish'. But it was soon clear that there was to be no final flourish. Preparing to go over the top, Robinson added, 'I got my men ready and shook hands with Major Redford a few seconds before he leaped out. He remarked as he did so: "See you later Robbie".'[52]

The first wave was cut down the moment it left the trenches. Lieutenant-Colonel Alex White, commanding officer of the 8th, went over with his men, wearing a chain and locket containing photographs of his wife and baby. He ran eight or nine paces before he was hit, fatally. Major Tom Redford also fell, shot through the brain. 'He died with a soft sigh and laid his head gently on his hands as if tired', wrote Corporal William McGrath.[53] One of the few survivors from the first wave, Sergeant Cliff St Pinnock, recalled that 'we got over and cheered but they were waiting ready for us and simply gave us a solid wall of lead'. As he explained, 'I was in the first line to advance and we did not get ten yards. Every one fell like lumps of meat . . . I got mine shortly after I got over the bank and it felt like a million ton hammer falling on my shoulder.'[54] Private Jack Dale, another survivor, had also made little headway before he was hit, writing later to his mother that 'the Turks opened up on us with murderous machine gun fire. It was terrific and I have never heard anything like it. Those of us who got over the very slight rise of ground were simply mown down'.[55]

At 4.32 a.m. the second wave went over the top. Captain Leslie 'George' Hore and his men had listened to the cacophony of fire that had met the first charge, and 'we knew we were doomed. We saw our fate in front of us but we were pledged to go and to their eternal credit, the word being given, not a man in the second line stayed in his trench'.[56] Suffering a flesh wound to his shoulder as he ran, Hore got within forty yards of the enemy trenches before he slumped down, taking refuge behind a dead Turk. Later, having been hit for a second time, he decided to inch his way back to the Australian trenches, and survived. With the 8th Light Horse, from Victoria, having been almost annihilated in the first two waves, it was now the turn of the Western Australians in the 10th. The regiment's commanding officer, Lieutenant-Colonel Noel Brazier, having witnessed the slaughter of the 8th, made haste to Brigade headquarters at 4.40 a.m. to have the attack called off. There he encountered the brigade-major, Lieutenant-Colonel John Antill, known to all and sundry as the 'Bullant' on account of his bullying and hectoring manner. Insisting that an Australian marker flag had been seen in a Turkish trench, signifying a breakthrough, he angrily rebuked Brazier and told him to 'push on'. Brazier returned to his line. 'I'm sorry lads', he said, 'but the order is to go'.[57]

'Goodbye cobber, God bless you', said Trooper Harold Rush, turning to his mate, and at 4.45 a.m. the third wave leapt from the trenches.[58] It too was shot down within moments. By now Brazier had found the brigade commander, Colonel Frederick Hughes, who appeared to dither. But even as he did so, Antill demanded that the fourth wave attack, and hearing the command relayed by a staff officer who inquired hotly as to why they had not gone, the right flank rose from the trenches and commenced its charge before it could be halted. It too was mown down; only then was the futile attack at last called off. Bewildered and dejected, Noel Brazier returned to the line, thinking for a moment that he was the sole survivor of his regiment, as he looked about his empty

AUSTRALIAN WAR MEMORIAL G01330

Lieutenant-Colonel John Antill, brigade-major of the 3rd Australian Light Horse, photographed in characteristic pose by the journalist Charles Bean at Rhododendron Spur, Gallipoli. Known as the 'Bullant' (after an aggressive species of Australian ant), Antill was the anti-hero of The Nek.

trench in amazement. But soon survivors began to trickle in, and he was relieved when he found those men from the 10th that happily had not participated in the final charge. Shortly after, the 9th Light Horse arrived to secure the otherwise defenceless Anzac positions against the possibility of a Turkish counter-attack. By any measure, the battle at The Nek was a catastrophe. The military authorities tried to play down the scale of the disaster, and for a while it was hushed up. But on 19 September the Perth *Daily News* broke the story. 'Grave news received from Gallipoli', it reported: 'Disaster to Light Horse'.[59]

He 'will get to Constantinople all the same'

While the traumas of Lone Pine and The Nek had played out, the fresh British 10th and 11th divisions had arrived at Suvla Bay, north of Anzac Cove, landing at night on 6 August. The initial plan, as noted previously, was to consolidate the beach area as a base from which future operations could be conducted, once the Sari Bair Ridge had been taken. But the ridge was never captured, and as the Australians and New Zealanders fought and died at Lone Pine, Chunuk Bair and The

Nek, so word reached them that the newly arrived British were idling on the beach, brewing tea. It seemed to confirm all they had heard about the hesitancy and inefficiency of the British troops – and the ineffectualness of their commanders – and so another part of the Anzac myth was born: the 'tea party' at Suvla Bay. In fact, as we know, the new British divisions had not been expected to support the Anzac assaults of 6 and 7 August. But in Anzac eyes the new arrivals had failed to come to their assistance in their hour of need. Private Melville Pethick, from South Australia, explained that what 'turned us against them was through our boys getting cut up at Gallipoli through the Tommies refusing to reinforce them'.[60] Private Stan Carbery, from Gilgandra in New South Wales, agreed, writing from Gallipoli in the aftermath of the Suvla Bay landings. 'Nothing is so welcome as a troopship loaded with Australians', he exclaimed, but 'My experience of the "Tommies" is that they are useless. They make wharf labourers out of them here'.[61]

Frustration with imagined British inertia was part of a wider exasperation that Hamilton's big push had failed to dislodge the Turks from the heights, and that after so much effort and so much bloodshed the stalemate at Gallipoli had been resumed. But still reinforcements kept coming. Private Eddie Cairns, for example, arrived at night on 10 September, going ashore the next morning at Watson's Pier, the improvised jetty at Anzac Cove. Within the first few hours he was introduced to the ubiquitous presence of Turkish sniper fire, as he recorded in his diary, and to the strange delight of bathing in the cove while shells whistled to and fro overhead. The following morning, Eddie and the other stretcher-bearers in his unit collected their kit, and made their way to the front. 'I will never forget the trip either', he wrote, astonished at the steepness and rugged nature of the ascent. As he put it: 'We had to go up a communicating trench in a ravine and it was heartbreaking work climbing the steep hills with a full pack, blanket, rifle, 150 rounds of ammunition, stretchers . . . and I was deadbeat when we got to the top'. Within hours, Cairns was busy at work. 'A Turkish sniper got a couple of chaps', he recorded, they 'were on top of the hill cooking their dinner and happened to be in his line of fire . . . Two from the 28th were shot dead, Bugler Colgate being shot through the heart'. With the help of his mate Joe Timperon, Eddie Cairns carried poor Colgate up to the 28th lines for burial in their impromptu cemetery.[62]

Snipers remained a constant threat in the days ahead. On the morning of 17 September, for example, Cairns and Joe Timperon went to collect firewood, and 'a Turkish sniper had a couple of shots at us, but did not bag any game'. Shortly after, C Company's commander, Captain J.W. Blacket, 'a very good officer' in Cairn's estimation, fell victim to a sniper's bullet. Lance-Corporal Mayman, standing alongside, was also killed. Shrapnel was likewise an ever-present problem, especially when the Turks shelled their position. 'Last night,' Cairns wrote on Wednesday 6 October, 'Evans from "D" Company was hit in the hand . . . About 9.30 this morning the Turks again shelled our camp, wounding 3 or 4 chaps'. As he reflected: 'Being a Stretcher Bearer is not necessarily a pleasant task . . . with bleeding men and bodies shattered . . . bullets whizzing around your ears'.[63]

Yet Eddie Cairns remained intensely positive and optimistic. 'My word', he wrote on Thursday 7 October, 'our boys have got a stiff proposition ahead of them and I am tipping that this war is not going to end too early'. Surveying the heights, he acknowledged the inherent strength of the Turkish positions at Gallipoli, describing 'the natural strongholds the Turks have in these hills'. But it was only a matter of time, he considered, before the Anzacs finally broke through. The formidable ridges that dominated the skyline 'make no difference to the Australian soldier', he insisted, 'he will get to Constantinople all the same even if the devil tries to stop him'.[64] The very next day, Friday 8 October, Eddie Cairns and fellow stretcher-bearer Harold Caseldine went to the aid of two soldiers hit by a burst of shrapnel. As they did so, a second shell landed in exactly the same spot, and Eddie and his mate Harold were killed instantly.

'I am very proud to say I am an Australian'

Alas, there was to be no breakthrough to Constantinople, and it became increasingly apparent that withdrawal was the only option. Harry McAufille wrote home to Dubbo in New South Wales on 22 October. 'I am still alive and kicking', he observed with the wry and fatalistic humour that had come to typify the Australian troops at Gallipoli, 'and I hope to be kicking for a long time yet. I am enjoying the best of health at present', he continued, 'but a fellow never knows when they will push him off the map'. As he explained, he was 'not 70 yards from the Turkish trenches. When they get a bit closer we will be able to exchange biscuits with them. They often send us a postcard in the shape of a bomb or shell, and they don't have to wait long for an answer'. McAuliffe also reported the marked change of weather, the heat of late summer having given way to the chill of autumn. 'The cold weather is setting in', he wrote, 'and we are told it gets fairly cool here. We are all comfortable in our underground homes, and have been supplied with Sheep skin vests, which are a valuable item here'. Yet he did not relish the prospect of Gallipoli in winter: 'I would like to be with you at Christmas, but I'm afraid I can't as Abdul and his friends wish us to be near them on that occasion'.[65]

Roy Perkins, from South Australia, had noted in late August that the 'days are getting very short and the nights very cold here. I don't know when winter sets in', he wrote, or when 'snow falls on the hills'. But he realized that it 'will be very hard for us then'.[66] Thomas Pedler, another South Australian, thought the same. 'The weather is becoming very cold here', he reported: 'We are told it snows here in winter, but as yet none has fallen'.[67] By the end of November, however, blizzards swept the Gallipoli peninsula. The prospect of maintaining the Allied toehold in such conditions was simply untenable. Lord Kitchener visited Anzac on 13 November, and decided the position was too precarious and too small to be held indefinitely. A new wave of sickness led to the evacuation of 16,000 incapacitated men, while others froze to death at exposed outposts or drowned in the now freezing sea.

On 7 December the word was given to pull out. Gradually, the troops were spirited away from Anzac and Suvla Bay, until only a rump of 20,000 remained to cover the two final nights of the evacuation. In an elaborate ruse to confuse the Turks, troops were landed constantly to give the impression of continual reinforcement, only to be taken off again at night. For the final moments of the evacuation, self-firing rifles were set up, their triggers set to activate automatically by attaching them to tins that would overbalance when heavy enough, having been filled drip by drip from other tins. As one soldier explained: 'We rigged up a can of water which dripped into another underneath and that was attached to the trigger of a gun. As it dripped down, the weight increased and it pulled the trigger. It sounded like continuous firing. You put more water in some than others so that it fired sooner'.[68] At

Anzac the last boat-load left the shore at 4 a.m. on 20 December 1915, the final one from Suvla departing slightly after 5 a.m. Altogether, 83,048 officers and men, 186 guns and 4,695 animals had been removed by stealth, with no casualties. Harry McAuliffe might not be home for Christmas but he and all his mates had managed to sneak away from the embrace of 'Abdul and his friends'. At Cape Helles they had to wait a little longer. The evacuation was not complete until 9 January, a close-run thing after a determined Turkish assault was beaten by the British just two days earlier.

Some 7,600 Australians had been killed at Gallipoli and 18,500 wounded, along with 2,400 New Zealanders killed and 5,000 wounded. Inevitably, the withdrawal was met with mixed feelings. It was a defeat, which hurt, and there was anguished disappointment that all that effort had been to no avail, that 'those narrow acres so hardly won and that all those graves of our people so long defended would soon be in Turkish hands'.[69] But there was also pride in the Australian achievement, and a feeling that the embryonic Australian nation had demonstrated its worth at Gallipoli, enhancing its place in the British Empire and earning the respect and gratitude of the mother country. For some, indeed, there was a newfound sense of undisguised supe-riority. As 'Wrinkler' Halliday wrote to his mother: 'I am very proud to say I am an Australian. The Englishman is all right and a very decent and plucky chap, but he hasn't got the spirit and freedom of the Australian'.[70]

Chapter Four

Half a World Away: Australia's Home Front

MORE THAN 10,000 Anzacs had been killed during the eight months of the Gallipoli campaign, just under 7,600 of them Australians, the remainder New Zealanders. A further 23,000 had been wounded, many of them seriously, leading often to permanent incapacity for men who had lost limbs or suffered other appalling injuries. For those who survived, there was the daunting prospect of further active service in other theatres of war in the months and years ahead. Britain's Prime Minister, Herbert Asquith, would later claim – despite the failure to dislodge the Turks or capture Constantinople, let alone eject Turkey from the war – that the Dardenelles campaign had been successful in its declared aim of supporting Russia in the Caucasus. And by tying down several hundred thousand Turkish troops, the Allied position in the Middle East had been made more secure, he argued, underpinning the subsequent 'favourable development of events in Egypt, Mesopotamia and Persia'. Indeed, he insisted, 'to describe the expedition as a tragedy and a catastrophe was a complete perversion of the case'.[1]

The 'ringing plains of windy Troy'

Asquith's was a version of events – in Australia, as much as in Britain, New Zealand and other Allied countries – that many clung to in justification of the terrible hardship and loss of life that had been endured.

For those whose loved ones had suffered, physically and mentally, or had been killed, maimed or captured, any positive gloss that could be put on the defeat at Gallipoli was eagerly embraced. Today, there are historians who argue that even an Allied victory in the Dardenelles would have had little strategic relevance, for the real, gargantuan strug-gle for supremacy was already being acted out between the increasingly vast armies of the Western Front. It was there that the war would be won or lost, with the Gallipoli enterprise – whether successful or not – inevitably a sideshow. Defeat in the Dardenelles merely accentuated the futility of the operation.[2] But this was not a view that many were inclined to accept in the wake of the withdrawal from Gallipoli, and there were those who found comfort instead in General Hamilton's romantic comparison between the heroic exploits of the Allies in 1915 and the Classical tales of Troy and the Trojan War, fought some 3,500 years earlier. 'You will hardly fade away', Hamilton told his troops at Gallipoli, 'until the sun fades out of the sky and the earth sinks into the universal blackness. For already you form part of that great tradition of the Dardenelles which began with Hector and Achilles'. In another few thousand years, he added, 'the two stories will have blended into one', the Anzac legend and the Trojan, a fusion that many in Australia found highly seductive.[3] It was a Classical allusion that added lustre to the Anzac myth, an echo of which could still be heard as late as the 1960s, when textbooks provided for primary schools in Western Australia carefully juxtaposed the tales of Gallipoli and Thermopylae. Here Persians had replaced Trojans as the enemies of Greek (Western) civilization, but the comparison was even more apt. Thermopylae, it was explained, was near the place 'many hundreds of years later that the Australians landed at Gallipoli', and although the 'gallant little band' of Greeks was overwhelmed by the Persian hordes, they 'had not died in vain', for eventually Persia was defeated – just as Turkey would be by Australia and the British Empire in the Great War.[4]

Comparisons like these helped mould the collective memory of Gallipoli as it developed over time, extending and modifying the Anzac story. But in the immediate aftermath of 1915, such elevation was a palliative, gratefully accepted by the bereaved and others anxious to validate and give meaning to their losses, and welcomed by politi-cians and military leaders who realized its importance in maintaining morale on the home front and sustaining recruitment to the armed forces. As the Methodist *Australian Christian Commonwealth* put it: 'Every drop of Australian blood that has stained "the ringing plains of windy Troy" was calling to its kindred blood to render certain that its shedding should not be in vain'.[5] In fact, recruitment had run strongly as the Gallipoli episode had unfolded, while home-front fundraising and other support activities had reached their apogee during 1915 and the early months of 1916. Thereafter, as we shall see in later chapters, cracks began to appear in the ostensibly united front presented by the Australian people, not least over the conscription issue. But, for the moment, the collective resolve remained strong, at least on the surface, although the naïve enthusiasm of late 1914 and early 1915 had been replaced now by a more sober estimation of the nature of war. The idea that warfare might be a great adventure, or a higher form of sport, had been quietly discarded, giving way to a more subdued and reflective sto-icism, a resigned acceptance that the war had to be fought and won.

The 'collision of the forces of good and evil'

At Moonta on South Australia's Yorke Peninsula a memorial service was held in September 1915 in the local Methodist church. 'We are gathered to lay wreaths, metaphorically at least', explained the min-ister, 'on the graves where our brave soldiers lie sleeping at Gallipoli'. The fallen, he added, 'nobly gave themselves in sacrifice for King and country, justice and righteousness'. But, responding to the changing public mood, he was also quick to point out that 'war is such a dire evil, yea the most fearful scourge that can come on a country'. Nonetheless, he continued, 'there are occasions when it is justified in defence of hearths and homes'. Indeed, detecting perhaps the first seeds of uncer-tainty or dissent in his own community, he was keen to emphasize that: 'Those who tell us that war has no justification, and that Christians ought never to engage in it, are forgetful of the sacred scripture'. He went on to insist that 'greater love hath no man than he [who will] lay down his life for his friends'.[6]

This was a message repeated in churches and chapels across Australia, and after the tragedy of Gallipoli it helped to steady resolve as well as to offer comfort. Although there were no formal links between Church and State in Australia, the Church – or rather,

churches – often took it upon themselves to speak on behalf of communities or to indicate paths of moral or civic duty to their congregations,
pointing the collective way for the nation. This was never more so than
in August 1914, on the outbreak of war, when churches and church-
men of all persuasions – Anglicans and Methodists, Presbyterians
and Congregationalists, even Lutherans and Catholics – were anxious
to explain the justice of the cause, urging men to enlist and encouraging women and children to assist in mobilizing the home front in
support of soldiers in the trenches. Clergymen detected God's mighty
hand behind the momentous events that had led to war, and considered that if He had allowed such terrible things to happen, then surely
the eventual outcome could only be good.[7] A better world would arise
from all the death and destruction, as good triumphed over evil, and
Australia was destined to play a prominent role in ensuring this positive
result. At Ballarat in Victoria a leading Presbyterian minister envisaged
post-war Australia as a 'fire-purged civilization, [in] which the King of
Kings and Lord of Lords shall rule'.[8] Likewise, the *Australian Christian
Commonwealth* insisted in January 1915 that 'this war, is one of the
most tremendous things in the history of the world. Not only is it a
colossal war, but a colossal event. We believe', the magazine continued,
that 'it will tell on the future history of the world as no event has told
since the birth of Jesus Christ. It will be epoch-making in a tremendous
way'.[9] It was an opinion that the *Australian Christian Commonwealth*
would maintain with unwavering faith throughout the conflict, observing in the moment of victory in November 1918:

> The present generation has witnessed the collision of the forces of good
> and evil on a scale surpassing everything known before. The war is
> more than the greatest military event in history. It is a climax of the
> moral realm. It is the greatest decision reached since Christ was cruci-
> fied and rose again nearly twenty centuries ago.[10]

Hand in hand with such rhetoric, churches became more overtly patri-
otic in their decoration and services became increasingly militarized.
For instance, at a memorial service at Moonta Methodist Church in
September 1915 the pulpit was swathed in the Union flag and at Uralla
Methodist Church, near Armidale in New South Wales, a service
attended by local government representatives featured a 'church parade

of the Commonwealth forces and rifle club'. Led 'by the local Salvation Army band, the troops marched to the church . . . [which was] decorated with flags of our Nation'. Appropriately, the 'service closed with the hymn "God bless our native land"'.[11] Increasingly, churches became the venues for farewell ceremonies for recruits bound for the front, or for welcome home services for the wounded and others returning from the war. They also became sites for fundraising and recruiting. When Private Harry Banfield, badly wounded at Gallipoli, arrived back in South Australia he conducted services for packed congregations at the Salvation Army barracks at Moonta Mines on several successive weekends, and as a practising Salvationist subsequently set off on a lecture tour of Eyre Peninsula where he raised some £50 for the Cheer-Up Society and Wounded Soldiers' Fund.[12]

Sacrifice 'will hallow all our Australian life'

Anglicans liked to imagine themselves the legitimate religious voice of Empire but, in Australia, Methodists were often especially vociferous in their support for the war. One famous exception was B. Linden Webb, the pacifist minister of Hay in New South Wales, but perhaps more typical in his attitude was Revd George Tregear, Methodist minister at Rochester in Victoria, who in October 1915 sent a white feather and inflammatory note to a prominent local politician said to be reluctant to enlist. Far from keeping his actions anonymous, Tregear was proud to defend his behaviour in public. Few clergy resorted to such extreme or controversial gestures, although as early as March 1915 the *Australian Christian Commonwealth* had suggested that compulsory conscription to the armed forces might be a good idea, a way of dealing with the shirkers, the cowardly and the hesitant. Presbyterians, too, embraced the rhetoric of the just war. For some, the appalling bloodshed might even have a cleansing quality, as W.H. Cooper, a prominent Presbyterian minister in Victoria, explained: 'if in this awful sacrifice of the nations we emerge unchastened, having made only pecuniary sacrifice, there is a danger of over-weening pride and boastfulness'. However, he continued, 'if with the brave fighters from the British Isles and Canada and India our soldiers mingle their blood . . . then sacrifice will hallow all our Australian life'.[13]

The Lutheran church, with its intimate connection with Australia's German communities, found it politic to echo the rhetoric of Empire patriotism (see pp.22–3), and indeed – as war memorials across the country attest – many Lutherans of German descent did indeed join the colours. When Revd J.G. Wright, a Methodist patriot, spoke at a rally at Angaston in the Barossa Valley early in the war, he was delighted to see so many potential recruits who 'owed their origins to German parentage. He refused to believe that these men were enemies of Britain, but believed that they were brothers proud to claim allegiance to the flag under which they had gained such prosperity'.[14] In South Australia, Lutheran churches tried to explain that their adherence to the German language and customs was 'nothing to do with the political goals of Imperial Germany', and Lutheran schools went out of their way to celebrate Empire Day in style in May 1915, with much saluting the flag and three cheers for the king.[15] Lutheran children were asked to write essays extolling the virtues of the British Empire, and were enthusiastic participants in the Australia Day events of 30 July 1915. Lutherans were also generous contributors to the South Australian Lutheran War Relief Fund, one of the many practical patriotic home-front organizations that had sprung up at the beginning of the war. But none of this prevented Lutherans from being the victims of suspicion and even violence as the war progressed. Lutheran churches were burnt down at Edithburgh in South Australia and at Murtoa and Netherby in Victoria, and at Quorn in the southern Flinders Ranges the church door was daubed a patriotic red, white and blue in punishment for the pastor preaching in German.

At least until the Easter Rising in Ireland in 1916 and the deepening conscription crisis – when new complexities and uncertainties were introduced into ethno-religious relationships in Australia – the Catholic church had matched the Anglicans, Methodists and others in its unqualified support for the war. Its rhetoric may have been more restrained, its clergy unconvinced by Protestant notions of blood 'sacrifice' and 'cleansing', but there was no doubting the Roman Catholic church's adherence to the Empire's cause. Like the Lutherans, Catholics found it politic on occasion to echo the rhetoric of war, disarming those ultra-Protestants suspicious of Papist 'disloyalty'. But, like the Lutherans, they were fundamentally committed to Australia's participation in the conflict. Even after 1916, when the Catholic hierarchy in Melbourne and the other metropolises became more equivocal, Catholics in the countryside often continued to lend their wholehearted support. Indeed, as John McQuilton has argued, it 'is not difficult to find Catholics who were prominent in the regional war effort'.[16] In north-eastern Victoria, for example, leading Catholic families, such as the Denchys at Rutherglen, were among the most vocal Empire loyalists. Margaret Denchy organized the concert at St Mary's Catholic school in December 1915, when boys in khaki uniforms paraded into the hall with the flags of Britain and Australia proudly held aloft. Such displays remained an integral part of school life at St Mary's throughout the war. Likewise, Catholics were often prominent in fundraising activities in support of patriotic causes. At Porepunkah, also in north-eastern Victoria, proceeds from the St Patrick's Day Sports in 1915 (and in subsequent years) were dispersed among local patriotic funds. Similarly, Catholic schools in the area held special events to raise money for the Red Cross, which was active in supporting soldiers at the front. In the same locality, the Dederang Racing Club in 1914 decided to split its surplus for the year between the new Catholic church and various patriotic organizations, an example followed by the Tallangatta Easter Sports. Perhaps not surprisingly, one cause that attracted particular support among the Catholic community was the Belgian Nuns' Distress Fund. Only the Catholic clergy found it difficult to embrace the various patriotic funds, perhaps because such organizations were usually Protestant-dominated, with local priests often asked to participate only as an afterthought.[17]

Patriotic Leagues

Patriotic Leagues and similar funds had sprung up across Australia almost immediately after war broke out when, as McQuilton puts it, 'the home front organised itself with amazing rapidity'.[18] At Beechworth in Victoria, for example, a Patriotic League was launched at a public meeting on 19 August 1914. Other regional centres in Victoria soon followed suit. Local councils led the way in making donations to the newly emergent funds. Beechworth Shire contributed £100, and neighbouring Yackandandah Shire dug deep into its coffers to find £100 for the local patriotic fund and a further £25 apiece for the Red Cross and the Belgian Relief Fund. At Moonta in South Australia a Moonta Patriotic Committee was formed shortly after the outbreak of war, to be followed by a Moonta Mines Soldiers' Aid League. The local Patriotic Fund was established at a meeting in the council chamber, the mayor presiding, and with representatives appointed from across the locality – from Moonta, Moonta Mines, North Moonta and neighbouring Cross Roads, as well as from outlying settlements on northern Yorke Peninsula such as Agery, Arthurton, Cunliffe and Tippara. The fund was dominated by local businessmen and politicians, a decidedly masculine approach to mobilizing the home front, but roles were found for women, not least in the activities of the Belgian Relief Fund where a committee meeting in the Moonta Institute in November 1914 attracted 'a good attendance of ladies'.[19] It was felt that women were especially adept at marshalling resources to comfort distressed civilians or wounded soldiers in distant lands, their sympathies and disposition humanitarian rather than martial. They were also good at getting things done. They organized a fundraising concert at Weetulpa, for example, a small agricultural community on Yorke Peninsula, and arranged for proceeds from performances of the Wallaroo Mines Dramatic Company to go to the local Belgian Relief Fund. In many areas women formed Ladies' Patriotic Committees, Women's Patriotic Leagues or Patriotic Sewing Guilds, the precursors of the Red Cross branches that sprung up across Australia in late 1914 and 1915. As Michael McKernan has observed, with no large-scale munitions factories in Australia and no acute shortage of male labour, Australian women had to carve out a niche of their own: they initiated what might almost be described as 'a completely new sector of the economy, the provision of "comforts" for the Australian troops and victims of war'.[20]

At first, as every community clamoured to set up its own patriotic fund of one sort or another, there was a multiplicity of new and varied organizations, and sometimes considerable duplication of effort. In a move designed to achieve greater efficiency and focus, the government intervened to prescribe the causes for which money might be raised – the Australian Patriotic Fund, the Soldiers' Relief Fund, and the Belgian Relief Fund – and the great many local funds across the country affiliated accordingly. To these was added the Red Cross, formed by Lady Munro-Ferguson, wife of the Governor-General, two days after the declaration of war as the 'Australian Branch of the British Red Cross Society'. Vice-regal and establishment backing accounted in part for the extraordinary speed with which branches appeared across Australia, but the desire of women to 'do their bit' was equally important. Central to the Red Cross ethos was the spirit of volunteerism, as women eagerly took on unpaid roles of all kinds, from knitting and sewing to management and administration and the acquisition of nursing and first-aid skills. By November 1914 there were already eighty-eight metropolitan Red Cross branches and 249 country branches in New South Wales. By August 1915 there were 462 branches in Victoria, fifty-four of these in Melbourne alone. Together, they produced thousands upon thousands of pairs of socks, mittens, mufflers, balaclava helmets, vests and even shirts and pyjamas for soldiers overseas. These 'comforts' were despatched to Red Cross headquarters in each state, and from there were sent off to Britain. Perhaps not surprisingly, Red Cross branches were especially active in more affluent areas. This may have reflected middle-class commitment to the war. But middle-class women often had time on their hands to devote to the Red Cross, while their working-class counterparts were fully preoccupied keeping home and hearth together.

The landings at Gallipoli in April 1915 precipitated a new upsurge in fundraising, and governmental attempts to channel funds through a small number of agencies broke down in the face of popular enthusiasm. In Northern Tasmania, for example, a Plum Pudding Fund emerged, presumably devoted to improving culinary provision at the front, while at Tallangatta in Victoria local people resorted to ever-more novel ways of raising funds – such as a charity football match where the players dressed as women. At Wallaroo Mines in South Australia a 'Gallipoli Fair' was held to raise money to support the troops at the front, and in July 1915 a garden fête was held at nearby Agery to aid wounded soldiers returning home. Twelve young girls performed a maypole dance, 'tastefully dressed in red, white and blue' according to one newspaper report, while an 'enthusiastic auction sale' raised gratifying amounts for a handmade quilt, half a ton of chaff, poultry, flowers, bacon, and a cigar.[21] Among the more curious fundraisers to appear in 1915 were 'the Mugs', groups of young men whose enlistment had been turned down on medical grounds or otherwise refused. In a parody of the numerous serious concerts that had already supported the war effort, the Mugs devoted themselves to intentionally inept performances, their clowning, poor singing and bad acting invariably bringing the house down.[22] Across the country, 30 July 1915 was designated 'Australia Day', earmarked for raising funds for sick and wounded soldiers. In some communities, the activities went on for three days but most, like Bright in Victoria, managed to squeeze a multiplicity of events into the official day. At Bright the celebrations commenced in carnival mood, with a street parade complete with floats, brass band and uniformed cadets, followed by a fancy-dress football match and, in the evening, concluding with a 'Mugs' concert and a dinner and dance. At Moonta in South Australia there was a similar procession, with children prominent in fancy dress, and cadets accompanying what was described as the 'Joffre Quick Firing Gun'.[23]

The Cheer-Up Society

One uniquely South Australian innovation was the Cheer-Up Society, formed by Alexandra Seager with the support of W.J. Sowden, editor of the *Register*. In November 1914, Alexandra Seager had visited her eldest son at the training camp at Morphettville, near Adelaide, where troops were being held prior to their embarkation. She was shocked by the apparent lack of public support for the soldiers as they waited their turn to go to war, and determined to do something about it. Sowden helped in publicizing her call for like-minded women to join her, and she became organizer and secretary of the Cheer-Up Society – as she dubbed it – a body founded to 'promote and provide for the comfort, welfare and entertainment' of soldiers and sailors.[24] High-minded and protective, the women volunteers of the Cheer-Up Society wished to shield the young soldiers from the seamier temptations of urban life, including alcohol. They visited army camps and hospitals, befriending lonely recruits often far from home, and arranged a variety of lively entertainments, such as free luncheon parties and concerts. In 1915 the Society erected a large marquee near Adelaide railway station, in which they dispensed refreshments and offered recreation for servicemen. This was followed swiftly by the construction of the Cheer-Up Hut, situated behind the Adelaide City Baths in Elder Park, financed by donations from the local business community (Alexandra Seager was herself a successful businesswoman, running a scholastic employment agency) and proceeds from fêtes and badge days. Opened on 14 November 1915, the Cheer-Up Hut provided free meals and free entertainments (such as billiards) for upwards of 200,000 soldiers, sailors and airmen over the next four years.

Departing troops were given tremendous send-offs, and the wounded returning from Gallipoli and later battles were greeted as heroes. Private Harry Banfield, arriving in Adelaide, was stunned by the extraordinary welcome he received from the enthusiastic young women in their long white uniforms and 'Miss Muffet' hats.

Alexandra Seager's youngest son, George, was killed at Gallipoli, but this only redoubled her determination and commitment. She launched the Violet Day Appeal, first held on 2 July 1915, which became a local remembrance day, and oversaw the expansion of eighty country branches across South Australia. At Murray Bridge the Cheer-Ups met troop trains and handed out refreshments, and at Burra in the mid-north the Cheer-Up Girls Band proved especially adept at fundraising – it also formed a mounted guard of honour for a visit to the town by the state governor.[25] The Cheer-Up work continued after the end of the war, as Australian troops began to arrive home in large numbers, but in 1920 the Hut was closed and the Society wound up. Alexandra Seager was remembered fondly as a 'petite, sweet-faced woman with blue eyes and great vivacity' who was 'loved by the Australian servicemen, especially by the young recruits who saw her as something of a mother figure'.[26] After the war, she went back to her business, and during the Depression years engaged in charity work in support of the unemployed and homeless. She eventually retired to Kangaroo Island, where she wrote poetry, as she had done during the war itself:

> Today we wear the clinging violet
> In memory of the brave,
> While ever thoughts of fond but proud regret,
> Come surging on the wave.[27]

'Petticoat power'

Among the upsurge of fundraising organizations that proliferated after Gallipoli was the Australian Comforts Fund (ACF), formed in 1916 and soon to rival the Red Cross in its appeal to women across the continent. Like the Red Cross, it co-ordinated the production of thousands of pairs of socks, along with other items of clothing for soldiers at the front, and provided tobacco and 'luxury' foodstuffs such as cakes, puddings and condensed milk. Sometimes working alone at home, or gathering together with friends and neighbours in sewing or knitting 'bees' (as they were known), women toiled long hours to produce their countless 'comforts'. Often they would place personal notes in among the socks or balaclavas, bringing a welcome touch of 'home' to the recipient, and forging a momentary intimacy between home front and battlefront. Frequently, if they gave an address, such women would receive grateful replies. 'The socks you so kindly sent have arrived', wrote Corporal John Dunstan Woon to Mrs Wearne at Moonta Mines, as he thanked her 'for your kindness to a soldier in need of socks'.[28] Others engaged in 'doorknock' activity, going from house to house to collect suitable items for despatch or to raise funds (doorknocks in North Sydney alone realized some £75 per month), and there were the usual fêtes and badge days, and even a cake shop in Sydney which reportedly did a roaring trade. So too did an ACF flower shop, also opened in Sydney. By the end of the war, the New South Wales branch of the ACF had collected over half a million pounds. Relying overwhelmingly on volunteers, its salary bill for the entire period was little more than £2,000.[29]

Not all women, however, were content with roles that seemed merely extensions of the domestic sphere, and some were anxious to move closer to the action. Some, indeed, especially those with existing medical experience or qualifications, were able to go overseas with the Australian Imperial Force (AIF) as nurses. They had served with distinction at Gallipoli, on Lemnos and at Cairo, Malta and elsewhere, and would do so again shortly on the Western Front. Others rallied to the call of Eleanor Jacobs of Stanmore, New South Wales, who proposed the creation of an Australian Women's Service Corps, designed to support the AIF in Britain and Europe or to release uniformed staff in Australia for active service overseas. These roles were politely declined by the government, but the Corps was able to busy itself in other activities, not least in helping to build 'homes for heroes' for returning soldiers at French Forest in New South Wales.[30] Corps members also volunteered as loyalist workers during the general strike in New South Wales in 1917, betraying the Corps' mainly middle-class composition and, perhaps, its political orientation. Other women directed their energies towards social reform, especially to combating gambling and drinking, both 'vices' being seen as subversive threats to the war effort. In particular, women led the early closing campaigns (a referendum in New

South Wales decisively supported a closing time of 6 p.m.), addressing rallies and lobbying politicians. They also, as we shall see (Chapter 7), played an important role in the conscription debate of 1916 and 1917, and in encouraging recruitment to the armed forces. Often overlooked, there was also a minority of women's organizations opposed to the war, such as the pacifist Sisterhood for International Peace, the Women's Peace Army, and the Women's Peace League, the latter a branch of the Victorian Socialist Party. Seemingly radical in their critiques of the conflict, such groups nonetheless espoused traditional gender-role and biological assumptions, arguing that the waging of war was contrary to the nurturing and peace-loving disposition of most women.[31]

There were those who hoped that the greater prominence in public affairs achieved by women during the war would be perpetuated into the ensuing peace, the *Red Cross Record* in October 1918 extolling the virtues of 'petticoat power' and arguing that the 'feminine influence is going to be the greatest power in Australia after the war'.[32] But it was not to be. Organizations such as the Cheer-Up Society and the Australian Comforts Fund were wound up after hostilities ceased, and even the Red Cross (shedding its 'British' prefix in 1928) assumed a more modest role. There had been an expansion in the employment of women from twenty-four per cent of the national workforce in 1914 to thirty-seven per cent in 1918. But this expansion was achieved mainly in the clothing and textiles industries and in food processing – areas of low pay and traditional female employment – with much of this growth being to meet the increased demand from the armed forces. After the war, many of these additional jobs were shed, although in some 'professional' areas – such as shop assistants and schoolteachers – increased participation achieved by women was sustained after 1918. Overall, however, penetration of the employment market by women in Australia was substantially lower than that in Britain, and the war did less to alter the place of women in Australian society than it did in the United Kingdom.

The 'circles of mourning'

For many women in Australia during the First World War, their principal preoccupation was with the fate of husbands, sons, brothers and other relations and friends at the front, with war work – whether voluntary or paid – at best a distraction from constant worry or a prac-tical demonstration of support for loved ones overseas. From Gallipoli onwards, women lived with the knowledge that close relations and neighbours were often in mortal danger half a world away, and they were in constant dread of the telegram boy at the gate or the clergyman on the doorstep. As casualty lists grew ever longer, so fewer and fewer women had not suffered some personal loss or knew someone whose kith and kin had been killed, wounded, captured, recorded as 'missing', or become desperately ill. Together, they created 'circles of mourning', as Annette Becker has described them, where the greater the losses sustained by families in a particular locality or precinct, the greater the sense of communal suffering and dislocation.[33] Isabella Rose, a doughty Scotswoman who had come to Australia as a child, inhabited one such 'circle'. She had lost her husband in a mining accident in 1905, and her eldest son Ernest had been electrocuted at the Ivanhoe mine at Boulder in Western Australia in June 1911. But she was proud when her other son, Reuben, known universally as 'Charlie', went off to war in 1916. She delighted in the letters he sent back, first from training camps in England, and then from France, and knew that her female neighbours, most with sons or husbands away, clamoured for any news from the front. Accordingly, it was always a red-letter day when one of Charlie's missives arrived home, and Isabella Rose would raise the Australian flag on a makeshift pole outside her cottage at East Moonta, a signal to her neighbours – her 'circle' – that she had put the kettle on and that they should call round to hear Charlie's latest news over a cup of tea and a piece of cake.

Alas, Charlie Rose, having survived the fearful Third Battle of Ypres in July 1917, when many of his mates in the 43rd Battalion were slaughtered or maimed, was killed in action on 28 August 1918 on the eve of the successful Australian assault on Mont St Quentin. News of his demise was tempered, perhaps, by the announcement that he had been awarded a posthumous Military Medal for his action earlier in the month at Hamel, when he had rushed his Lewis light machine gun to outflank and silence a German machine-gun position, allowing the capture of an important artillery field gun. A fulsome letter of condo-lences from the Base Records Office in Melbourne informed Isabella that her son, Lance-Corporal Rose, had won the admiration and sympa-thy of the King himself, and that Charlie's 'conduct on the field of battle

AUSTRALIAN WAR MEMORIAL P07723.001

Hilda Pollard, pictured here on her wedding day, was one of those who mourned. Her husband Herbert, from near Dunolly in Victoria, was killed in action at Fromelles in France on 19 July 1916. He never saw his baby daughter Agnes. Hilda wrote to the military authorities to ask 'if anything might be done to find if my husband . . . is a Prisoner of War in Germany' but the later return of Herbert's identity disc by the Germans confirmed that he had been killed. In 2008 the remains of Herbert George Pollard were found in a mass grave at Fromelles.

has helped earn for our Australian soldiers a fame which will endure as long as memory lasts'. The accolade may have comforted Isabella Rose in her bereavement. But the illusion of personal concern for her late son was shattered a few years later when the same Base Records Office wrote to say that a mistake might have been made in the inscription of his memorial plaque, which read 'Ruben Charles Rose'. Although there was not the slightest evidence to support the claim in Charlie's service record, the Base Records Office insisted that 'some doubt exists regarding the correct spelling of the first Christian name'. Cynically, Isabella was asked to confirm the correct form but also warned that, if indeed there had been a mistake, 'some considerable time must elapse' before a replacement plaque could be produced. For those whose sons or husbands lay in graves that, in all probability, they might never have the opportunity to visit, the memorial plaques were tangible reminders of the fallen, eagerly awaited and highly cherished. Sadly, Isabella replied that the correct spelling was 'Reuben' but that, in the circumstances, she was prepared to accept the plaque as currently engraved.[34]

The tale of Isabella Rose, a widow who had lost her son in battle and subsequently suffered the ignominy of official indifference, is an insight into the agonizing and often bewildering experiences of women on the home front. Among her 'circle of mourning', at least in the

geographical sense of being in the same neighbourhood, was Mary
Anne Quintrell at nearby Moonta Mines. She too was a widow and,
of her thirteen offspring, five had died in childhood. Of her remaining
adult sons, three – Clarence, John and Richard – went off to the war,
and none returned. Richard was reported 'missing' after the Battle of
Fromelles in July 1916, and the community hoped that he had been
taken prisoner and would 'turn up safely after the war'.[35] But the Red
Cross, dutiful and exhaustive in its enquiries, ascertained that Richard
Quintrell was not a prisoner of war in Germany. Later, on Armistice
Day in 1918, Red Cross representatives interviewed one of Richard's
mates, Sergeant C.F. Lewis, who explained that he had seen Quintrell
'running from one part of the trench occupied to a shell hole when a
burst of machine gun caught him, and he dropped, apparently killed.
This occurred about 7.30 a.m. 20th July 1916'.[36] More than two years
after the event, Mary Anne Quintrell at last knew the truth, and any
lingering hope that Richard might yet be alive was finally extinguished.

Meanwhile, in December 1916, John Quintrell had been buried
alive in an explosion on the front line in France. Despite his pre-war
occupation as a miner, John was so unnerved by the experience that
he lost the power of speech, permanently. Suffering from what his
service documents described as 'shell shock and aphonia', he was
evacuated to England, where it was reported that he 'sleeps and eats
poorly', is 'very costive' (constipated), has a 'heaving cardiac' and
'general debility'. It was decided to return him to Australia, but he
died en route of 'inflammation of the liver' on 1 September 1917, and
was buried at sea.[37] It was a bitter blow for his mother who, as one
local newspaper reflected, had been 'anxiously looking forward to his
home-coming with no small amount of pleasure . . . the residents of
the district were stunned at the news'.[38] Alas, Mary Ann Quintrell's
third son, Clarence, had already been killed at the battle for Mouquet
Farm on 16 August 1916, less than a month after Richard had fallen
at Fromelles, completing the cycle of death experienced by this unfortunate mother and adding further to the sense of perpetual mourning
that lay over the community. Such loss was intensely personal, yet
in sharing and expressing the pain within the wider community, the
burden might be spread, the bereavement cushioned. One frequent
means was the placing of In Memoriam notices in local newspapers,
often with touching verses designed to convey and perhaps assuage the

stinging sense of loss. Not all possessed the gift of poetic composition, of course, but such memorial rhymes were available 'off the shelf' and could be altered to meet personal needs:

> Could I, his mother, have clasped his hand,
> The son we loved so well,
> Or kissed his brow when death was near,
> And whispered 'My son, farewell'!
>
> I seem to see his dear, sweet face,
> Through a mist of falling tears;
> But a mother's part is a broken heart,
> And a burden of lonely years.[39]

Or, equally poignant:

> When the flags are o'er the roadways,
> When the troops are marching home,
> When the sisters lean to bless them,
> And the mothers to caress them,
> Oh God, have pity for the watching ones,
> Whose boys will never return.[40]

'Feminine wiles?'

To the anguish suffered by those whose sons were at the front should be added the no-less traumatic experiences of young women who suddenly found themselves bereft as sweethearts and would-be husbands left to join the forces. Anxieties were increased by news that many members of the AIF overseas were marrying British girls – the so-called 'English brides', as they were described through gritted teeth – and that even if these soldiers survived the perils of the trenches, it might be the last their erstwhile Australian girlfriends would see of them. The anxiety was all the more acute when, during the emotional days of pre-embarkation leave in Australia, a girlfriend had unintentionally fallen pregnant, and faced the prospect of being left quite literally 'holding the baby' and with the social stigma of having borne an illegitimate child. W.H. 'Billy'

Hughes, as Prime Minister, sympathized with the predicament of such unfortunate women, and attempted to introduce a marriage-by-proxy scheme in which members of the armed forces would be allowed to marry their Australian girlfriends without actually being present at the ceremony, even if serving overseas. Ingenious, pragmatic and humane, marriage-by-proxy was nonetheless anathema to the churches, which saw it as a licence for pre-marital sex. Other critics attacked the scheme as a means by which unscrupulous girls might secure regular allotments from their absent husbands, and pensions should they be killed. Under such pressure, Hughes let the idea quietly drop, although he did try briefly and unsuccessfully to raise it again in 1917.

But if many young women were distressed by the prospect of their boyfriends going off to war, there were others who positively encouraged their young men to join the colours. To be seen on the arm of a soldier or sailor in a smart uniform was to invite admiration and envy from less fortunate girls, and it was comforting to know that one had done one's bit in support of the war effort by persuading a loved one to enlist. Sometimes this enthusiasm for recruitment was extended to all the available young men in a locality, with single young women shaming them into joining up, not least by the widespread means of sending or presenting a white feather to those deemed reluctant to enlist. At Wangaratta, in Victoria, one wag remarked on the supposed sharp rise of bald chickens in the area, so commonplace was the practice.[41] However, while such motivation was no doubt often genuine, there was also considerable moral pressure placed on women to act as unofficial recruiting sergeants. At public meetings women were exhorted to urge their menfolk to join the forces, and there were attacks in the press against those who appeared tardy in their efforts. 'Feminine wiles' were seen as legitimate weapons in the armoury of the recruitment campaign, and the promise of female attention or even sexual favours was a powerful inducement for many young men. In this way, women, often unwittingly, were co-opted into the recruiting process.

'Busy Bees'

Children, too, were not immune to co-option, and their prominence in events such as concerts and parades, sometimes as cadets or boy scouts or in other uniformed guises, where they were seen to be 'doing their bit', was also an important contribution to moral persuasion, a means of encouraging their elders to enlist. Schoolchildren were also drawn into other aspects of the home-front war effort, and were often engaged alongside the grown-ups in the production of 'comforts' for troops in the trenches. The South Australian Children's Patriotic Fund, for example, encouraged such activity, awarding war service medals (with bars, as appropriate) in recognition of individual achievement. Such medals were sported proudly at public events, a very visible measure of a child's personal contribution to the war effort but also a means of shaming those grown men who had yet to don a uniform. Under supervision at school, children produced items such as 'billy-cans', much desired at the front, extremely versatile utensils which could be used for carrying water, brewing tea, boiling food, and any number of other functions. Often packed tightly with other comforts, from mouth organs to shaving kits to bars of chocolate, the arrival of billy-cans was the cause of much genuine glee. Gunner Frederick Teo wrote home to Australia from Cairo on 5 January 1916, thanking a young schoolgirl, Ilene Andrewartha, for her welcome parcel. 'My Dear Friend Ilene', he wrote: 'Just a few lines to let you know that I received your Xmas billy with thanks and I can assure you it was beautiful. There was a lot of fun when chaps got their billys to see who had the best'. Most were hoping for mouth organs, he explained, but 'I was pleased with my billy as there were lots of things I was greatly in need of'. Teo assured young Ilene that he was now 'your sincere friend', and, on receipt of his letter, no doubt she felt a tinge of personal pride as well as the thrill of intimacy with the AIF in distant Egypt.[42]

In Victoria, the State Schools' Patriotic Fund entrusted fundraising to the local school Inspectorates, which rose to the challenge magnificently. The Beechworth Inspectorate, for example, had already raised £114 by early October 1914, and went on to contribute £13,000 to the State total of £100,000 accumulated by 1916, when schoolchildren in Victoria were given a half-day holiday in recognition of their achievements. Competition between and within schools was keen, and drove the fundraising campaign. Teachers made regular contributions to the funds, and so did the pupils' parents, who were encouraged to make weekly donations. But it was the children themselves who made the most visible effort – gathering firewood, selling flowers, raffling poultry, collecting rabbit skins, growing vegetables, staging concerts and sporting events, and making 'comforts'. Some of the more enterprising even collected 'tiger' leeches, much sought-after by local chemists who paid a fair price for good specimens. In 1917 the Young Workers' Patriotic Guild was established in Victoria, a means of recognizing outstanding effort by individuals. Those children who had raised £1 were presented with a War League Certificate and a 'Busy Bee' badge, and further 'seals' or endorsements were added to the certificate as more money was raised. Again, there was stiff competition between and within schools, and especially in individual grades where class members strove to outdo each other.[43]

Children, like women, were often also closely involved in 'farewell' ceremonies, when new recruits, their training completed, received lavish send-offs from their home communities before embarking for overseas. Sunday Schools were popular venues, where 'old scholars' or teachers who had joined up might be bade farewell by the pupils, the departing soldiers presented with gifts such as a pocket Testament or Bible, for many as vital a trench comfort as socks or mittens. At other times, children and young people were expressly invited to join 'farewells', such as that in the Council Chamber at Kadina in South Australia in July 1915 when thirty members of the Kadina Young Men's Club were summoned to listen to the mayor's stirring address to the four local recruits destined for the front. Their presence, an indication of youthful approval, validated the recruits' decision to enlist. But it worked both ways, for the youngsters were now also exposed to the pressures that in the fullness of time would urge them to join up themselves.

'God Bless Our Splendid Men'

Such 'soldiers' farewells', then, as the press dubbed them, served several purposes. They existed principally to fête those about to leave for the front, presenting them with gifts and showering them with fine words. But they were also an opportunity to demonstrate community solidarity, to show support for recruiting and fundraising campaigns, and to indicate cross-gender and intergenerational involvement in patriotic activities. In particular, they provided important platforms for local worthies – ministers of religion, politicians, business leaders – to articulate that solidarity and to remind the community where its duty lay. Reported extravagantly in the regional press across Australia, these farewells were a vital component of the home-front war effort and, at least until the conscription crisis and divisions of 1916 and 1917, were significant in binding communities together. Reuben 'Charlie' Rose, the ill-fated son of stoical Isabella, noted earlier, had been 'farewelled' at an especially memorable gathering at the Moonta Mines Recreation Grounds pavilion in April 1916. He was one of a dozen new recruits, most of whom would be dead or seriously injured within a year or two. They represented the continuing high level of enlistment that existed on the eve of the Battle of the Somme, a rate that the worthies who spoke at such events were keen to perpetuate, not least by lauding the many excellent qualities of the new recruits and encouraging others to follow their lead.

The Revd H.A. 'Harry' Gunter, for example, a local Methodist minister, declared confidently in his farewell speech to 'Charlie' Rose and his pals that 'they would quit themselves like men [and] play the game', drawing upon the repertoire of patriotic rhetoric that he had developed over recent months on similar occasions. Earlier, during March 1916, Gunter had delivered what was reckoned in the press 'an interesting and forceful address', a prelude to what proved to be an evening 'of a most enthusiastic character'. 'God Bless Our Splendid Men' sang the audience, as Mrs Gunter – Harry's wife – handed out a 'sleeping outfit' to each of the departing soldiers. Gunter himself presented them with trench periscopes, made locally in the mines' workshops, now recognized as an indispensable part of a soldier's survival kit at the front. A week later, and Harry Gunter was again in full flow at the pavilion, 'farewelling' yet another group of recruits, dispensing the usual sleeping outfits, periscopes, balaclavas, socks, mittens, and other comforts, including 'a little Testament, suitably inscribed'.[44]

Although such authority figures might later find their influence curtailed as the conscription controversy raged, for the moment Harry Gunter and others like him basked in their status as local opinion-leaders. Another favourite speaker at farewell socials in South Australia was Hon. John Verran, only recently State Premier, a virulent anti-German who used such platforms as propaganda opportunities, whipping his audiences into frenzies of xenophobia. Although he too gave out the obligatory periscopes, trench comforts and pocket

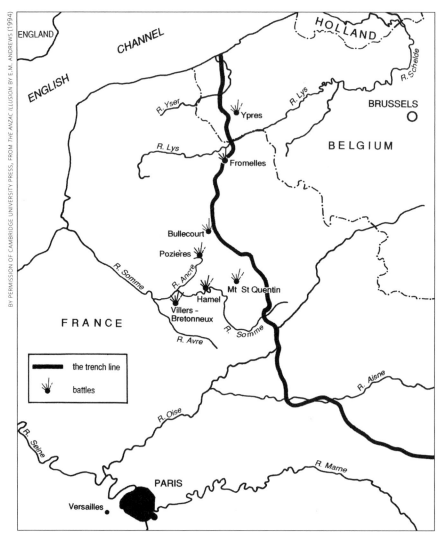

BY PERMISSION OF CAMBRIDGE UNIVERSITY PRESS, FROM *THE ANZAC ILLUSION* BY E.M. ANDREWS (1994)

The Western Front 1916–18: a simplified composite map of the Western Front trench line, indicating the principal battles in which the Australians participated.

Testaments, his principal aim was to leave all those who heard him – recruits as much as those who had gathered to say farewell – in no doubt that Germany was an evil colossus, and that only superhuman effort and limitless sacrifice could bring it down. Verran wished to frighten his audiences but he also wanted to inure them against what lay ahead, a titanic struggle with the German war machine that would make Gallipoli appear the sideshow that it really was. On one occasion, in the midst of his farewell speech, Verran turned suddenly to fix a new recruit with his steely gaze. He commanded him 'to put aside sickly sentiment and destroy as many Germans as he could', predicting grimly that 'the last German he would see in his travels would be a dead one'.[45] It was an uncompromising message, with no hint of mercy or compassion for an enemy that deserved no quarter, and Verran knew that he was preparing people for what lay ahead – a long and bloody road to victory. Indeed, by 1916 the centre of action for Australian forces had shifted decisively to France, and it was on the Western Front that the AIF would now make its full contribution to the Allies' gigantic war effort.

Chapter Five

Fromelles, Pozières and the Somme

MIRED IN CONTROVERSY – and the mud in which 150,000 men of the British Empire lost their lives – the Battle of the Somme, in all its horror, remains vivid in the collective memory of Australia and the other combatant nations of the Great War. Fought on a scale that still remains difficult to comprehend, the Somme has long been considered a disaster of unparalleled proportions, its appalling death and destruction an indictment of the unimaginative and self-serving generals who squandered the lives of young innocents in futile offensives that were bound to fail. The pig-headed incompetence of the generals, who persisted in their hopeless war of attrition, was – and is – one of the enduring myths of the First World War. First articulated in volume three of Winston Churchill's monumental six-volumed *The World Crisis*, published in 1927, the myth swiftly gained popular currency across the anglophone world. More than a million copies were sold, and the book was periodically reprinted (most recently in 2007), ensuring its continuing familiarity to the reading public throughout the twentieth century and into the twenty-first. Churchill's partial view rapidly became the conventional wisdom, shaping the opinions of subsequent generations and perpetuated by leading historians, such as A.J.P. Taylor who, in his *The First World War*, published in 1963, concluded simply that the 'war was beyond the capacity of generals and statesmen alike'.[1]

The 'generals who caused us to suffer such torture'

Struggling to grasp the enormity of the Somme, readers – in Australia as elsewhere – were persuaded that the battle was a costly failure, a catastrophic error of extraordinary proportions for which the generals, in their ineptitude, should be held perpetually to account. For those who had fought and suffered on the Somme, and searched for meaning for all they had endured, the narrative of senseless slaughter and callous irresponsibility was a powerful one, an explanation that allowed them to give full vent to their anger and to express their continuing traumas. As Lyn Macdonald observed in 1983 in the preface to her book *Somme*, the 'very horror of their experience has given birth to a widely held emotional view of the war in which every Tommy wears a halo and every officer above the rank of captain a pair of horns'.[2] 'I cursed, and still do', recalled one private soldier, 'the generals who caused us to suffer such torture, living in filth, eating filth, and then, death or injury just to boost their ego'. 'It was pure bloody murder', said another: 'Douglas Haig should have been hung, drawn and quartered for what he did on the Somme'.[3]

Douglas Haig, Commander-in-Chief of the British Empire's forces on the Western Front, including the Australians, was, inevitably, the main target for such attacks, for he had directed the Battle of the Somme. Honoured after the war, his reputation collapsed following his death in 1928, hastened by Churchill's scathing assessments and later by the damaging personal criticisms in Lloyd George's war memoirs, published in 1933–6. So loud and so widespread was the condemnation that few thought to question the accusations and, even today, despite important correctives from the pens of Gary Sheffield and others, Field-Marshall Earl Haig remains something of a bogeyman in the collective imagination of the anglophone world. John Terraine was one of the first to interrogate the 'Somme myths', as he termed them, and in so doing began the long rehabilitation of Douglas Haig, such as it is. Far from being the intransigent and unbending dullards of popular fancy, Haig and his generals proved remarkably flexible, argued Terraine, as they quite literally learned on the job, responding to rapid and often unforeseen developments in modern, industrial warfare that would have overwhelmed lesser men. Technical advances posed new challenges, from the advent of military aviation to the invention of the tank, while chemical warfare (poison gas and napalm), the ubiquity of the internal combustion engine, the application of wireless telegraphy, and unprecedented levels of mass production, mass logistics and mass administration, taxed even the most expansive of minds.[4]

Moreover, as Gary Sheffield has argued, Haig was an important architect of the final British Empire and Allied victory in 1918. Not only had Haig played a leading role in reforming and modernizing the British army before 1914, preparing it for the trials that lay ahead, but between 1916 and 1918 he had transformed the Empire's forces into a war-winning machine capable of confronting and then defeating German military might.[5] Here Haig's performance should be judged not merely on his handling of the Somme offensive but on the subsequent unfolding of the war on the Western Front. Likewise, as William Philpott has argued, the battle of the Somme itself should be assessed against the wider backdrop of the war and its eventual outcome. The Somme, he maintains, was the tipping-point in the First World War. Far from being 'futile' or 'a defeat', the battle challenged and at length unravelled the intrinsic superiority of the German army, so evident in the opening months of the conflict, and set the Empire and its Allies on the inexorable if bloody road to victory in November 1918.[6] In this view, the war of attrition was not an aimless squandering of men and material, but was a necessary prerequisite in the deadly struggle between two massively equipped opponents. The sacrifice on the Somme made possible the final 'decisive blow' of which Haig – as Commander-in-Chief – had never lost sight as the ultimate goal. As early as March 1915, Haig had made his case quite plainly: 'we cannot hope to win until we have defeated the German Army'.[7] It was, John Terraine argued fifty years later, a defeat that could only be inflicted through prolonged, unrelenting struggle and the attendant terrible loss of life. 'Was there no other way?', he asked rhetorically. His answer, reluctantly, was 'that there was not'.[8]

Lessons learned

As William Philpott makes clear, innumerable painful and extremely costly lessons were learned the hard way on the Somme. Early in the war, as he has explained, military theorists had 'stressed the élan and morale of the infantry',[9] and this view prevailed in the early days of the Somme, where undue confidence was placed in the dash and determination of the infantryman in the face of barbed-wire, fortifications, massed artillery and machine guns. The catastrophic first day of the Somme, with its misplaced optimism in what the infantry might achieve – not to mention its vast casualties – was overwhelming evidence of the shortcomings of such a doctrine. But lessons were learned and, as a new attritional strategy was devised, so it was increasingly understood that 'the artillery conquered and the infantry occupied'.[10] Moreover, in occupying ground won by bombardment, the infantry learned to wed initiative and intellect to élan, applying new tactical techniques, such as mopping up pockets of enemy resistance or outflanking and silencing machine-gun nests. The infantry was also taught to work alongside engineers and how to engage in 'all arms' operations, where tanks, aircraft, artillery, mines and other offensive components could combine to bring overwhelming force to bear against the enemy.[11] As Philpott makes plain, the Australians – who in the early months of the Somme had suffered alarmingly from over-confident belief (including their own) in their dash and élan – went on to become supreme practitioners of 'all arms' operations, acquiring their reputation as the 'shock troops of the British Empire' and their enviable battlefield skills, including consistent tactical superiority over the Germans.[12] As Lieutenant-General Sir John Monash, commander of the Australian Corps on the Western Front in 1918 would write later, summing up his own interpretation of the emergent doctrine, of which he was part-architect and peerless practitioner:

> I had formed the theory that the true role of the infantry was not to
> expend itself upon heroic physical effort, not to wither away under
> merciless machine-gun fire, nor to impale itself on hostile bayonets,
> nor to tear itself to pieces in hostile entanglements . . . but on the con-
> trary, to advance with as little impediment as possible; to be relieved
> as far as possible of the obligation to *fight* their way forward; to march
> resolutely, regardless of the din and tumult of battle to the appointed
> goal, and there to hold and defend the territory gained; and to gather,
> in the form of prisoners, guns, and stores, the fruits of victory.[13]

Perhaps it took an Australian to explain the doctrine with such simplicity and clarity of vision. But such levels of sophistication and insight were not available in the early days of the Somme, when the Australians suffered inordinately on the battlefield. Not surprisingly, therefore, Australia has its own version of the 'Somme myth', where, having already endured the pointlessness of Gallipoli, Australian troops were now needlessly expended by British generals in wanton displays of military hubris and vanity. A recent example is Patrick Lindsay's *Fromelles*, published in 2008. Describing the Battle of Fromelles, fought on 19–20 July 1916, Lindsay mused that 'there can be few more stark examples of the futility of war'. He contemplated with a mixture of anger and sorrow, he said, 'the lost potential of the young men destroyed by the stupidity and the cavalier indifference of the High Command . . . because of the ineptitude and the callous glory-seeking of their British commander'.[14] There can be no doubt that Fromelles was a dreadful calamity, as Lindsay makes clear, and that serious mistakes were made in its planning and execution, the outcome so appalling that it was effectively hushed up for years. Yet the battle needs to be understood in the wider context of the developing conflict on the Western Front, and to reduce it to the incoherent whim of a half-witted 'brass hat' is to deny its inherent complexity and its place in the pattern of lessons learned through experience, tragic though these were. In a telling observation of the changing fortunes of the war, historian John Williams has noted that the Bavarian regiment which gave the Australians such a drubbing at Fromelles, itself met its nemesis only four months later, when it was effectively destroyed on the Somme in the October – 'dragged along in the darkness and night' – while the 5th Australian Division, having licked its wounds, was subsequently back in business and went on to greater things.[15]

'How excited these French people were over us Australians'

The first Australians to disembark in France, the men of I ANZAC Corps, had arrived at Marseilles on the Mediterranean coast on 19 March 1916. They had sailed from Egypt earlier in the month, where they had been training and reinforcing (and guarding the Suez Canal) since the withdrawal from Gallipoli. Forced route marches in the fierce desert heat and the ubiquity of sand and yet more sand had begun to tell on the Australians, who longed to be off somewhere new. Private

Albert Cross wrote home to South Australia in early 1916, complaining that he had 'been in Egypt about three months now, and have seen just about all the sights there are to be seen here; so things are getting a bit stale'. As he put it: 'We want a change of scenery'. But he also noted that 'they are drilling us fairly hard now; they are getting us ready to have a go at the Germans', and predicted (correctly) that he would be in France or Flanders by April.[16] Sergeant Harold Campbell, writing to his parents as the troopships sailed from Alexandria, was more direct: 'Thank God we were able to say good-bye to that Cursed Egypt, the Land of Deserts & the home of the Coon or Gyppo'.[17] The Australians were equally thankful when they arrived at Marseilles. They marched through the town to the strains of 'Australia Will be There' and the 'Marseillaise', and were greeted by cheering crowds who showered them with rose petals and, when the opportunities arose, plied them with beer and wine. Lieutenant Hugh Knyvett could hardly believe it. 'How excited these French people were over us Australians!', he wrote: 'They pelted us with wild flowers and sweets, and while no one objected to the embraces of the girls, we thought it a bit too much when the men as well threw their arms around us and kissed us on both cheeks'.[18] As Knyvett observed, French customs would take a bit of getting used to.

Over the next few months, the remainder of I ANZAC arrived in France, a constant stream of troop trains taking them across country to the front. Sergeant Edgar Rule was delighted by the prospect of Marseilles. 'Rough mountainous scenery greeted us as we steamed into Marseilles harbour', he wrote, but the 'ruggedness was softened by the many lovely houses which clung to the hillsides . . . Churches or monasteries crowned most of the heights. To me it was a glimpse of paradise'. The long train journey through the heart of France, to reach the trenches in the north-east, was no less entrancing. 'The next morning', Rule continued, 'we were entrained and moved off on the most wonderful journey I have ever made'.[19] Their progress through the French countryside had an almost mystical quality, as Rule mused:

I have often wondered why it was that this trip through France left an impression on our men's minds which has never been erased – a memory which men fondled to themselves, certain that no greater joy awaited them in the years to come. It was the month of June, and everything was radiant. Perhaps we were suffering the reaction of our experiences in the desert. For sixty hours we forgot we were on a deadly mission, and in imagination lived within the pages of Grimm's fairy-tales. Mansions nestling into the folds of hills, and old castles perched on crags, over-looked the verdant valleys, while the beautiful River Rhone was never out of the picture in the early stages of the journey.[20]

'The farms were the envy of us all', Rule confessed: 'Everything was so peaceful that the existence of a state of war was almost incredible'. At the various stations en route, 'maidens handed out refreshments, chatting and laughing the while. Few understood them, but that did not matter. Eyes were sufficient'. Indeed, after the vicissitudes of the broth-els of Cairo and Alexandria: 'Men had almost forgotten, till then, what decent women looked like'.[21] Lee and Will Pomeroy, writing to their parents in Australia, were similarly enthused. 'We were travelling for some fifty hours', they reported, 'and have seen some of the best scenery in the world'.[22] Harold Williams agreed. 'The beautiful South of France passed before our eyes in a series of panoramas which astounded us', he wrote: 'Everywhere seemed to be running streams, avenues of trees and fields ablaze with scarlet poppies, blue cornflowers and white margue-rites'. As he concluded: 'Perhaps there are more beautiful countrysides than the South of France in the month of June, but to us it seemed not possible'. As the train continued its journey, he added, 'women left their work in the fields and came to the railway line to throw kisses, clap their hands, and call out *"Vive l'Australie"*'. Like Edgar Rule, Harold Williams delighted in these women: 'After the squalor of Egypt these deep-bosomed, sun-kissed daughters of France seemed to us to vie in beauty with their flower-decked fields'.[23]

But the illusion of peace and beauty could not last. 'After a two days' journey', recorded Edgar Rule, 'the 14th Battalion detrained just outside Bailleul, and marched off into billets. The weather had changed and rain began to fall. No sooner had the train stopped than the rumble of artillery could be heard, and through the pitch-black night the quivering flashes of the guns played up and down the horizon'. It was a sobering moment, and for 'some reason or other, everyone was quiet and serious'.[24] The joyous interlude was over, and the unknown dangers of the trenches awaited them. As Harold Williams put it, 'on the morning of the fourth day we reached our journey's end at Thiennes. We stood up as a battalion in the zone of the British Army of the

Western Front'.[25] Yet, for those who found themselves in agreeable billets, there was a sense of welcoming comfort. Lee and Will Pomeroy wrote that they were 'not very far from the front – close enough, in fact, to hear the big guns and to see some shots fired at the aeroplanes. We are billeted in farm houses', they added, 'which are very nice and warm, and are very different from the sandy desert of Egypt'. The brothers enjoyed the 'opportunity to see this pretty country', they added, and 'would not mind coming back here to work after the war'.[26] Sergeant George Vercoe, writing to his parents, also extolled the attractions of the landscape. The 'walks are glorious', he explained, 'the nice white undulating road with lovely big green trees on both sides . . . thousands of lovely little yellow buttercups, with their beautiful satin petals, peeping up amongst the green sward'. There were 'cornfields and the beautiful red poppies', and quaint villages with glorious rose gardens and friendly cafés where they drank beer and wine and coffee with the locals, sharing their bread. George Vercoe wrote his letter home on 5 July 1916, just a few days after the start of the Somme offensive, and even as he revelled in the wonders of the French countryside, he knew that much of it faced imminent destruction, as the war intruded on the lives of the civilian population. He had also seen the first victims of the Somme. 'The train-loads of wounded that come down every day are appalling', he wrote, 'yet often we envy these fellows who have done their bit and now taste the well-earned fruits of rest'.[27]

'Daddy Plumer's Army'

Initially, I ANZAC, commanded by General Birdwood, was sent to a quiet sector of the front near Armentières, to be followed shortly by II ANZAC under Lieutenant-General A.J. Godley. Here the Australians and New Zealanders were attached to General Sir Hubert Plumer's British Second Army, becoming an integral part of the British Expeditionary Force, and contributing nearly one-third of Plumer's 338,000 men. Considered a 'nursery' area, where there had been little hard fighting for months, the sector was deemed ideal for introducing new troops to life in the trenches on the Western Front. The Anzacs – or 'diggers' as they were increasingly known, an allusion to their experiences at Gallipoli but also an echo of the gold rush days of the

1850s when the term had first emerged – were delighted to be there. As Sergeant Cyril Lawrence noted in his diary, 'to men who went through Anzac [Gallipoli] this scrap is fine'. At Gallipoli, he said, 'there was no escape from shells and bullets, you were in it every day and night'. By contrast, in the line at Armentières, 'if you are not on duty you can get back into towns and villages, buy what you like and enjoy a certain amount of civilization, for the women and children live right up almost into the firing line itself and only leave when they are blown out'. The trenches themselves were comparatively safe, he added, with the enemy positions a good distance away: 'the trenches in our area, the nearest they approach each other is 200 yards and it is more often 400, whilst at Anzac 5 yards was the distance and 200 yards the extreme'.[28] The comparison with conditions at Gallipoli also impressed Sergeant Roy Denning: 'There were no girls at all to talk to on Gallipoli, and no beer, or white or red wine'.[29] Looking back later on those early weeks at Armentières, many Australians remembered them fondly as halcyon days, a veritable calm before the storm. 'I had the best of times in the trenches and wish I was back again', wrote Sergeant Cec Baldwin, 'I did 3 hours work laying wire at night, and the rest of the 24 hours to myself. It suited me down to the ground'.[30]

If the 'nursery' conditions agreed with the Australians, as they settled into conditions on the Western Front, then so did their status as part of Plumer's Second Army. As Godley wrote to George V's private secretary, his men were delighted at 'having gone to Plumer's Army, as he had so much to do with the Australians and New Zealanders in South Africa, and knows and likes them and they know and like him'.[31] According to one story, a British Tommy called out to an Australian battalion as it marched past in northern France, 'Where are you off to Aussie?' Without a second thought, the answer shot back: 'We don't know, but thank God we're going to Daddy Plumer's Army'.[32] As Godley had explained, the Australians and New Zealanders had fought under 'Daddy' Plumer in the Boer War, and they had got on well with their commander. Geoffrey Powell, Plumer's biographer, considers that 'Plumer had . . . a better understanding of these fine troops than any other senior British general'.[33] Leading a motley collection of colonial units, such as the Queensland Imperial Bushmen and the New Zealand Mounted Rifles, Plumer had forged a working relationship based on mutual respect. One particular incident stands out. Having completed its tour of duty, an Australian unit was told at the eleventh hour that it was needed for one last operation, to assist a column that had found itself in trouble. On hearing the news the men grew mutinous, and their mood was not helped by the condescending speech of a British general sent to order them. Plumer intervened, and on parading the unit told them bluntly that he would be there at 7 a.m. the next morning and so would they. The Australians broke into cheers, and fell in the next day as instructed.

Although few of those arriving at Armentières had actually served under Plumer in South Africa, he remained a legend among the Australians, and there was much goodwill. But life in the 'nursery' was not always as easy as some had hoped. On 5 May 1916 the Germans unexpectedly mounted a raid on the Australian line, inflicting more than 100 casualties and taking ten prisoners. Two supposedly 'secret' Stokes mortars, a new weapon in the British Empire's arsenal, were also taken in the raid, to the fury of Plumer and Haig. It was apparent that the Germans were gradually asserting an offensive superiority in the area, and in response the Australians launched a raid of their own on 5 June. They managed to kill a few Germans in the lightly manned enemy trenches, and took one prisoner. As the raiders returned to their own trenches, they were located by the German artillery, causing thirty casualties. Three weeks later, during another raid, 18-year-old Private William Jackson became the first Australian on the Western Front to win the Victoria Cross, when he took a German prisoner, brought in three wounded men under fire, and went back to search for more, despite being badly hit in the arm by a shell fragment.

Raid and counter-raid

Turning up the pressure on the enemy, such attacks became more frequent. Edgar Rule described the preparations for a raid on 2 July. The raiders 'certainly looked a queer lot', he wrote, 'more like pirates than soldiers. To hide their identity from the enemy . . . they had discarded their Aussie uniforms for British tunics; faces were blackened so as not to show up in the light of flares, and instead of hats, they wore dark woollen caps'.[34] Some were armed with rifles and blackened bayonets, others carried pistols, and still others knobkerries, ideal for hand-to-hand trench warfare. Lieutenant Harold Wanliss, a public-schoolboy from Ballarat in Victoria, led the raid, for which he was subsequently awarded the Distinguished Service Order. When the raiders reached the German wire, they found to their dismay that it had not been flattened by the preceding barrage, but they somehow made it to the enemy trenches where they reckoned to have inflicted fifty or so casualties. Sergeant Jack Garcia, one of the raiders, later described his encounter with a 'big Hun' in a dugout. The German threw up his hands, begging for mercy: 'Me father of fourteen children'. Then, said Garcia, 'It's time you were b***** well dead', whereupon he shot him.[35] Ten minutes later, the raid completed, the Australians dashed for their own lines, only to be caught by enemy machine-gun fire, with numerous casualties. As Plumer observed laconically: 'The Canadians and Australians were both cock-o-hoop when they first came to this front, but all of them now have had their lesson. Even the Anzacs have learnt that they do not know everything, but they are excellent at raiding'.[36]

The 'nursery' little by little had become a nightmare of raid and counter-raid, and the Australians' first taste of trench warfare on the Western Front had become bloodier and more harrowing than many had been led to expect. The welcoming land of pretty girls and *estaminets*, where the soldiers would repair for their beer and wine, had gradually assumed a more sinister face. It is not clear when the Australians adopted their own version of the British Tommy's favourite, 'Mademoiselle from Armentières', but it seems likely to date from this time. Strangely sentimental, and surprisingly mild compared to some extremely bawdy British versions, the Australian song captured the changing mood of the European spring and early summer of 1916. It tells its own story of loss of innocence, from the Australians' carefree early days in the benign 'nursery' town, including the inevitable romance between digger and 'Mademoiselle', to the tragic moment when the Anzacs suddenly melted away:

Mademoiselle from Armenteers [*sic*], parlez-vous,
Sang the diggers between their beers, parlez-vous,
And the soldiers' chorus and ballad gay,
Rang through the old estaminet,
Inky pinky parlez-vous.

Men from Wagga and Gundagai, parlez-vous,
From Perth, the Towers and Boggabri, parlez-vous
From Sydney city and Dandenong,
Sinking their sorrows in wine and song,
Inky pinky parlez-vous.

Mademoiselle enjoyed the din, parlez-vous
She tripped around with the bock and the vin, parlez-vous,
And Mademoiselle in an innocent way,
Trolled a stave of a ribald lay,
Inky pinky parlez-vous.

One young digger, tanned and lean, parlez-vous,
From Darling Downs or the Riverine, parlez-vous,
Set her heart in a rapturous whirl,
When he vowed that she was his dinkum girl,
Inky pinky parlez-vous.

They laughed and loved in that old French town, parlez-vous,
And her heart spoke out of those eyes of brown, parlez-vous,
But the time went by and there came the day,
When he and his cobbers marched away,
Inky pinky parlez-vous.

Maybe on a field in France he fell, parlez-vous,
No word came back to Mademoiselle, parlez-vous,
But a little French girl with eyes of brown,
Prayed for him still in that war-swept town,
Inky pinky parlez-vous.[37]

By early July, as the battle of the Somme developed, it was feared that raiding would no longer be sufficient to keep the attention of the Germans deployed near Armentières. Something far more elaborate would have to be undertaken if the enemy was to be prevented from moving units to reinforce the epic struggle unfolding some fifty miles to the south. On 7 July, I ANZAC was itself ordered to the Somme, while II ANZAC remained in the north to try to stem the anticipated leaching of German troops from the sector. On 13 July 1916 it was reported with alarm that nine enemy battalions had already relocated southwards, and plans for a more convincing Allied show of force in the north were hastily drawn up. This was to be a feint conducted by two divisions – the 61st (South Midlands) and the 5th Australian Division – at Fromelles. Its architect was Lieutenant-General Sir Richard Haking, commander of XI Corps in General Sir Charles Monro's First Army, a British officer of the old school who, like many of his contemporaries, believed absolutely in unswerving commitment to offensive action, in which the élan and verve of the infantry would be the deciding factor in any battle. 'There is one rule which can never be departed from', he insisted, 'and which alone will lead to success, and that is always to push forward, always to attack'.[38] Putting his conviction to the test, he had only recently launched a two-battalion assault in the sector, resulting in over a thousand casualties, which had singularly failed to take its objectives. The experience, however, according to Haking, was not wasted on his troops, for it would improve their fighting quality, ensuring that their performance would be better next time round. Elan was everything, he continued to believe.

'Hopping the bags' at Fromelles

The Sugarloaf, a German salient projecting into the Allied positions, was the objective in the plan that emerged. Haking had hoped for massed artillery to support the attack but Plumer could only provide the inexperienced and partly trained artilleries of the 4th and 5th Australian divisions. Moreover, of the twelve infantry battalions of the Australian 5th Division earmarked for the attack, six had been in the front line opposite Fromelles for only two days when they received their operation order, and the remainder had not even arrived. The 61st Division, meanwhile, had been badly battered in recent raiding, and was undermanned and poorly equipped. The omens were not good. Additionally, the interdivisional boundary between the South Midlanders and the Australians lay just beyond the Sugarloaf, confounding military doctrine. The join between one division and another was inherently weak, it was stressed, where communication and co-ordination might easily collapse in the heat of battle. Boundaries, therefore, should not be located at critical points – but this is precisely what Haking had arranged at the Sugarloaf. Observing that the Sugarloaf objective lay 420 yards across open ground, Brigadier-General Harold 'Pompey' Elliot, commander of the 5th Division's 15th Brigade, had expressed grave misgivings about the enterprise, and was careful to place this on record years later as details of what had happened at Fromelles began to emerge. But Elliot's superior officer, Major-General James McCay, another Australian, was keen for the plan to go ahead, and looked forward to committing his men to the battle. As new to the Western Front as his troops, he had no experience of warfare in this environment and, like Haking, believed in the overwhelming power of the offensive. He was excited that his division, the last of the Australians to arrive in France, would be the first to see major action, an opportunity to display their superior skill as infantrymen.

Haig had also expressed misgivings about the proposed attack, wondering whether the artillery was sufficient, but gave his cautious approval conditional on receiving assurances that the support was adequate. At the same time, Haig's staff began to reassess the transfer of German units south to the Somme, and suggested that the action at Fromelles might not be necessary after all. Haking was keen to press ahead regardless but poor weather caused him to seek a postponement. By now Haig's staff had already reversed their opinion, and were anxious for the assault to begin as soon as possible. The attack was scheduled for 19 July 1916, by which time the battle-hardened 6th Bavarian Reserve Division opposite the Australian trenches, having observed the preparations, was fully appraised of what was about to happen. But Haking remained supremely confidant, and so did the Australians. Even as the massive bombardment opened on the German lines, a prelude to the imminent assault, some of the Australians indulged in a last-minute drink. 'We entered an estaminet', wrote one soldier, 'and found the place crowded to overflowing . . . The men were in the best of spirits and looked forward to the attack as if it were a football match'.[39] At 6 p.m., in the evening light of a glorious summer day, the British and Australians finally went over the top – 'hopping the bags', in Australian parlance. The 61st Division was swiftly defeated (in Haking's opinion it was 'not sufficiently imbued with the offensive spirit'), and although the 'Australian infantry attacked in the most gallant manner' – as Haking admitted – it too was badly mauled, many succumbing to the relentless German fire.[40] Sergeant Martin, from Dulwich in New South Wales, later gave an account of the battle that, as Bill Gammage has observed, 'well outlines Fromelles'. According to Martin:

> We lost some men going over to the enemy's lines and you could hear the moans of the wounded and dying wherever you went. I got over the parapet . . . made for a big hole and rested there while we got our breath . . . after that we made a dash but had to drop into any sort of hole we could find for machine guns were turned on us and the bullets were just skimming over our heads . . . We got to Fritz's front line trenches eventually . . . and stayed there till 5.30 a.m. when we were forced to retire . . . we had to make a bolt for it and a good few were hit coming back . . . the bullets happened to miss me somehow or other.[41]

As Martin's summary indicates, there were those who penetrated the German lines. But they were soon bogged down in mud, as water poured in from a main drainage ditch that had been breached and clogged by shellfire. In the early hours of the following morning, 20 July, the Germans counter-attacked, and shortly after first light the order was given for the Australians to withdraw. In the manner described by Sergeant Martin, the Australians stumbled back to their lines as best they could, and many were shot down as they leapt from one shell hole to the next. Wounded men were 'calling out for their mother', Martin recalled, while others, shell-shocked out of their wits, 'were blabbering sentences one could not make out'.[42] As the survivors reached the comparative safety of their own trenches, they realized the full enormity of what they had just experienced. 'Our senses gradually returned to normal', wrote Corporal Harold Williams, 'and we looked around us like men awakened from a nightmare'. The ordeal 'was plainly visible on all the faces', he added, 'ghastly white showing through the masks of grime and dried sweat, eyes glassy, protruding, and full of that horror seen only upon men who have lived through a heavy bombardment'.[43]

Sergeant William Mair, from Argyle in New South Wales, writing home to his wife Ellen, explained that from the moment they had climbed over the parapet, 'we were met with such a deluge of shells and machine gun fire it seemed almost impossible for human beings to have the nerve to face such a fearful blast'. Yet they did, as Mair reported, 'and got right in among the "Boches"'. Some of them were mere boys, he said, 'sitting in the dugouts and crying', but in the second German line

Australians of the 53rd Battalion, moments before 'hopping the bags' at Fromelles on 19 July 1916.

AUSTRALIAN WAR MEMORIAL H16396

the Australians encountered what they imagined to be 'big Prussians and Brandenburgers', whose officers urged them onwards.[44] William Mair was one of those hit in the German counter-attack:

> That was when I was bowled over, and Ellen, the man that carried me back to the rear was Dan Ryan from Cootamundra, and he had half his face shot away. I will always say that Dan Ryan saved my life, because you know I would have lain there all through the night, and would surely have been blown to pieces. The stretcher-bearers were all killed or wounded so you can see I am a lucky man.[45]

'Don't forget me, cobber'

Corporal Elliott, from Newtown in New South Wales, also lent a helping hand among the wounded stranded in No-Man's Land. From the Australian lines, he heard a soldier crying out. Taking a volunteer with him, Elliott cautiously climbed over the parapet and crawled out to the injured man, who had been hit in both legs by machine-gun bullets. But the moment they tried to lift him, the Germans opened fire. One round went through Elliott's hat, grazing his scalp, and the Australians decided that it was sensible to leave their comrade until he could be recovered safely under darkness. They gave him cigarettes and matches and, before setting back to their trench, promised to have water and food sent out as soon as possible. As Elliott recorded, 'I was a bit narked at not getting him in, but it would have been suicidal to attempt any further'.[46] But Elliott's actions won the admiration of his colleagues. Harold Williams was full of praise for 'Skinny' Elliott, and added that after dark 'Skinny' went out once more, with two others, and brought the wounded man in. 'Only those who witnessed this performance and Skinny Elliott's particular pals knew of this exploit', Williams confided: 'The corporal of No.9 Section was very proud of his punctured hat, and guarded it like a family heirloom'.[47] Likewise, Sergeant Simon Fraser, a farmer from Victoria, was successful in his determined efforts to rescue the wounded marooned in No-Man's Land. Altogether, he estimated, 'we must have brought in over 250 men by our company alone', and he explained their technique: 'You had to lie down and get him on your back then rise & duck for your life with the chance of getting a bullet in you before you were safe'. In the early morning fog, Fraser and his mates scoured the battlefield and found 'a fine haul of wounded'. Finally, as he brought in a soldier with 'a big wound in his thigh', he heard another sing out: 'Don't forget me, cobber'.[48] As Peter Pedersen has rightly observed, the 'cry became part of Australian folklore'.[49]

The watchful Germans did their best to prevent or at least hinder these rescue operations, and many of the wounded who might have been saved died of their wounds or were killed by the vigilant enemy. As Harold Williams wrote, those 'trying to crawl back to us . . . made of themselves a target for German machine-gunners'. The wounded called out unceasingly for help and water. 'The sun and flies persecuted them', he said, and those 'who were able to crawl were sniped at by the Germans'. One such man, pulling his badly injured pal with him, inched his way to the Australian line: 'He got within a few yards of our parapet when he was fired upon by a German sniper'.[50] A blinded soldier was seen to stumble around in No-Man's Land for several days, before the Germans shot him – observers could not decide whether this was an act of malice or compassion, killing a defenceless man in cold blood or putting him out of his misery. Another wounded Australian, disoriented on the battlefield, mistook the German lines for his own, and with superhuman effort crawled almost to the enemy trench, where he was bombed by its occupants. In all, the Australians suffered 5,333 casualties at Fromelles – almost a quarter of all their losses at Gallipoli – and the 5th Division was finished as a fighting force for the time being. 'Pompey' Elliott wept when he learned the scale of the defeat, one officer later recalling that he would 'always have before my eyes the picture of Pompey . . . the morning after Fromelles, tears streaming down his face, shaking hands with the pitiful remnant of his brigade'.[51]

Haking, while acknowledging the courage of the Australians and praising their penetration of the German lines, decided that 'they were not sufficiently trained to consolidate the enemy's position'. This was why they 'were eventually compelled to withdraw and lost heavily in doing so'.[52] Some Australians admitted their inexperience. R.A. McInnis, a surveyor from Brisbane, Queensland, lamented sadly that 'we were mere recruits, and have had our full education in one day'. But not all were so forgiving. Harold Williams insisted that they had been 'sacrificed on the altar of incompetence'.[53] Pompey Elliott blamed Haking, as well he might, but many Australians pointed their accusatory fingers at McCay, their divisional commander, and his conduct of the battle. He earned the contempt of his own staff officers, and became known as the 'Butcher of Fromelles'. Others were swift to pour opprobrium on the British, considering that they had let the Anzacs

Wounded Australian prisoners of war at a German collecting station on the morning of 20 July 1916, after the battle of Fromelles.

AUSTRALIAN WAR MEMORIAL A01551

down at Fromelles, just as they had done at Gallipoli. Indeed, it was pointed out that 61st Division had lost far fewer men, 1,547 in all, and that this was evidence of their half-hearted and lacklustre performance. But the South Midlanders had gone into battle at half-strength, so the comparison was not entirely fair. Nonetheless, as Lyn Macdonald has observed, the damage had been done, 'and it created a breach between the Australian fighting troops and their British comrades, which would never be completely closed'.[54]

'It is very hard for a Mother'

The story of Fromelles has an added poignancy, in that the dead Australian and British soldiers were recovered from the battlefield by the Germans, and interred in a mass grave behind enemy lines that remained undiscovered until July 2008. The subsequent exhumation of the fallen of Fromelles caused a sensation across Australia, and for many families at last answered questions about the fate of loved ones. In 1916, not knowing had been an intolerable burden. Sarah Briggs, for example, had been informed after the battle that her son Clarence was 'missing', and in December learned that he had been 'killed in action'. Thereafter there was silence, and in April 1917 she wrote from Adelaide to the Base Records Office in Melbourne, 'asking if you could give me a little information concerning my son'. As she explained: 'It is very hard for a Mother to take for granted she has lost her son just on the word of a cable . . . I feel very anxious & would be grateful to you if you could let me know anything at all about him'. The military authorities replied that there was no further information to hand, although the Germans eventually returned, via the Red Cross, Clarence's identity disc, together with his notebook, papers, letters and some photographs. But Sarah never did find out that her son's lifeless body had been dumped onto a light railway wagon by the enemy, and taken for burial to a freshly prepared mass grave.[55]

There was also much uncertainty about the nature of the battle. First news came from a German communiqué, widely reported across Australia in the metropolitan and regional press. The *Queensland Times*, *Newcastle Morning Herald*, Launceston *Examiner*, and numerous other newspapers repeated German claims that the 'English attacked with considerable forces our positions west and north of Fromelles but were thrown back by our counter-attacks from points occupied'.[56] There was no mention of Australian participation – 'English' was a generic term as far the Germans were concerned – and few papers made the connection until Charles Bean, the official war correspondent, arrived on the scene. The Hobart *Mercury* and other newspapers were then able to offer clarification, explaining that the 'battle in which the Australians took part on Wednesday was fought on a two-mile front at Fromelles'. To this was added Bean's account. The shellfire was heavier than anything experienced at Gallipoli, he said, while many of the Australians 'were untried previously, yet the manner in which they carried it through seems to have been worthy of all the traditions of Anzac'.[57] But Haig, anxious to play down the scale of the reverse and, as he saw it, to put it in context and proportion had, in his own communiqué, reduced the battle (located vaguely somewhere 'south of Armentières) to merely 'some important raids'. In Australia, this was interpreted by a puzzled *Warrnambool Standard* to mean 'extensive raids'.[58] The Darwin *Northern Territory Times & Gazette*, with similar uncertainty, published two unconnected reports in the same edition (27 July), one on 'Australian raiding', the other on the action at Fromelles. It had not occurred to the editor that the events might be one and the same. By the end of the month, some eyewitness reports had reached the press. The *Weekly Times*, published in Victoria, carried an account by an unnamed sergeant, currently in hospital in England, who explained that the Australians had had to advance over 450 yards of open ground 'under a hail of shells and bullets from machine guns', and that he had been hit 'simultaneously' by a shell fragment and a bullet. He was also 'absolutely convinced' that German snipers had tried to 'deliberately pot the wounded'.[59]

However, the true enormity of Fromelles was hidden from public view, the full scale of the losses and the lapses in military planning not appreciated until long after the war was over. Moreover, events on the Somme were fast-moving, and popular attention in Australia was soon fixed on the battle for Pozières Ridge, initiated only a few days after Fromelles. Bewildered by the pace and unable to distinguish Fromelles from the wider picture, the *Yorke's Peninsula Advertiser* reported incorrectly on 28 July 1916 that the 'Pozieres battle is the first pitched engagement in which they [the Australians] have taken part in

France', an opinion that typified the continuing confusion.[60] Later, in the October, when the *People's Weekly* published a letter from Richard Ritter, it did not realize that it was reporting the battle of Fromelles, seen through the eyes of the 5th Division's ill-fated 32nd Battalion. 'I have been in action and our Coy [Company] had rather a bad time', Ritter confessed:

> The boys were game enough, but there were not many who came back. . . . We were out of our trenches and got across no-man's land alright. Personally I did not expect to get back. It was a terrible experience. I do not want to spend another such night. The Germans turned water into the trenches and it was up to our wastes [*sic*] deep. Then, they used gas and liquid fire on us. Some of the boys were badly burnt and others suffered from shell shock . . . I lost all my mates.[61]

The haze and uncertainty that obscured Fromelles militated against objective analysis, although the Melbourne *Age* did try to make some sense of the engagement. 'At the very least', it opined optimistically, 'the Australian assault may be expected to detain an equally large [enemy] force in front of the Anzac sector, and to that extent contribute towards the operations on the Somme'.[62] It was not a view that survived later scrutiny, where conventional wisdom came to insist that the battle was pointless and irrelevant. However, more recent research has suggested that the *Age's* assessment was essentially correct, that the Australian action at Fromelles pinned down six German divisions for up to nine weeks, preventing their transfer south to the Somme. As Gary Sheffield has observed, if that was the case, then perhaps Fromelles could be counted a strategic success after all, despite its many shortcomings and the appalling losses.[63]

The assault on Pozières

In the early hours of 23 July 1916, just four days after Fromelles, I ANZAC Corps, having arrived from Armentières earlier in the month, went into action at Pozières, on the Somme. In contrast to the feint at Fromelles, Pozières Ridge was a critical strategic objective, key to unlocking the capture of Thiepval, itself a significant prize in the unfolding Battle of the Somme. Indeed, when Thiepval eventually fell to the Allies on 27 September that year, the effect on German morale and self-confidence was devastating, contributing to the gradual erosion of the enemy's sense of martial superiority. Earlier attempts by the British to take Pozières had been unsuccessful but by 6.30 a.m. on 23 July, the Australian 1st Division was already celebrating the capture of its initial objectives. The onslaught had been devastating, the preceding artillery barrage so disorienting the enemy that their first trench fell swiftly to the advancing Australians. Some Germans surrendered rather than fight but those who refused to cross No-Man's Land to the Australian lines were simply shot. The Anzacs had 'tasted blood', said one observer, and they rushed onwards 'like a pack of hungry dogs', capturing further ground.[64] The right flank, however, encountered stiffer opposition, and was pinned down by Germans bombers 'using a longer range bomb than ours'.[65] To break the impasse, Private John Leak rushed forward, braving heavy machine-gun fire at close range, and hurled three bombs into the midst of the enemy. Following up his attack, he bayoneted three unwounded survivors. For his action he was awarded the Victoria Cross.

Born in Portsmouth, England, 'Jack' Leak had enlisted in Rockhampton, Queensland, and had been briefly at Gallipoli before being evacuated with dysentery. Less than a month after his gallantry at Pozières, he was shot in the back and sent to England, where, at Wareham in Dorset, recuperating from his wound, the feisty streak that he had exhibited on the battlefield got him into trouble. For the crime of 'entering sergeants mess & demanding drink', and refusing to leave when ordered to do so by the Regimental Sergeant Major, he was sentenced to fourteen days detention. Worse was to come. Back in France, he was court-martialled in November 1917 for absenting himself 'from the line' for six days while 'on active service', for which crime he was sentenced to penal servitude for life (in the British Army, he might have been shot). This was reduced to two years, and then suspended altogether, recognition no doubt of his distinguished record. Yet there were further punishments for being absent without leave, and for 'insolence to an NCO'. Wounded three times and gassed before his eventual repatriation to Australia in 1919, John Leak VC demonstrated an individualism and independence of action that made him an outstanding soldier on the battlefield but a constant thorn in the side of the military establishment.[66]

AUSTRALIAN WAR MEMORIAL H06716A

Private John Leak, 9th Battalion AIF, who won the Victoria Cross for his outstanding courage and presence of mind at Pozières.

Following Leak's heroic action, the advance at Pozières was further hindered by machine-gun fire and, at 1.30 a.m., the Germans counter-attacked, forcing the Australians back. But it was a temporary reverse, for in an outstanding display of initiative and courage, Lieutenant Arthur Blackburn, in civilian life a solicitor in Adelaide, led more than half-a-dozen charges that regained the lost ground. In doing so, he won the second Victoria Cross of the night. By first light, the Australians were in Pozières village, mopping up resistance and consolidating their positions. The Germans counter-attacked again at about 5.30 a.m., this time in strength. According to one Australian, they 'came towards us like swarms of ants . . . In our trench each man full of fight and confidence lined the parapet and emptied magazine after magazine . . . The machine-guns caused great losses and artillery, which had been brought up, tore great gaps in the oncoming lines. The attack just melted away'.[67] By 6.30 a.m. it appeared to be all over, with souvenir hunters wearing the much sought-after *pickelhauben* spiked helmets, others sun-bathing or smoking or eating a leisurely meal. But in reality it was a temporary lull, for the Germans were also acutely aware of the strategic significance of Pozières Ridge. In the ensuing hours and days, they brought in fresh troops and subjected the Australians to prolonged bombardment of appalling intensity. Those who endured it, wrote Edgar Rule, 'looked like men who had been in hell . . . each man looked drawn and haggard, and so dazed that they appeared to be walking in a dream, and their eyes looked glassy and starey'.[68]

As the battle developed, the Australians committed their reserve battalions to the fray, rotating those in the front line. Private Fred Russell, a signaller in the 22nd Battalion, 6th (Victoria) Brigade, recalled that:

> Our Brigade came in and we had to take over from where the 1st Division were to carry on the fighting and go as far as we could. The place by this time was a shambles of destruction – a wreck. Our headquarters, where I was with the C[ommanding] O[fficer] of the Battalion, was in a fort called Gibraltar. It was a German concrete dugout with a six-foot tower above the ground, right in the centre of the village of Pozieres and all the rest of the houses round it were absolutely smashed to bits . . . We weren't in there ten minutes when a shell landed on top of it. There were about twenty or thirty fellows down below in there – and down fifteen or twenty feet in a very solid concrete-lined job. But the compression was terrific. All night long they were calling for stretcher-bearers. Every time a salvo came over, after the explosion, you could hear these calls going up outside, 'Stretcher-bearer! Stretcher-bearer!'.[69]

By dawn of 5 August 1916, the crest of Pozières Ridge was finally occupied by the Australians. Private Russell's 22nd Battalion had played a critical part in its capture, securing its left flank. But the Germans, rattled and infuriated at having lost this vital position, were to make one last desperate attempt to recapture it. They intensified their shelling so that, as Edgar Rule put it, 'even . . . the greenhorns [knew] that something was in the wind'. On 7 August the enemy barrage lifted, and the counter-attack began. Rule watched the action through his field glasses. He could see some Australians standing up and firing point-blank at the advancing hordes, while others were at work with their bayonets. 'It was one of the queerest sights I've ever seen', he wrote: 'Huns and Aussies were scattered in ones and twos all along the side of the ridge. It was such a mix-up that it was hard to tell who were Huns and who were Aussies. Each Aussie seemed to be having a war all of his own, and the issue was not long in doubt'.[70] Soon streams of prisoners were arriving at the Australian lines, seemingly happy to be out of the war, and then the stretcher-bearers came in, bringing the wounded. Rule was dismayed to find that among the injured was Albert Jacka, the man who had won a Victoria Cross at Gallipoli.

Wearing his captured German spiked helmet, 'souvenired' in the fighting at Pozières, an Australian soldier shaves in a back area. The leather satchels are also spoils 'liberated' from the enemy.

Jacka had been in a deep dugout when the Germans attacked. A bomb was rolled down the stairway, killing two of the occupants. Jacka rushed up the stairs, firing his revolver as he went, killing the German sentry at the top. He then encountered four enemy in a shell hole. As Jacka himself explained:

> All I could see were their heads, shoulders, and rifles. As I went towards them, they began firing point-blank at me. They hit me three times and each time the terrific impact of bullets fired at such close range swung me off my feet. But each time I sprang up like a prize-fighter, and kept getting closer. When I got to them, they flung down their rifles and put up their hands. I shot three through the head and put a bayonet through the fourth. I had to do it – they would have killed me the moment I turned my back.[71]

Jacka killed a further German, shooting him in the stomach, before collapsing. A stretcher-bearer found him, removed his tunic and dressed his wounds, and left to find a stretcher. But the ambulanceman never returned. Jacka imagined that he was about to join the many wounded left to die on the battlefield, and somehow found the strength to stagger towards the Australian lines. When he was brought in it was found that he had suffered no fewer than seven wounds, and those who had seen him in action reckoned he had killed twenty Germans that day. Men marvelled that Albert Jacka had survived, and speculated that he would receive a bar to his VC. In the event, he received 'only a Military Cross', as Rule put it.[72]

'Australians are recognised as the most dashing of all British troops'

In marked contrast to the public confusion over Fromelles, Australians at home were swiftly made aware of the great victory at Pozières. The high price paid would become apparent soon enough, but for the moment there was only pride in Australian achievement. A few days into the action, for example, the *Yorke's Peninsula Advertiser*, quoting the august opinion of the New York *Tribune*, announced proudly that now 'the Australians are recognised as the most dashing of all British troops'. The *Sydney Morning Herald* admitted that the 'Australian attack on Pozieres . . . came as a surprise to most people' but went on to quote another American paper, the *New Yorke Globe*, whose admiration for the Australians was 'because they closely resemble the Americans', a flattering comparison of which the *Herald* evidently approved. The Launceston *Examiner*, bristling with self-congratulation, was delighted that the 'Australians were chosen to attack Pozieres', a tacit recognition of their superior fighting skills, while the *Bathurst Times* reported the 'Australians' thrilling deeds'. Across Australia, editors reached for superlatives, competing to outdo one another in their choice of gushing and telling phrases. 'Pozieres falls after desperate resistance', said the *Barrier Miner*. 'Our boys achieve a dashing success', recorded the *Brisbane Courier*; 'Australians prove themselves', thought the Perth *West Australian*; and 'gallant fighting wins the day' was the opinion of the *Townsville Daily Bulletin*. 'Anzacs win renown for Australia' was the *Ballarat Courier's* verdict, while the *Mildura Cultivator* was pleased to note that the German 'defenders of Pozieres were practically

AUSTRALIAN WAR MEMORIAL P07670.003

Australian machine-gunners, probably from the 46th Battalion, in action at Pozières. Taken (illegally) by Corporal Robert Nenke, a despatch rider in the 1st Divisional Signal Company, this photograph was found among the personal effects of Sergeant Norman Pontin, from Richmond, Victoria, who was killed in action at Bullecourt on 11 April 1917. Robert Nenke, from Nurioopta in South Australia, one of many Australians of German descent to enlist, died on 10 August 1918 of wounds received two days earlier in the battle of Amiens.

exterminated'. This was just as well because, as the *Geelong Advertiser* informed its readers, 'Huns drink ether, then, maddened, kill the wounded'. The Adelaide *Chronicle* heaped praise on the 'Australian super-men', while the Perth *Sunday Times*, looking for a new angle, had a stern message for those male readers uncertain whether to join up: 'Don't be a slacker. Don't let the girls murmur "cold feet" when you pass by. Read what the Australians did at Pozieres'.[73]

Initially, it was reported that casualties had been comparatively light. But soon the bad news came rolling in. William Pomeroy wrote home shortly after the battle. 'Just a few lines to let you know I am safe and well', he explained to his parents, 'after the great charge we made . . . I dare say by now you have heard of our great victory'. He had gone into action with his Lewis light machine gun, he added, 'and had a few narrow escapes. We can all shake hands with ourselves in getting out so lucky'. But others were less fortunate, and Pomeroy mourned the loss of his good friend Joe Keen. 'Poor Joe Keen was killed', he wrote, 'so if you see his mother tell her from me that he fought . . . and died the death of a gallant soldier'.[74] Fanny Keen had received the inevitable telegram, delivered from the post office by the local Methodist minister, informing her that her son had been killed in action. But there was no further word – no explanation of how he had died, or where he had been interred – and the silence became unbearable. On 30 November 1916, unable to take the strain any longer, Fanny Keen wrote to the Base Records Office to try to learn more. 'I have heard nothing since I received the cable', she said, 'I feel it deeply to have had no particulars yet'. The military authorities responded in their usual fashion, to the effect that there were no further details available, although in due course Fanny Keen did receive the pitifully few items of her son's personal belongings, sent home from France: his identity disc, some letters, some coins, a scarf, a wallet, five photographs, two brushes, and some cards.[75]

'Mucky Farm'

Having held the crest on Pozières Ridge, the Australians' next objective in the push towards Thiepval was Mouquet Farm. Strongly held by the Germans, Mouquet Farm – 'Mucky Farm' or 'Moo-cow Farm', as it was known to the Australians – proved a formidable obstacle. The first assault was made on the evening of 8 August 1916, a prelude to dreadful days of attack and counter-attack, as the Australians tried to inch their way towards the Farm. 'I have been to HELL and have had the luck to get back again', wrote Captain Harry Armitage to his parents, describing the brutal fighting of mid-August 1916.[76] The Australian 1st Division was relieved by the 2nd Division on 22 August, as the battle continued. The 2nd was replaced in turn by the 4th Division, and on 27 August bombing parties from the 4th Brigade renewed the assault. Edgar Rule was in the 'stunt', as he called it, and almost lost his life. Unobserved by Rule, a German officer prepared to shoot him, until 'little Billy Mayne' spotted the enemy and 'put a bomb at his feet'. Mayne was later killed at Bullecourt, and Rule always considered 'that I owe my life to him. He was one of the nicest little fellows we had, and as game as a bull-ant'. In danger now of being overwhelmed by German bombs – 'I could hear the Huns yelling "Ja! Ja" as they heaved them' – Rule was hit in the hand and legs by fragments. When the bomb exploded, he recalled, 'I had the impression that someone had stabbed me with hot pins down my legs, and I felt blood running down my hand. It knocked the breath out of me, and I remember staggering around for a while'. Retreating now, Rule's party made its way back to brigade headquarters. Lieutenant Dean, another of the attackers, arrived at about the same time. 'Here we are, here we are again', he exclaimed jovially. But a bullet had lifted the top of his skull, inflicting a wound from which he died shortly afterwards.[77]

By now heavy rain had turned the battlefield into a quagmire. Nevertheless, the 13th Brigade almost succeeded in taking Mouquet Farm on 3 September. As Signaller T. Allen wrote to his wife, penning his note in the aftermath on the 4th, he and his mates had gone 'into the trenches at 12 o'clock on Saturday night, September 2, and worked all night digging ourselves in under heavy shell and shrapnel fire'. The Germans bombarded them steadily for eight hours, he said, 'but there was no shifting our boys'. At dawn Allen's unit made its attack. As he explained, 'our lads hopped over and captured one of their best strongholds, called Moquet [sic] farm, and two lines of trenches the other side of it'. Inevitably, 'Fritz counter attacked, but to his great surprise got driven back with heavy losses'. The Australians had taken up to 500 prisoners, Allen reckoned, and many were glad to surrender. 'Mercy, comrade, we no want to fight', they cried, throwing up their hands. 'You can bet', however, said Allen darkly, 'that we are getting a little of our own back now'. Allen trumpeted Mouquet Farm as 'a great victory over the enemy' but the reality was that, even as he penned his letter to his wife, the Australians were again driven back.[78] It was to be their last attempt at this tantalizing objective, for on 5 September they were relieved by the Canadian Corps. Ironically, Thiepval fell to the Allies *before* the Canadians finally took Mouquet Farm, attacked from another direction.

For the exhausted Australians, the happy days of Armèntieres seemed a lifetime away. When visited by senior officers and staff, they sang gently 'Take me back to Daddy Plumer's Army', a yearning to return to the 'nursery' but also a charmingly insubordinate commentary on what they had been made to endure at Pozières and Mouquet Farm. They had sustained some 23,000 casualties, not far short of the total at Gallipoli.[79] In the event, I ANZAC was moved to a relatively quiet sector, this time at Ypres in Belgian Flanders. 'Let me tell you it's a home here compared to Pozieres', wrote Lance-Corporal Richard Daw to a friend in Australia, 'you might not believe me when I tell you that at Pozieres there were more shells fired in a day than bullets here'.[80] Private Les Bishop, writing to his sister, experienced the same sense of relief, and was comforted that the 'Belgian people speak our language more fluently than the French'. Looking back, he could hardly believe that his nerve had not cracked at Pozières. 'While you are under shell fire it is not too bad', he confessed, 'but after it is all over there is a kind of reaction, and you feel yourself going, and it is then that you have to pull yourself together'.[81]

The end of the Somme offensive

Sadly, the Ypres sojourn proved to be all too short, and after its brief respite I ANZAC was ordered back to France, taking over the Allied front line between Flers and Gueudecourt from 21 October 1916, in what were to be some of the final moves of the Somme offensive. Here the scene was one of complete devastation, of endless mud and waterlogged shell holes and unburied corpses, while fresh water was scarce and food was rarely hot. And here, in this unpromising environment, the Australians were expected to attack the ominously named Maze. As they did so, they sank into the quagmire that was No-Man's Land, as did the Germans who charged out to meet them. As Captain Gordon Maxfield observed, 'the absurd position was created of scores of attackers and defenders bogged up to their waists in mud only a stone's throw apart'.[82] These assaults caused another 2,000 Australian casualties, and there might have been more if, following the capture of Beaumont Hamel and Beaucourt by the British Fifth Army, the Inter-Allied Conference on 16 November had decided not to call a winter halt in the Somme offensive.

Although, as ever, Haig remained optimistic and confident of final victory, the Australians who had fought in the terrible Somme battles could have been forgiven for wondering what on earth all the sacrifice was for. It was not yet clear what had been achieved. Many took heart, not from the breezy self-confidence of the senior officers, but from the exploits and tenacity of the ordinary digger. They delighted in the story, therefore, of Private Isaac MacLean, from Wallaroo in South Australia, who was said to have been awarded the Military Medal for 'playing the mouth organ whilst going over the top at Pozieres'.[83] It was not quite true – he had also killed a German and wounded and captured eight others – but it was a good yarn, and appealed to the Australian sense of humour.

Chapter Six

The Seat of Empire: Australians in Blighty

O
N CHRISTMAS DAY 1917, Kit Dodsworth, a nurse in the British Voluntary Aid Detachments (VAD), was on duty in Dyke Road Hospital in Brighton, Sussex, looking after wounded Allied soldiers. VAD members, such as Kit, were drawn from the Red Cross and the Order of St John, and although they worked in military hospitals – in Britain and in France – they retained their civilian status. But they were subject to strict discipline. Fraternization (as it was called) with the wounded they tended and the soldiers they served alongside was strictly forbidden, and their matrons behaved like 'Victorian headmistresses'.[1] Skirts might not be shortened, for example, even in the interests of saving material for the war effort, and the VADs were watched closely for any signs of over-familiarity with their charges, or any other impropriety. For some of these VADs, the strictures were impossible, and despite the eternal vigilance of their superiors, friendships and even romances blossomed. But for Kit Dodsworth the rules were a welcome safeguard. As she later explained, she had had an exceptionally sheltered upbringing. The daughter of a successful Yorkshire lawyer, she had been cosseted throughout her adolescence. Until the age of eighteen, she had lived in the schoolroom in her parents' substantial house, being allowed down for the occasional tennis party (where her job was to pick up balls) before being sent back upstairs. She had been permitted to 'come out' at the Yorkshire Hussars Ball but was 'petrified with shyness', and devoted her time to tidying her room, sewing, attending tea-parties, helping out with fêtes and bazaars, and teaching Sunday School children.[2]

Being 'set on by dozens of men'

Before Kit Dodsworth was appointed to Dyke Road Hospital, she had
served in France, where she was exposed to the realities of the Western
Front and of nursing wounded males. But she remained prim and reticent, and concerned above all to observe the many rules and regulations
that governed her life as a VAD. On Christmas morning 1917, therefore, she was 'very taken aback' when she and other nurses attending
the early service in the hospital chapel were 'literally set upon by dozens
of men'. Emboldened by the festive spirit, the convalescent soldiers tried
to kiss each of the nurses in turn, and the VADs were 'pushed from one
man to another'. Kit was 'absolutely appalled and dreadfully upset . . . I
was in tears and felt terribly humiliated'. But worse was to come. Later
in the day, 'raiding parties' came round the wards, and half-a-dozen exuberant Australians, one with his face blackened, insisted that they would
kiss every sister and nurse in the hospital. While they accosted the other
VADs in her ward, Kit quietly slipped away to take refuge in the bathroom, hoping that she had not been spotted. But she had not escaped
the attention of the roving Australians, and to her horror discovered
that there was no lock on the bathroom door. She tried to hold the door
shut but was no match for her enthusiastic pursuers. 'They came in',
she recalled, 'and, having trapped me there, started discussing in loud
joking voices whether they should do it in the ward or in the bathroom'.
Deciding that it would be more fun to perform in front of an audience in
the ward, they swept Kit off her feet and carried her from the bathroom.
'They set me down', she continued, 'and the black-faced man kissed me
vigorously, leaving a filthy black mark on my face. My own men felt it
was beyond a joke and protested like anything, but that didn't stop the
Australians'.[3]

After her ordeal, Kit Dodsworth 'felt too awful for words and I cried
for hours about it'. But, as she reflected later, she had 'heard afterwards that some English boys had told the Colonials that English girls
expected to be kissed on Christmas Day'. The gullible but irrepress-
ible Australians 'meant no harm', she conceded, but nonetheless she
objected to their behaviour: 'We didn't so much mind being kissed', she
explained, 'although we didn't like it a lot – it was the way that they
did it'. To the crude manners of the Australians was added their lack of
respect for authority, and their inherent indiscipline. Colonials needed a

firm hand, it was thought, but 'Matron was on leave, and the Assistant Matron was rather a weak character, or it would never have happened'.[4]

Although Kit Dodsworth did not say so, such Australian high spirits were reminiscent of their earlier antics in Egypt and the Wozzer (see pp. 38–9), an exhibition of the larrikinism that both admirers and detractors saw as typical of the Anzac soldier. But for every British observer, male or female, who took exception to the Australians, there were others who warmed instantly to their forthright egalitarianism, their pragmatism, common sense and lack of humbug, as well as their sheer attractiveness. Kitty Kenyon, another VAD, had more than a soft spot for the Australians, and had enjoyed their company. Completing her diary entry for 9 August 1918, while stationed at Camiers in France, she recorded her delight in making the acquaintance of two new arrivals at the hospital. 'I was thrilled when I saw two khaki, mud-stained Aussies in shorts and without hats come in', she wrote: 'It was like old times!'[5] The easy informality of their attire, which might have offended British military sensibilities, was part of the Australians' allure, as Kitty made plain, and it was not only to women that Australian no-nonsense appealed. Edmund Blunden, the British war poet, described his affection for the Australians in his autobiography, *Undertones of War*, first published in 1928. Sent on a rather dull signalling course in France, he explained, he discovered that it was attended by various Allied officers, and many 'of them, to my joy, were Australians, at whose resourceful wit and confidence one refreshed the parched mind'. He instantly made friends with them. 'I still hear the gay and easy Captain Bath', Blunden continued, 'reciting the "Nancy Brig", or offering sermons on the Uncertainty of Life'. He recalled Bath's 'towzled hair, bright eyes, and vinous flush as jolly as Bacchus must have had. I hear also his laments for Adelaide, while we were wandering through benighted farm buildings in performance of "a scheme"'. As Blunden concluded, in admiration: 'His [Australian] companions were worthy of him, and they revealed every day that it is possible for an army to be highly efficient without a sign of pedantry'.[6]

'A Colonial's joke'

If British attitudes to the Australians varied widely, then the ambivalence and uncertainty was reciprocated. As we have seen, the Anzacs blamed the Tommies for their supposed shortcomings at Gallipoli and Fromelles (see p.83 and pp.127–8), as they would later for alleged British failings in the face of the German 'spring offensive' in 1918. Private Melville Pethick, writing home to Australia in January 1916 from Monte Video Camp in Weymouth, Dorset, explained that there 'is not much love between the Tommies and the Colonials here'. He blamed the continued ill feeling on the 'Suvla tea-party' saga, when British troops were imagined to have let down their Anzac counter-parts at Gallipoli. Indeed, he added, there had 'been many a battle with them, and the authorities have had to shift the Tommies away from these parts on that account'.[7] Initially, the Australians had been wel-comed to Weymouth, and early misdemeanours were dismissed with a patronizing smile. When one Australian stole a horse and wagonette, in the normal course of events a fairly serious offence, it was treated lightly as 'A Colonial's joke', and the culprit walked free with a gentle admon-ishment from the bench. So too, when two Australians were said to have 'liberated' a cask of stout from a local public house; they were sent away from the court amid much laughter. And when a Tommy accused an Australian of stealing his bicycle, magistrates at Weymouth tried to persuade him to drop the charge. But the British soldier refused, a measure of the ill will detected by Private Pethick. Reluctantly, the bench fined the Australian £1.[8]

Antipathy between 'the Tommies and the Colonials' simmered beneath the surface at Weymouth, while the Australians continued to find themselves in one sort of trouble or another. In August 1917 the arrest of an Australian soldier, accused of using foul language and assaulting a police constable, was a cue for a hundred other Anzacs to come angrily to his rescue. On Christmas Eve that year festive celebra-tions turned sour when up to 400 Australians and civilians ran amok in Weymouth, causing much damage to property. Even when the ringlead-ers were arrested, the riot continued, the local police station besieged by Australians who would not disperse until the military police were called. The perpetrators were each sentenced to three month's impris-onment, evidence that patience was beginning to wear thin, the local mayor warning the Australians that their reputation was beginning to suffer. Yet when, in 1919, the last of the Australians marched away, the people of Weymouth were sorry to see them go, reflecting that there had been remarkably little crime or upheaval, given that some 127,000 had passed through the town during the war years. The Australians had also done their bit for the local economy. 'We've all had a good time here in England while it lasted', admitted Melville Pethick, 'I understand most of the boys have got through £100 each . . . and most of them have drawn all their back pay'. Indeed, Pethick had himself run out of money, and had had to wire his father in Australia for more funds to be sent across. Pethick also observed that the bad blood between the Aussies and the Tommies did not extend to the local women. 'Talk about girls', he exclaimed, 'that's about all that's left here now', complaining perhaps about the lack of other amusement in provincial Weymouth, and noting that many Australians had spent their money on the fair sex: in fact, 'a good many have been married over here'.[9]

As the Weymouth episode indicated, the experience of Australian troops in Britain and Ireland was complex and often paradoxical. They came to the United Kingdom on leave, to be treated in hospitals for sickness or wounds, to convalesce, or to train in the vast military camps such as those at Weymouth or on Salisbury Plain. They found themselves in contrasting parts of the United Kingdom, not only southern England – nearest to France and home of the military camps – but in Ireland, Scotland, Cornwall and other far-flung localities. Likewise, their relations with the British people were ambivalent, many Australians – a good number of whom had actually been born in the UK – instinctively thinking of Britain as 'home' were often surprised to find how different it was from Australia. Sometimes there was disappointment, and the hostility that had grown up between the Tommies and the Anzacs would occasionally colour relations with civilians. At first, there was novelty, newly arrived Australians delighting in the curious blend of the familiar and the unfamiliar that they encountered, and the British were likewise enchanted by their Colonial cousins. But in time the freshness wore off, Australians finding aspects of British life tedious – not least in camps on the windy Dorset heaths or Salisbury Plain – and the British themselves deciding that those Aussie traits that they had once found so endearing were now merely irritating. Michael McKernan has put the case straightforwardly, arguing that in 'the British imagination the Australians had been transformed from heroes to criminals during their stay in Britain from late 1915 to late 1919'. But this seems too wide a generalization, for the experiences of the Australians – and their British hosts – varied enormously from one individual case to another. As E.M. Andrews mused in his *The Anzac Illusion*: 'Reactions were intensely personal, depending partly on the man concerned, and partly on experiences'. And as he concluded: 'At first the men had high expectations of the land they had been taught to love at home and in school. But reality, and the mischances of life, changed many of their views'.[10]

'Three days from England now'

By 1916, most Australian soldiers arriving in Britain had sailed directly from Australia, a long and often boring sea journey that served to heighten the anticipation of being in the 'mother country' at last. That the route was usually by way of British possessions – Ceylon, South Africa, Aden, Gibraltar, and so on – enhanced the sense of Britain's global reach and her omnipotent Empire. Private Fred Verran wrote home to Australia from Salisbury Plain in June 1916, with the wonders of Gibraltar still fresh in his memory. He enthused over 'that marvellous far-famed place, Gibraltar' and admitted to being 'so impressed with the rock' as they approached by sea: 'the glorious picture which opened to the view holds you, if you have a spark of British pride, spellbound. The bay, sparkling in the awakening morning, is crowded with shipping of all description, but you notice the old Union Jack predominates'.[11] It was an exciting display of British imperial and naval power, and Verran had longed to be in England itself. Private Edward Lynch, who had sailed from Sydney in the transport *Wiltshire* in August 1916, felt the same. 'Three days from England now', he wrote, and was much impressed when three torpedo boats of the Royal Navy came out to escort them through the western approaches. 'We're proud of them and cheer as they close in and the sailors wave and cheer back', he wrote: 'We're safe from submarines with three watchdogs of our great British Navy guarding us. Good old British Navy. We thrill with unspoken pride of our Empire's Navy'.[12]

'Almost to England now!', Lynch continued: 'Great cliffs of old England show up ahead and we anchor in Plymouth Harbour . . . Our sea voyage of twelve thousand miles is over and we're in England at last'.[13] Private Lloyd Pollard was similarly impressed. Writing home to South Australia in July 1916 from Larkhill camp, on Salisbury

Plain, he explained how he and his mates had been ferried ashore in launches from their ships in Plymouth Sound. He had gazed at the Hoe in wonder, he said, 'where Francis Drake was playing bowls when the Spanish Armada was sighted', and, being of Cornish stock, was excited by the close proximity of Cornwall. Landing at Devonport, he explained, the 'first thing I had to eat was three good Cornish pasties, on the wharf – boys selling them for 3d each', and he 'could see a piece of Cornwall just over the River Tamar, which divides Cornwall from Devonshire'. Military bands greeted the disembarking Australians with strains of 'Land of Hope and Glory', and many Anzacs experienced the 'mysterious attraction' – as one Norman Hale put it – 'of actually going to land in the "old country"'.[14] At Devonport station the newly arrived Australians boarded waiting troop trains to take them to their training camps, usually on Salisbury Plain. Lloyd Pollard marvelled at the splendour of the railway system. 'The Great Western is the flyer here', he exclaimed: 'They are lovely engines, and are spick and span, as if got up for imperial inspection'. Such trains could do sixty miles per hour and more, he explained, but the 'London South-Western Railway was to take us to camp, and we had a rather slow ride, which, however, was in our favour as it gave us a good chance to view the passing scene'.[15]

Impressed as he was by this first taste of Britain, Private Pollard was also intrigued by its difference. He was bewildered, he admitted, by the seemingly vast numbers of people inhabiting the tightly arranged housing. 'I have often wondered how so many people could be packed into this small island', he admitted, and 'now I understand'. The troop train took them high above the little streets of Devonport, the working-class area of Plymouth adjacent to the naval dockyard, and Pollard 'had a good view of the town'. As he gazed down from his window, he could see that the 'houses are joined to each other for the length of a street; a wall seems to divide these houses in half from end to end. One family lives on one side', he thought, 'another crowd the other, so you can imagine how many live in one little street'. In some respects, it was a dreary scene: 'These streets run back tier after tier, there must be millions of houses in this spot, and all with slate roofs'. However, the urban greyness of Plymouth was soon left behind, as the train skirted the wild grandeur of northern Dartmoor. At 'a town called Exeter', Pollard continued, the Lady Mayoress greeted the train, and handed out to each Australian a bottle of tea and a bun, complete with a little note of welcome. From there, the train made its way slowly through the gentle West Country landscape of east Devon, Dorset, Somerset and Wiltshire, and Pollard feasted his eyes on the glorious panorama as it unfolded. 'I couldn't believe they had hedges to divide up these lovely fields', he exclaimed, the 'passing scenes were indeed lovely to behold'. He espied pretty villages, he said, each with its ancient parish church, and saw 'ruins of old castles'. He was also struck by the general absence of men from the countryside, another contrast with Australia he thought, and was interested to see women at work in the fields, 'and, in fact, at every occupation . . . the men having gone to the front'. Earlier in the war, before the recruiting for 'Kitchener's army' had taken effect, and before conscription, the wounded arriving in Britain from Gallipoli had been 'amazed', according to one soldier from New South Wales, 'to see the number of young fellows not in khaki who came to look at them while they themselves had travelled thousands of miles to fight for King and country'.[16] Now, however, all that had changed.

At last, at 7 p.m., the Australians arrived at Amesbury, and marched the final four miles to camp at Larkhill, just one component, as Pollard explained, of the vast military infrastructure that comprised Salisbury Plain. He was astonished by its extent: 'You cannot imagine how extensive this camp is. It is said they could accommodate two million men on these plains'.[17] But Amesbury itself was quintessentially English, exactly as Lloyd Pollard had imagined, 'a quaint little village'. Some of the houses were more than 200 years old, he wrote, 'with thatched roofs, all two storeys high, but very low, with little windows overlooking the street'. There was a village pump, walls made of flint, and a ruined abbey, together with the vicar's wife who always made herself available 'to explain the meaning of all the relics' to curious Australians. Moreover, Pollard had studied the American poet Henry Longfellow at school in Australia, and was delighted to stumble across the 'old village blacksmith's' of Longfellow's verse: 'Just fancy . . . coming to England and seeing the spot that gave Longfellow his wonderful inspiration!' He was also thrilled to learn that the 'Druid Temple' of Stonehenge was in the same vicinity, and felt privileged to be in the midst of this classic landscape, with its many historic, archaeological and literary associations. July of 1916 was warm and sunny in southern England, and Lloyd Pollard basked happily in its luxuriousness, with its long evenings and very un-Australian lingering twilight. He looked about contentedly. 'England will do me', he said.[18]

Had Pollard arrived in winter, when Salisbury Plain was often wet and windswept, and sometimes carpeted in snow, and when the wooden camp huts let in every icy draught, and water froze in the taps, his judgement might have been different. The Dorset heathland, also exposed and bleak in winter, was no better. Melville Pethick complained in January 1916 that 'it is getting too cold for me here', and although he thought Weymouth 'a pretty spot', the endless training, drills and duties – much of it conducted out of doors in inclement conditions – wore him down. He wrote dejectedly that 'I'm on picket [duty] tonight in the town of Weymouth', glumly anticipating the long hours of boredom and freezing darkness. Succumbing to the weather, Pethick went down with double pneumonia, and was ill for some time before, at last, he was shipped to France. He was glad to be off. As he put it, 'I'm about fed up with England now'.[19]

Yet, whatever the depredations of camp life in England, there was a great sense of camaraderie among the Australians. Australian battalions were recruited and reinforced from particular geographical localities, so very often men who had known each other since childhood joined up together, and then travelled to Britain, trained, and fought and sometimes died side by side. Private Leonard Harvey, for example, was a mate of Lloyd Pollard and, like his friend, enthused about the historical and literary connections of the countryside around Larkhill, where he too was posted. Writing to his father, he explained that he had visited Stonehenge, and waxed lyrical about Tennyson and Longfellow. There were some things about England that grated, he admitted. 'Fruit is very dear at present', he complained, and it is 'a terrible place here for pennies and half pennies. I have not had a 3d. given in change yet'. And, like Lloyd Pollard, he disliked the terraced housing and overcrowding of the cities. 'No harm in having plenty of room around the house', he thought: 'I don't like them too close. Have seen too much of the closeness over here'. But generally he admired what he had observed so far, and looked forward to visiting London, Scotland and Cornwall. He added that he and his pals from Australia stuck closely together for companionship, making camp life bearable, even enjoyable. 'This letter is being written with Bert Grummet's pen and Charlie Rose's pad', he said: 'I am down in their hut'.[20]

Ireland and the Easter Rising

Whether on leave from camp (or from the front in France or Belgium), or convalescing in Britain from wounds or sickness, Australians looked forward to their expeditions to the capital or the provinces – sometimes alone but, preferably, with their chums. Some, with Irish roots, found themselves in Dublin during the Easter Rising of 1916, when a minority of nationalists, frustrated at Britain's unwillingness or inability to grant even a modicum of Home Rule, resorted to armed rebellion in pursuit of an independent republic. Like thousands of Irishmen, many Australians of Irish-Catholic descent had willingly taken up arms in defence of the Empire of which they were all a part and, specifically, to safeguard the rights of small nations, believing that Home Rule for Ireland would be a just reward for loyalty when at last the war was won. Indeed, many had imagined that self-government within the Empire, such as had been achieved by the several Australian colonies before Federation, was a natural model for Ireland, and that loyalty to the British Empire was by no means incompatible with Irish nationalism.[21] The Easter Rising, then, caught Australians by surprise, and those in Dublin were perplexed by the complex interplay of loyalties, identities and enmities that they observed on the city's streets. Some felt that they were neutral observers, on neither side, but were swiftly disabused when Irish rebels took pot-shots at them – they were wearing the King's uniform, and were considered legitimate targets. In the longer term, the Easter Rising – and in particular Britain's savage reaction – affected Australian public opinion, especially over the conscription crisis. But, for the moment, for those who had gone to Ireland to seek out relations or to visit places with family connections, or just to sightsee, the violence – and its repudiation of Empire – was disconcerting, to say the least.[22]

Two Australians, Privates George Davis and Bob Grant, both convalescing from illness contracted at Gallipoli, had decided to visit Ireland over Easter 1916. On Easter Saturday they had gone to view the lakes at Killarney, meeting up with two Australian VADs, and generally having a good time. But arriving back in Dublin they found the city in uproar. Drawn by the sound of gunfire, they made their way towards the commotion. Civilians urged them to take cover but Davis and Grant insisted that they were merely tourists, and that this was not their fight.

However, explained Davis, 'walking towards Parliament Street, we were brought to our senses by a rifle bullet which struck the kerb nearby, and was followed by a quick succession of shots'. He continued: 'I ducked into a doorway as a bullet struck the concrete pillar close to my head, the chips stinging in my face. My pal [Bob Grant] dodged round the corner, and knowing discretion to be the better part of valour, I followed'. Later, they reported to the local barracks where they were issued with rifles and ammunition, and told to defend the building if necessary. Meanwhile other Australians had become embroiled in the defence of Trinity College, sharp-shooting from the university's roof, where they accounted for at least one rebel despatch rider. According to an eyewitness account: 'It was wonderful shooting . . . Three [bullets] found their mark in the head of the unfortunate victim. Another of the riders was wounded and escaped on foot. The third abandoned his bicycle and also escaped'.[23]

In the aftermath of 1916, as British rule began to crumble, Ireland became a popular destination for those Australians anxious to desert from the AIF. Irish public opinion increasingly embraced the republican cause, and deserters from the Empire's forces were welcomed and sheltered. In Britain, the police kept a sharp look-out for those intent on taking absence without leave or deserting permanently. But in Ireland it was easier to be invisible, to become anonymous. 'Perhaps that is why most [absconding] diggers make off to Ireland', pondered George Davis: 'Most deserters are reported dressed in mufti [civilian clothes] and favour Ireland, where they evidently get more sympathy'.[24] It is not clear whether deserting Australians (especially those of Irish-Catholic descent) were drawn ideologically to the republican cause, and there appears to be no evidence of any taking up arms in its support. For most would-be absconders, the attraction was simply that Ireland was remote, where close scrutiny by the authorities was impossible, and where the local population turned a blind eye or actively colluded, especially if there were family or other links.

The 'Cousin Jacks'

Another remote but popular location was Cornwall. Writing in 1927, Harry Pascoe, contributing to a book published in the Cornish capital,

Truro, nostalgically recalled the war years 'when scores of Australian khaki clad soldiers sought out remote corners of the County to visit for the first and last time the homes of their fathers'.[25] Among their number was Private Leigh Lennell, who had lost an arm at the battle of Lone Pine at Gallipoli (see pp.78–9) and was in London to have an artificial limb fitted at Fulham Military Hospital. Lennell explained in a letter to his mother that 'we have been having the time of our lives', and that the British 'simply idolise our boys and take us for motor rides all over the country . . . I have visited many beautiful spots, and have been to some wealthy people's places for tea'. From Fulham he moved to a convalescent home in Putney, where he was having 'a jolly time' despite difficulty in adjusting to his new arm. But most exciting of all, he said, was the prospect of a visit to Cornwall, accompanied by his pal Art Trenwith, another Australian soldier. Soon Lennell was writing home again, this time from the Tywarnhayle Hotel, Perranporth, on the north coast of Cornwall. 'You will see by the address that I am down with the Cousin Jacks [the Cornish]', he exclaimed, 'and as soon as the people knew we were Australians and of Cornish descent, they crowded around us and talked for hours'. No less than the Irish, the Cornish were anxious to claim their own among the visiting Australians. They were 'making us Cousin Jack pasties', Lennell reported, and he and Art Trenwith were taken to all the local beauty spots and historic sites. As they travelled around Cornwall, they met people with familiar family names, to whom they imagined they might be related, and at Penzance had the curious experience of bumping into erstwhile neighbours from South Australia. Cornwall felt like a home from home, said Leigh Lennell: 'I shall be very sorry to leave'.[26]

Leonard Harvey was also keen to visit Cornwall in search of relations. Like many Australians, he found himself in 'Blighty' (as they invariably called it) on several occasions. He was, as we have seen, at Larkhill on Salisbury Plain in 1916 before deployment to France. He was back in the summer of 1918 (recovering from 'gassing'), first at the Burdon Military Hospital at Weymouth and then at No.4 Hurdcott Command Deport near Salisbury. Finally, after the war, he was in England again in the spring of 1919, awaiting repatriation to Australia. It was on this latter occasion that he at last made it down to Cornwall, travelling with his chum Jack Pyatt. They were met at Camborne railway station by Jack's aunt, Mrs Bennett, and, like Leigh Lennell and Art Trenwith, were driven all round Cornwall by local people, who remained as welcoming as they had been earlier in the war, when other Australians had visited. Leonard Harvey and Jack Pyatt were also taken to a rugby football match between Cornwall and New Zealand (a 'Win for New Zealand', despite Cornish passion), an unexpected insight into Cornish life that fascinated the two Australians. 'So you can see', wrote Leonard Harvey to his father, with the sense of an ambition at last accomplished, 'I have now had a look at the land of "Cousin Jacks" and Pasties'.[27] The Cornish had also had an opportunity to look at their Australian cousins, and liked what they saw. As one budding poet put it:

> There'll be many an Australian soldier
> Linked with some sweet Cornish girl.
> Who would blame them? Not the writer.
> He would e'er their flag unfurl.[28]

To see 'all the places in London'

Despite his obvious affection for Cornwall, it was London that really captured the imagination of Leonard Harvey and his pals. The capital was in easy reach of Salisbury, unlike Ireland or Cornwall, and visits could be organized at short notice, without much planning or expense. 'The Tube railways are a splendid thing', Harvey revealed, and the buses were cheap. During short leave periods, he and his chums 'went to all the places in London that we had time to visit', taking in St Pauls, the Tower of London, London Bridge, Westminster Abbey, and a captured German submarine moored on the Thames as a tourist attraction. There were also, he added, a great many YMCA huts all over London, 'which are worked by woman [sic] who do it voluntary, and they can't do enough for the Australians', cheerfully handing out cups of tea and other refreshments to the grateful Anzacs.[29] Some Australians, particularly from the bush, found London mystifying, even intimidating. There were stories of Anzacs at busy mainline railway stations having to ask policemen for directions to find the exits, and likewise there were tales of terror about the 'moving stair-ways' or escalators that diggers encountered for the first time on the Underground. W.D. Gallwey, an impressionable 18-year-old, described his unnerving experience. Observing that even women seemed to cope with escalators, he felt that he too should be able to manage them. Unaware of the dangers, he unwittingly stood on the division between one step and another, so that as the escalator began its descent, he was almost propelled head-over-heels. A young woman took his arm to steady him but as he stepped off at the bottom, he 'spun like a top' and nearly pulled her over. 'An Escalator now is a nightmare to me', he concluded.[30]

Leonard Harvey, however, appeared to have none of these difficulties, and soon had the measure of London in all its complexity. He began to appreciate its extent, to understand its topography, and to discern the relationship between class and locality, to tell the poor areas from the wealthy. The social divisions intrigued him, as he explained in a letter home:

> We had a look around Richmond and Rotten Row, where all the heads [upper-class] live, it is a lovely place and a good many fine buildings are to be seen. From Richmond we went to the Eastern part of the city, where a poorer class of people are met with. The smell of the market place is simply terrible, but we didn't stop there too long.[31]

As Harvey realized, class in England was a many-nuanced thing, and, like other Australians, he found it increasingly irksome. In the unspoken divisions of the English system, the socially superior – including military officers – frequented the smarter restaurants, while lesser folk and other ranks knew instinctively to go elsewhere. But Harvey, like most Australians, took the view that he could venture anyplace, so long as he had the means to pay. Thus:

> Four of us went into a 'Café' to dinner, and found ourselves dining with frock coated gentlemen and officers of the English Army. We were taken very good stock of but I don't know the opinion that was formed. I overheard one lady say that she didn't think we were every-day soldiers at any rate she passed the time of day to us when she was going out.[32]

It was a common experience. W.D. Gallwey and a chum, both sporting the 'high rank of Lance Corporal', entered the exclusive Comedy, a society restaurant frequented by senior officers, who evidently disapproved of these upstart Colonials. But, despite the murmurs and glances, Gallwey and his mate stood their ground, enjoyed their meal, paid the bill, and left: 'as we went out we overheard many funny remarks about us'. As Gallwey observed, in civilian life he was a gentleman, so why should he not act as a gentleman when wearing the King's uniform? It was an attitude that would have struck many Australians as fair enough, scandalizing though it was to class-conscious Englishmen and women.[33]

'It was the womenfolk who fascinated me'

Australians had also acquired a reputation as 'pushy', asserting themselves in social situations where the English might be more reticent. Private Harold Williams, on 'Blighty Leave' (as he deemed it) in the spring of 1917, went first to AIF Headquarters in Horseferry Road, to have his pass checked, to hand in his rifle and kit, and to draw his pay. Then all London was at his beck and call! 'It was the womenfolk who fascinated me', he recalled later: 'Slowly it dawned upon my bewildered senses that these girls, with their fresh faces and happy gait were of my own race, that any one of them could talk my language'. Moreover, he said, 'the realization of this made me long to make any one of them understand that I was a lone Australian who for months past counting had lived the life of an animal corralled in a landscape of mud and beastliness'. One morning, while waiting for his mate Bob, Harold Williams was sitting in the foyer of a smart West End hotel. He had already espied an attractive girl, dressed in grey, who had responded to his glance with a look of undisguised disdain. When Bob turned up, Williams pointed her out. 'Gee, she's a stunner', Bob exclaimed. Emboldened by his friend's assessment, Williams walked over to the table where the young lady was sitting. 'Pardon me, but may I sit down?', he asked. Affronted by his forward behaviour, the woman regarded him contemptuously. Pushing his luck further, Williams sat down anyway. 'Look here, Australia', she said firmly, 'what do you take me for?' Leaning across the table, he replied: 'The prettiest girl that I have seen in London'. Expressionless for a moment, she then threw her head back and laughed. 'There is no doubt about you Australians', she chuckled, 'your effrontery carries you through'. She added: 'Well as long as you do not take me for one of these women who frequent these hotels to be picked up by you Colonials, we know where we stand'.[34]

Reluctantly at first, the girl in grey agreed to go with Harold, Bob and another Australian, Bert, to a show that afternoon in the Coliseum. In the evening, the foursome went out to dinner, where the girl asked questions about army life, and the Australians responded with amusing tales of France and Egypt. The next day followed a similar pattern but, on the third afternoon, the young woman was due to join her parents in the south of England. Harold accompanied her to Paddington station. In the taxi, she was strangely quiet, until she blurted out that she had detected, in among the Australians' cheery anecdotes, 'a hideousness that you do not speak of, for it is in your eyes in your unguarded moments'. She had enjoyed the last few days immensely, she said, but now she feared for Harold and his friends as they prepared to return to the front. At the station, Harold went with her to the platform. There was a 'quiver on her lips', she called him 'cheeky Dick', and he kissed her before she sprang into her carriage. 'One little wave from the moving train and she had gone', Williams wrote much later, 'but down all those years I still remember the freshness of her youth with her dark head and eyes of limpid brown'.[35]

Written with the sentimentality of hindsight, Harold Williams' account of the girl in grey is nonetheless refreshingly honest, with its admission of the yearning for female company and the awful omnipresent knowledge – as apparent to the girl as to the soldiers – that leave is but a fleeting dream, a brief respite from the reality of the front. Williams' sojourn also took him to Scotland, where he had promised to pay his respects to Agnes, sister of his friend Peter Duncan, who had died in France. He found her working in an ammunition factory in Glasgow, and here was a different kind of female company, with Agnes dressed solemnly in mourning black when they went out for dinner, her self-control and apparent calm concealing her grief. Together they visited Peter's mother, at Fairlie on the Clyde, and Williams could see that her son's death had affected her deeply. They met one of Agnes' friends, betrothed to an officer in a Highland regiment, who quizzed Williams about life at the front, including the brothels and the 'horrible tales of houses where you soldiers visit women'. Searching for the right words, Williams said that men drank heavily or went with women as temporary relief, knowing that they would shortly return to the line. She seemed satisfied with the explanation. At any rate, Harold Williams returned down south armed with gifts of chocolates, a box of Scottish shortbread and a bottle of Scotch whisky.[36]

In the third of these almost allegorical encounters with women, Williams was accosted by a girl – about twenty years of age, he thought – as he and his mates were about to enter a lounge bar in Shaftesbury Avenue, London. Some establishments forbade the entrance of unaccompanied women, and this was one of them. 'Take me in, Aussie!' implored the girl in a broad Glasgow accent. 'Yes, Scotty, come in and we'll buy you a drink', he replied obligingly. Inside, Harold realized that 'Scotty' was good-looking, with 'hair of silky fineness and the colour of honey . . . her eyes large and dark brown, her teeth . . . even and white'. Later, they lunched at an Italian café, and in the afternoon went to Madame Tussauds waxworks 'in a rather mellow state'. In the evening they dined at a restaurant in Piccadilly, and after midnight, as they made to leave, Scotty, 'who had been showing signs of feeling the weather', suddenly collapsed. 'The female portion of the platoon is down', said Bert, Harold's friend, and there followed a desperate series of events as they revived the now sobbing Scotty, managed to hail a passing taxi, and with good fortune found a card in her handbag with her address, allowing them to return her home safely. The next morning, with barely ten shillings left, Harold boarded his leave train. At Folkestone, as the channel steamer set sail, 'I could not bear to look back on the receding coast', and that night, back in France, having supped on bully-beef and biscuits and weak tea, 'we turned into our blankets, seeking only unconsciousness'.[37]

The poignant charm of Harold Williams' memoirs, even if coloured in the telling, is for us an important insight into the significance of leave in Britain for the Australians. Although many had relations in the British Isles, and considered the United Kingdom at the very least a surrogate 'home', few had real homes to go to, and there was an urgent intensity that drove them to make the most of their time away from the trenches. Even for those in Britain for longer periods, on extended leave, or in convalescence or training, female company was much sought after. As Williams suggested, part of the appeal was that women seemed so 'fresh faced' after the 'mud and beastliness' of the front. That English was their natural tongue lent them a wholesomeness, it was imagined, that contrasted with many of the foreign women the Australians had encountered in Egypt and France. The desire for cleanliness, after the filth of the trenches, extended beyond a longing for newly laundered sheets and tidy lodgings, to encompass attractive, neatly turned out women. It was a fantasy, and sometimes reality did not match the ideal. Sergeant Cyril Lawrence, for example, had gone on leave to Scotland with a mate. They met two local girls, and persuaded them to come on a trip to Loch Lomond. 'We caught our train and off we went', Lawrence explained, and in the privacy and cosiness of their compartment, he began to turn his attention to the young lady who had especially caught his eye. 'After about 10 minutes', he continued, 'I summed up enough courage to have a screw [closer look] at her'. He was in for a shock. 'Help! For scrimey! Shades of hades!', he exclaimed: 'Her face was just perfect, profile etc. fine, but her ears, full of dirt, her neck ditto, and her nails supporting enough black for the whole army'. As Lawrence concluded: 'How I hate and detest one speck upon a girl . . . During the whole afternoon I felt the dirt near me. Thank God the trip as regards scenery was glorious'.[38]

The 'longings, desire and frustrations of all men'

Of course, not all were as fastidious as Cyril Lawrence, and Corporal Roy Denning admitted to 'the longings, desires and frustrations of all men'. He explained that previously, in Egypt, France and London, he 'hadn't availed myself of the opportunity of promiscuous sex', mainly through 'fear of infection'. In London, he continued, he met Shirley. 'Shirley was a decent, good girl, full of fun and mischief. She liked to be kissed and cuddled but drew the line there', he said: 'She was broadminded but honest'. Nonetheless, on his last day of leave, before returning to the front, they spent the afternoon in a long farewell. As he put it, coyly: 'To dwell in detail about the goodbye would be "to tell tales out of school"'.[39]

For those Australians who merely wanted to pick up girls, there were plenty of opportunities, as Sergeant Joseph Maxwell observed. Piccadilly, he wrote, was 'a jostling pack of party girls, a gust of assorted talcum and heated flesh, a whirl of wet scarlet lips, a flash of white teeth and lecherous smiles that held in them the promise of devilry before dawn'.[40] Further north, in Scotland, Gunner Arthur Howell encountered the 'Aberdeen Flappers', as he termed them, girls 'who want so much amusement as they can get but are quite anxious to make the Australians welcome. And I must say I didn't let *all* opportunities slip'.[41]

Prostitution flourished in such an environment, and some Australians claimed to have been routinely propositioned in the street, on buses, and in restaurants and bars. British prostitutes did not always conform to idealized notions of cleanliness and wholesomeness, and in many cases were infected by soldiers who had picked up diseases in Egypt or France. Venereal disease (VD) had long between the scourge of barrack towns in the British Isles, and as early as 1864 the Contagious Disease Act had attempted to contain VD in localities such as the Curragh in Ireland and Aldershot in England, making medical inspection and treatment compulsory. But the proliferation of military camps and vast numbers of military personnel during the First World War made treatment of VD an increasingly uphill battle. VD was reckoned at the time to be the biggest threat to military efficiency in the United Kingdom, with the Australians and New Zealanders identified as the worst offenders. It was estimated that the rate of Australian and New Zealand troops admitted for treatment for VD was 128 and 130 per 1,000 respectively, compared to just 24 per 1,000 for British soldiers.[42] Failure to declare VD was a punishable offence, and so Australian service documents are full of those who had no choice but to own up and seek treatment, sometimes repeatedly so. The Anzacs knew the risks – posters were prominently displayed in the camps, and there were frequent lectures – and (in direct contrast to British policy) condoms were discreetly made available. But many were reluctant to use these 'dreadnoughts', and were prepared to run the risk of catching or spreading a sexually transmitted disease or causing an unwanted pregnancy – or both. Some men were careful but others managed to get their British girlfriends 'into trouble' (to use the contemporary euphemism), a number being responsible for multiple pregnancies with various women during different leave periods. Alfred James Angove, from Cross Roads in South Australia, in England recuperating from injuries at Wilton House, near Salisbury, was one of those mortified when he found out that his girl was 'expecting'.[43]

Men in such situations often 'had to get married' (to use that other colloquial expression, popular at the time), either of their own volition or as a result of familial pressure. How many were reluctant to walk down the aisle it is impossible to say, although only a small minority of marriages contracted in Britain are likely to have been the result of coercion. Most Australians were proud of their 'English wives', although courtships were often brief, sometimes recklessly so. One couple was reckoned to have wed after only six hours acquaintance, while the Australian who married a Dorset nurse after just six weeks was perhaps not atypical. The desire to wed was understandable, many men being desperate for the security of a formal relationship, an antidote to lone-liness and a comfort when they returned to the trenches. In all, some 5,626 members of the AIF eventually returned to Australia with 'English brides'. Some soldiers had married nurses they had met while recovering from wounds or sickness in British hospitals. In 1915, for example, Percy Brokenshire found himself in hospital in Fishponds, a suburb of Bristol, where he met his bride-to-be, Ethel Comley. Brokenshire survived the war, and in 1919 he returned to Australia, accompanied by his wife and young child. Likewise, William Pomeroy was evacuated from France to the London General Hospital in October 1916, having been severely injured with gunshot wounds to the head, left hand, right leg and right thigh, and was later treated at No. 2 Birmingham War Hospital. In London he met Rosamond Gridley, and they married in February 1919, shortly before his repatriation to Australia.[44] Another Australian wrote home bashfully to explain that while 'in Hospital at Camberwell I met a very nice nurse . . . affection has grown on both sides . . . I think I have found the right one'. He added that he had made it very clear that he could not settle in England, because of the cold, but 'she is quite satisfied to . . . come out to Sydney. I informed her that you would all be pleased to welcome her out to Sydney and make her feel at home'.[45]

Most 'English brides' were adjudged 'respectable' women, although there was often suspicion on both sides, women at home in Australia feeling that their menfolk had been 'poached' or 'stolen', while similar jealousies informed male opinion in Britain. 'Tommies' felt especially aggrieved, resenting the popularity of the Australians with British women, and envious of the Anzacs and their six-bob-a-day pay, and even their Colonial slouch hats, which were thought to have sex appeal. There was also suspicion that some British women had deliberately lured Australian servicemen into marriage. Edward Heron-Allen, who lived in Sussex, kept a journal during the First World War, and in its pages was deeply critical of the these 'war marriages', as he disparagingly termed them. According to Heron-Allen, in exchange for 'housekeeping' a woman would marry her victim and show him 'a good time' while he was on leave, in the hope or expectation that he would be killed at the front and she would receive his pension. Should he survive, then they could simply get divorced after the war – she would give him plenty of cause! Similarly, Heron-Allen was contemptuous of those cads 'in khaki and Sam Browne belts' who 'hurried girls into marriage', and he fretted especially for 'the really portentous number of girls who have "married" Canadian and Australian soldiers, who simply disappear and return home – many of them being married already'.[46] Alas, there was some evidence to support Heron-Allen's prejudice, notably in the high-profile case of one soldier, originally from Scotland and already married, who had fought in Gallipoli and France, and had 'married' for a second time when in England in February 1916. His new 'wife', a mere nineteen when she wed, had no idea that she was entering a bigamist relationship. When the matter was uncovered and brought to court, she had already borne one child by her 'husband' and was pregnant with a second, the judge offering his sympathy to the young woman now burdened with two illegitimate offspring.[47]

Few Australians displayed such cynicism, irresponsibility or manipulative behaviour. But gradually the Anzacs' reputation began to suffer, aggravated by reports of riots and rowdy behaviour at Weymouth and elsewhere, and occasionally by serious allegations, such as the attempted rape of a VAD at Salisbury. Added to this, as the war dragged on, was increasing dissatisfaction among Australians that their feats of arms, so conspicuously reported in the British press in the days of Gallipoli, were now routinely glossed over as 'British' victories, especially in the heady days of 1918 when Australian forces played a disproportionate role in the defeat of Germany. Ironically, the London *Daily Mail*, a popular paper reflecting popular prejudices, complained of the 'reticence of British military censorship' to mention the exploits of English units, while 'recording the deeds of Scottish, Irish, Canadian and Australian regiments'.[48] Suspicion, it seemed, could work both ways. New Australian recruits continued to arrive in Britain as late as 1918, full of wonder and excitement at the prospect of being in the 'old country', just as their predecessors had been earlier in the war. But, for those who had experienced the shortcomings of Blighty, as well as its delights, there was no doubt that Australia was 'home', and that Australia was best. Perhaps it was not surprising that many sang:

> Take me back to dear old Aussie,
> Put me on the boat for Woolloomooloo,
> Take me over there, drop me anywhere,
> Sydney, Melbourne, Adelaide, for I don't care;
> I just want to see my best girl,
> Cuddling up again we soon will be;
> Oh, Blighty is a failure, take me back to Australia,
> Aussie is the place for me.[49]

Chapter Seven

Trouble at Home: The Conscription Crisis

Iɴ Nᴏᴠᴇᴍʙᴇʀ 1916, in a ceremony to 'farewell' a newly recruited soldier bound for the front, Councillor Sweeney – a local politician on South Australia's Yorke Peninsula – compared 'the advantages we have of living in Australia' with those of other countries, 'even England'. Unlike Britain, where conscription of eligible males had been introduced in January 1916, in Australia recruitment into the armed forces remained entirely voluntary. 'Everything in Australia was voluntary', Sweeney explained, and this was among Australia's manifold advantages. Like other Australians, he was especially proud that theirs was a volunteer army, composed of men eager to do their duty for king and country, while that of Britain was increasingly full of the unsuited and the unwilling, individuals who were coerced and often made poor as well as reluctant soldiers. In Australia, therefore, Sweeney insisted, it was easier to 'do homage to those who had gone, and honour those who will not return'.[1]

'Everything in Australia was voluntary'

Councillor Sweeney was a self-confessed imperialist but he also shared in the growing mood of Australian nationalism. The Gallipoli landing, he had explained on an earlier occasion, 'was the most glorious [military action] in British history to date', a historic event 'which has written in blood Australia's name high in the annals of fame'.[2] His opposition to conscription was then a matter of patriotism, of pride in Australia's superior volunteer army and its disproportionate contribution to the British Empire's cause. But it also reflected pride in the voluntary principle itself, which Sweeney saw as fundamental to Australian democracy. His position was shared by many other Australians, and helps to explain the strong opposition to conscription that emerged after the idea was first promoted by Prime Minister 'Billy' Hughes during 1916. Sweeney's opinions also indicated the inherent complexity of the conscription debate as it emerged. As we shall see, anti-conscriptionists were often dismissed by their pro-conscription opponents as unpatriotic; 'shirkers', cowards and subversives who shrank from their duty to king and country. But, as Sweeney's opinions revealed, it was perfectly possible to be strongly in support of Australia's participation in the war, yet also to oppose conscription. However, as we shall also see, there were indeed those who opposed the conflict on ideological grounds, and who found in the conscription debate a welcome opportunity to express views that earlier in the war were untenable in the public domain. In this way, the conscription crisis served to undermine the façade of unity that had characterized Australian society until at least late 1915, while reopening and aggravating divisions that already existed below the surface. Religious sectarianism was reinvigorated and issues of ethnicity made more pronounced, while the Labor Party across Australia was split down the middle, marginalizing it for at least a decade.

Andrew Fisher, by nature a consensual leader, was replaced in October 1915 by 'Billy' Hughes as Labor Prime Minister, altogether a more combative and potentially divisive figure.[3] Within a week of taking the reins, Hughes had dropped plans for a referendum seeking the transfer of greater powers to the federal government from the several states, a central tenet of the Labor programme, despite his earlier earnest enthusiasm for the proposal. The *Australian Worker* had welcomed Hughes' appointment as Prime Minister, extolling him as 'a great man, with great services still to perform for Australia'.[4] Yet less than a month later, the socialist *Labor Call* was warning darkly that it was 'the calm before the storm', and that Hughes' u-turn over the referendum could never be forgiven or forgotten: 'a man who deliberately breaks his pledge is a traitor to the cause he represents, and can never again be trusted by the people'.[5] It was a prescient insight.

In December 1915, in what many imagined to be a precursor of conscription proper, the Hughes government required all Australian males between the ages of eighteen and forty-four to register their willingness (or otherwise) to volunteer, and, if reluctant or unable to enlist, to explain their reasons.[6] When the plan was first unveiled, the *Daily Herald* had published a critical article, warning sharply of 'Conscription: A Sure Poison for Unionism'.[7] But for the moment recruitment remained buoyant, driven by the rhetoric of Gallipoli, reaching a very satisfactory total of 22,000 for the month of January 1916. Yet by May of 1916 this had fallen dramatically to 10,500, reaching a low of 6,000 in the July. This may have reflected an encroaching war-weariness, as the reality of the failure at Gallipoli began to sink in, yet the drastic decline was noticeable even before news of the dreadful Somme losses understandably made young men think twice before volunteering. A more likely explanation is that the pool of available eligible men was already running dry, many of those who remained being employed in strategic industries such as mining, agriculture and transport. And when the losses at Fromelles, Pozières and Mouquet Farm did become known, it was apparent that the available reinforcements could not make good the numbers required. Some 2,800 men were 'poached' from the 3rd Division, still training in England, as a stop-gap, and in August 1916 the British Army Council announced the manpower requirement from Australia for the next three months – 16,500 per month, plus a special draft of 20,000 to bring all units up to full strength. By now 'Billy' Hughes had already made his mind up – conscription was inevitable, if Australia was to meet its obligations.

At the invitation of the British government, Hughes had left for London on 15 January 1916, ten days before the introduction of conscription in Britain (but not Ireland) for single men, a measure that was extended to married men in the March. It seems likely that the British initiative helped convince Hughes that conscription was necessary in Australia, not only to meet manpower demands but also to show good faith with the mother country. But Hughes was by no means humbled by the British War Cabinet, and the decision to embrace conscription was his alone, rather than the result of British pressure. Indeed, for Hughes, the London-born Welshman, those months in the imperial capital were 'days of glory', as K.S. Inglis described them: 'The poor emigrant boy returned as imperial statesman. He rebuked the patrician [Prime Minister] Herbert Asquith for his conduct of the war and helped

AUSTRALIAN WAR MEMORIAL P03155.003

The Right Honourable William Morris 'Billy' Hughes, Prime Minister of Australia, enjoying the company of nurses from the Australian Army Nursing Service. Popular with Australian servicemen and women, Hughes was especially keen to enlist the support of women in his conscription referendum campaigns.

fellow Welshman, Lloyd George, on his climb towards 10 Downing Street'.[8] Hughes was no sycophant, and there was an Australian nationalist edge to his rhetoric. In London in 1916 and later at the Versailles Peace Conference in 1919 he opposed Japanese designs in the Pacific and in consequence he and Lloyd George 'descended to abusing each other in Welsh'.[9] Indeed, at Versailles he began to craft what looked like the beginnings of an independent Australian foreign policy. When, after his first triumphant sojourn in Britain, Hughes arrived back in Fremantle on 31 July 1916, he was met by cheering, flag-waving crowds. But the *Australian Worker* delivered a sombre warning. 'Welcome home to the cause of anti-conscription', it announced: 'Let him not mistake the popping of champagne corks for the voice of the people'.[10]

Undying 'hostility to conscription of life and labour'

Campaigns for and against conscription had already emerged by the time of Hughes' return to Australia. Ostensibly, the divisions that appeared were on class lines – the middle-class generally supporting conscription, the working-class against it – but the reality was more complex. The Labor Party, in particular, was in imminent danger of splitting on the matter, with a range of opinions and sometimes divided loyalties evident within its ranks. In some areas there was a clear division between town and country, and in rural communities the controversy was frequently more bitter, as the protagonists often knew each other personally. There were variations between and within states, and sometimes there were important regional issues at play, together with religious and ethnic dimensions. Even before Hughes had arrived home, institutions had begun to line up on one side or the other. The United Service League, the Australian Natives' Association and the Australian National Defence League (which Hughes had helped to found in 1905) were all in favour of conscription, as were the Liberal Party, most chambers of commerce, and even some trade unions. On the anti-side, the potential for division and conflict was already apparent. Labor conferences in Victoria and New South Wales passed resolutions against conscription, and a hastily convened Australian Trade Unionism and Conscription Congress declared 'its undying hostility to conscription of life and labour'.[11] The Labor Parties in Queensland, South Australia and Tasmania also came out against conscription; only Western Australia remained equivocal.

Meanwhile, on 30 August, Hughes had announced a national referendum on conscription, scheduled for 28 October 1916. So convinced was he that the country would return a 'Yes' vote – he even hoped that the referendum would 'not excite the turmoil that surrounds an election' and might avoid an 'outburst of public feeling' – that he had ordered a preliminary call-up in September 1916 of all single men between twenty-one and thirty-five who would be eligible for compulsory enlistment, should the referendum succeed.[12] At Border Town in South Australia, 128 men duly reported for registration. Each was examined medically, and ninety-four were classed as fit for enlistment. Four decided to join up there and then, but no fewer than eighty-seven claimed exemption under the terms of the call-up. Across South Australia as a whole, some 14,000 men had been examined by 12 October 1916, of whom 8,548 were declared fit for service – of these, a colossal 6,065 sought exemption. The pattern was reproduced across the country. Rarely did a claim for exemption reflect ideological or conscientious objection. More usually, claims were entirely practical, based on sensible arrangements that had already been made privately within families. Samuel Hedley Phillips, for example, aged twenty-five, had agreed to stay in Australia as sole support for his sisters – one of whom was 'delicate', the other still at school – while his brother joined up instead. It was an explanation that failed to impress, and his bid for exemption was turned down. Likewise, Isaac Joseph Dunstan, aged twenty-nine, was a miner (a strategically important occupation) and had stayed at home to look after his widowed mother, while his brothers went off to war. His claim too was rejected.[13] No doubt the bewilderment and ill-feeling caused by such decisions added to the weight of the 'No' vote in the referendum, when it came.

Popular opinion among the pro-conscriptionists was that those seeking exemptions were probably 'shirkers' and 'slackers'. As early as August 1915, W.A. Holman, Premier of New South Wales, a Labor politician but firmly in favour of conscription, had unwisely made a belligerent recruitment speech at the Sydney Stadium before an assembly of 16,000 people attending a boxing title fight. He had insinuated that there were 'young loafers' among their number, indolents who would rather attend sporting fixtures than join up to serve their country. Holman was 'counted out' by the incensed crowd, a measure of the strong feelings already being aroused.[14] A year later, and these sentiments had hardened considerably. The Methodist *Australian Christian Commonwealth* magazine, echoing the position adopted by the Methodist church in Australia, published a satirical 'Anti-Conscriptionist Song' in October 1916:

We don't want to fight,
But by jingo if we do,
We'll stay at home and have our fun
And send the brave Hindoo!

We don't want to fight,
Perhaps the Russians do:
Then let us hire the poorer types
For just the Russian screw.

Or look to Africa,
The lusty, large Zulu;
Let him be trained to fight the Huns
Instead of me and you.

We're in an awful funk,
Believe us, friends, 'tis true;
Before this close conscription call
We kept it out of view;

And now unless the 'Nos' –
The rash, red-raggers' crew –
Can show them how to save their skins,
What will the Slackers do?

We do not want to fight
We are a peaceful crew;
To races, pubs, and movey shows
We'll stick, dear pals – like glue.[15]

A 'callousness and frivolity among the people'

In condemning 'races, pubs, and movey [sic] shows', the *Australian Christian Commonwealth* was linking the pro-conscriptionist cause to long-standing Nonconformist hostility to betting, alcohol, and self-indulgence in general, dismissing 'shirkers' and 'slackers' as selfish moral degenerates. This attitude was echoed across Australia by individual Nonconformist ministers – Methodists, Baptists and others – such as the Revd David Morgan, pastor at the David Lloyd Memorial Congregational Church at Wallaroo in South Australia. Criticizing the shirkers and slackers, he 'in strong terms denounced what he regarded as callousness and frivolity among the people', exhorting them to 'live worthily' and to raise their 'moral standard' so that they would be deserving of the sacrifice made in their name by young soldiers from the district.[16] The contrast between those who had already given their lives and those who chose instead a life of leisure at home was all too apparent to many, especially to those who had lost loved ones in distant lands. The *In Memoriam* notice for Private Fred Willard, killed at Pozières, was typical of many:

He was no coward or shirker,
He fought for honour's sake;

He fought hard in muddy trenches
For the pride of Britain's race,
And our darling now lies cold
In a soldier's grave in France.[17]

In embracing the conscriptionist cause, Methodism adhered to the
rhetoric of patriotism and Empire. 'Australia more than any other place
on the globe', thundered the Queensland *Mount Morgan Chronicle* in
October 1916, 'is the ultimate aim of Germany's dream of colonial
expansion', a position that many Methodists would have endorsed
uncritically.[18] Such was the level of controversy that at Binginwarra, in
Gippsland in Victoria, the local Methodist minister became embroiled
in a public brawl, when eggs were thrown. But Methodist commitment
to conscription was redoubled as Irish-Catholic opinion in Australia
hardened against conscription in the aftermath of the Easter 1916
rising in Ireland itself. Here, Methodists imagined, was opposition to
conscription that differed from both Councillor Sweeney's patriotic (if
misguided) adherence to Australian 'voluntarism' and the cowardly
shirker's avoidance of enlistment. Here, instead, was an altogether more
subversive and dangerous opposition which, it was thought, threatened
the war effort and the integrity of the British Empire.

Mannix, Catholic opinion and the first referendum

Although Catholic opinion generally, including that of Australia's Irish
community, had supported the war, there had been those who were
lukewarm or equivocal. When, in Easter 1916, the rebellion in Dublin
by a handful of republicans had been savagely repressed, its leaders
summarily executed, there had been outrage in Australia as well as in
Ireland. In Ireland, this proved to be the revolutionary turning-point,
when many Irish nationalists, hitherto supporters of the war and aspir-
ing to Home Rule (rather than independence), swung now behind
the separatist militant republicanism of Sinn Féin. In Australia, Irish-
Catholic misgivings were voiced by Dr Daniel Mannix, the Roman
Catholic Coadjutor Archbishop of Melbourne. Mannix had arrived
from Ireland in 1913 and, although relatively few Irish-Australians had
actually been born in Ireland, most being second-generation at least,

he swiftly assumed the role as their mouthpiece. Although, he said, he regretted the Easter Rising, he understood its origins and had some sympathy for the rebel cause, Ireland having long suffered at the hands of British misrule. In saying this, he effectively married the cause of Irish nationalism to that of anti-conscriptionism, casting doubt on the Empire's war aims and, in the estimation of his critics at least, on the legitimacy of Australia's participation in the conflict. On 16 September 1916, the Catholic weekly *Advocate* carried a speech delivered by Mannix at a church fête at Clifton Hill in Melbourne. 'I am as anxious as anyone can be for a successful issue and for an honourable peace', reported the *Advocate*, publishing his words verbatim, but 'I hope and believe that peace can be secured without conscription in Australia'. He continued:

> For conscription is a hateful thing, and is almost certain to bring evil in its train. . . . I still retain the conviction that Australia has done her full share – I am inclined to say even more than her fair share – in this war (Applause). Her loyalty to the Empire has been lauded to the skies, and the bravery of her sons has won the admiration of friend and foe alike . . . It seems, therefore, truly regrettable that Australia should be plunged into the turmoil of a struggle about conscription, which is certain to be bitter . . . Australians, brave as they have proved themselves in the field, are a peace-loving people. They will not easily give conscription a foothold in their country. (Applause).[19]

Although Mannix was careful to avoid mention of Ireland, and attributed to Catholics freedom of conscience in this as in other issues, he used his authority as Coadjutor Archbishop to imply Catholic opposition to conscription. 'There will be differences among Catholics', he allowed: 'But, for myself, it will take a good deal to convince me that conscription in Australia will not cause more evil than it would avert'. He also noted Protestant advocacy of conscription. In particular, 'I notice', he said, 'that certain authorities of the Anglican Church have given their public support to conscription'.[20] Again, he acknowledged their right to voice a different position but the inference was clear, that the conscription debate was acquiring a religious dimension. Mannix spoke publicly only twice on the subject during the first referendum campaign but he was seen, then as now, as having struck the most significant chord in the 'No' vote chorus. He insisted that he had expressed his opinions as a private individual, and other prominent Catholics (such as the Archbishop of Perth) certainly opposed his stance. But it seems likely that his intervention, and his personal charisma, did much to consolidate Catholic support for the 'No' vote in the referendum of 1916.

Mannix had chosen his words carefully, gently cajoling his Catholic flock. But, according to K.S. Inglis, 'the wilful ambiguity of his rhetoric only heightened the anger of imperial patriots'.[21] Perhaps, but there were other Irish-Australians who were prepared to go much further than Mannix. The Revd Maurice O'Reilly, for example, was rector of St John's, the Catholic College at the University of Sydney. Born in Ireland, he had been a loyal supporter of the war, and had even written a patriotic poem in praise of the heroes of Gallipoli. However, the Easter Rising and its repression 'turned him into an active anti-conscriptionist and hater of Empire'.[22] Likewise, a certain Father O'Keefe, speaking at Bowen in Queensland, was alleged to have told his listeners that 'I hope that the hands will wither of all those who vote for Conscription; that God will turn all those from voting for Conscription'. Indeed, he added, if 'Conscription is granted there will be Civil War in Australia, and I will fight with the rebels to the last drop of my blood'.[23] Pro-conscriptionist propagandists were eager to seize upon such intemperate remarks. J. Fihelly, Minister for Justice in the Queensland government, was reported to have told the Queensland Irish Association in September 1916: 'No Irishman should have the impertinence to apologise for the rebels [of Easter 1916] . . . every Irish Australian recruit means another soldier to assist that [sic] British Government to harass the people of Ireland'. Moreover, 'England was the home of cant, humbug and hypocrisy', Fihelly was reputed to have added, and in Easter 1916 she 'had murdered people whose compatriots were fighting for her by the hundred thousand'. Instead of contributing to local patriotic funds in Australia, he concluded, people should be sending money 'to relieve the distress in Ireland'.[24]

Added to the more extreme Irish nationalists, in the imagining of the pro-conscriptionists, were the activists of the Industrial Workers of the World (IWW) – the 'Wobblies' – whose advocacy of internationalist socialist revolution was anathema to supporters of the war effort. The IWW forbad its members from joining military forces, and in New South Wales especially was seen as a powerful influence on the left of the Labor Party. As far as Billy Hughes was concerned, all anti-conscriptionists were disloyal and a threat to Australia. In his eve of referendum appeal to the electorate on 27 October 1916, he told his 'Fellow Australians' that 'advocates of the "No" vote include every enemy of Britain open and secret in our midst. They include the violent and the lawless, the criminals who would wreck society and ruin prosperity. Will you dishonour Australia by joining their company?'[25] The next day Victoria, Tasmania and Western Australia voted 'Yes' to Conscription but in New South Wales, Queensland and South Australia the vote went the other way. Overall, across Australia, 1,087,557 had cast their vote in favour, while 1,160,033 were against. By a relatively narrow margin of 72,476, the people of Australia had voted 'No' and rejected Conscription.

The Labor Party split and the Second Referendum

In the political turmoil that ensued, Billy Hughes resigned from the Labor Party, irrevocably split as it now was, taking with him four federal government ministers and twenty-six other pro-conscription Labor MPs to form a new National Labor Party. In the several states, other prominent Labor pro-conscriptionists followed suit, including Crawford Vaughan, Premier of South Australia, and Jack Scaddan in Western Australia. At the federal level, the National Labor Party, with Hughes as leader, clung on to power (with Hughes as Prime Minister) with the backing of the Liberal Party. In February 1917 the two parties merged formally to become the Nationalist Party, with Hughes continuing as leader and Prime Minister. The rump of the Labor Party – marginalized, disillusioned and in disarray – was comprehensively defeated in the following general election in May 1917, when the Nationalists swept into power. Thereafter, as Dean Jaensch has observed, within the Labor Party 'most of the Protestant influence resigned, leaving the Irish-Catholic component with a controlling vote. The party moved to the Left in rhetoric, ideology and policy'.[26]

Recruitment dwindled further during 1917, and Hughes, with the democratic legitimacy afforded by his election triumph, decided on a second referendum, no doubt hoping that his recent victory would translate into a comfortable 'Yes' vote in favour of conscription. On 7 November he announced the new referendum, to be held on 20 December 1917. He chose a subtle form of wording, designed, according to his detractors, to ensnare the unwary: 'Are you in favour of the proposal of the Commonwealth Government for reinforcing the Australian Imperial Forces overseas?'[27] Mannix, by now promoted from his assistant (Coadjutor) position to full Archbishop, was appalled. 'Mr Hughes and his party', he exclaimed, 'had framed a question from which the word conscription was wholly eliminated'.[28] The *Australian Worker* condemned the new proposal as 'The Lottery of Death', complaining that 'Conscription is to take the form of a lottery. Lives are to be drawn for on Tattersall principles: souls to be made the subject of a hideous sweep'. Indeed, it concluded, if 'Australia accepts the scheme of military compulsion formulated by the Prime Minister . . . it will . . . reduce its citizens to the level of cannibals drawing lots for an obscene feast'.[29] All the rhetoric of the previous year was resurrected and deployed afresh, often in the most vociferous and lurid terms. The pro-conscription *Australian Christian Commonwealth*, for example, continued to rail against the enemy within. 'The venomous snakes of treason raise their heads in many parts of our wide-flung dominion', its editorial opined, 'but their warmest, most crowded nests are in Ireland and Australia'.[30] It offered clear advice to its readers:

> Speak plain at the next Referendum
> >   Reply by a thunderous 'Yes'!
> And show Dr Mannix' Sinn Feiners
> >   They cannot – yet – answer for us.
>
> Show those who would hoodwink the workers,
> >   The manifold pro-German crew,
> That tricks for betraying the soldiers
> >   Have no inch or quarter with you.[31]

For his part, Mannix had dropped the more cautious language of the first referendum campaign. After the 'No' vote of 1916, Catholic opinion – including that of leading clerics – had swung more firmly behind him, strengthening his position. He felt able now to speak more forthrightly on the Irish question. As the Melbourne *Argus* reported, his 'strong advice to the Irish people was to say, "Now or never" . . . If they did not get Home Rule during the war they had faint hope of getting it when England was out of her present difficulties'. To his opponents, this was uncomfortably close to the traditional nationalist dictum 'England's difficulty is Ireland's opportunity'. And there was more. Mannix insisted that Sinn Féin was aiming 'not at revolution' but 'to have government of Ireland by the Irish people in the interests of Ireland . . . Ireland was no longer to be ruled by Englishmen and in the interests of England'. To those who asked 'Will this serve the interests of the British Empire?', Mannix had responded: 'The men of Ireland today were determined that the paramount consideration in the judgement of every question should be did it or did it not serve Ireland. The Empire would have to take second place'.[32]

This was dangerous talk – there had already been calls for the government to deport Mannix – and Mannix compounded his offence, in the eyes of his detractors, by appealing especially to Catholic working-class voters. He told them that the war was a 'trade war' between competing capitalist nations, and lent support to socialist anti-conscriptionists campaigning for a 'No' vote. Again, this confirmed the worst fears of his opponents. During 1917 there had been a marked increase in labour unrest in Australia, culminating in the 'great strike' in New South Wales in August 1917. The latter had its origins in a dispute at the Randwick tramway workshops, where workers had objected to 'speed-up' efficiency measures. Their strike won widespread sympathy, and soon some 76,000 workers in New South Wales (fourteen per cent of the workforce) had also walked out, creating severe disruption in transport and shortages of food and fuel. Individuals from the middle classes volunteered to keep services going, adding to the sense of class antagonism that already permeated the dispute. Members of the Australian Women's Service Corps were among those who volunteered, adding a gender dimension to the class divisions. Middle-class women, especially, had been wooed by Billy Hughes, who had held 'women only' rallies where he appealed directly to their feminine patriotic sensibilities. Yet anti-conscriptionists, appealing in turn to women's nurturing and peace-loving instincts, warned that conscription would mean them being forced into men's jobs at home, just as they had been in Britain, where Australian soldiers had expressed distinct disapproval of their employment as tram-drivers, ticket-collectors and the like.

'One Conscript Equals Five Tons of Wheat. Which Will We Send?'

Billy Hughes had the task of holding together the new Nationalist Party and government (in reality still a coalition of disparate interests), and did so by deliberately perpetuating the atmosphere of crisis and confrontation. Against the background of increasing numbers of strikes and industrial conflict (sometimes violent) across the country, Hughes took on the trade unions and declared the Industrial Workers of the World illegal, imprisoning over one hundred 'Wobblies' and deporting others. It was in this context of suspicion and turmoil that the pro-conscriptionist Reinforcement Referendum Council issued its infamous handbill, entitled *The Anti's Creed*, in which the anti-conscriptionsts were accused of everything from welcoming the sinking of the *Lusitania* to advocating the surrender of Australia to Germany. It was, perhaps, the most extraordinary propaganda document of the whole debate:

I believe the men at the Front should be sacrificed.

I believe we should turn dog on them.

I believe that our women should betray the men who are fighting for them.

I believe in the sanctity of my own life.

I believe in taking all the benefit and none of the risks.

I believe it was right to sink the *Lusitania*.

I believe in murder on the high seas.

I believe in the I.W.W.

I believe in Sinn Fein

I believe that Britain should be crushed and humiliated.

I believe in the massacre of Belgian priests.

I believe in the murder of women, and baby-killing.

I believe that Nurse Cavell [shot as a 'spy' by the Germans] got her desserts.

I believe that treachery is a virtue.

I believe that disloyalty is true citizenship.

I believe that desertion is ennobling.

I believe in Considine, Fihelly, Ryan Blackburn, Brookfield [all anti-conscription agitators], Mannix, and all their works.

I believe in egg power rather than man power.

I believe in holding up transports and hospital ships.
I believe in general strikes.
I believe in burning Australian haystacks.
I believe in mine-laying in Australian waters.
I believe in handing Australia over to Germany.
I believe I am worm enough to vote No.

Those who DON'T Believe in the above Creed will VOTE YES.[33]

Such vitriol was repeated endlessly in the national and regional press as the second referendum drew closer. An advertisement in the *Yorke's Peninsula Advertiser*, for example, insisted that those campaigning for a 'No' vote were men who were 'playing Germany's game in our midst, Sinn Feiners, members of the I.W.W. . . . men of the type responsible for the strike which paralysed Australian industries, men responsible for the rebellion in Ireland, the kind of men who, to-day, are in Russia and are offering Germany a separate peace'.[34] These were by now familiar accusations. But many anti-conscriptionists refused to be drawn by such taunts. Instead, they redoubled their own arguments. There was real fear, for instance, that conscription would rob strategic industries of vital manpower, a concern that increasingly affected agricultural communities. Australian agricultural produce was a significant contribution to the war effort, it was contended, especially to feeding Britain, and it would be folly to jeopardize this important role. As one anti-conscription advertisement inquired: 'One Conscript Equals Five Tons of Wheat. Which Will We Send?'. Or, put another way: 'To equip a transport carrying troops from Australia to Europe means sacrificing tons of dead-weight cargo space for each man carried'. The powerful message was that support for the anti-conscription cause was neither unpatriotic nor anti-Empire but advocated instead the optimum use of Australia's resources to help win the war: 'Keep Australia Free. Send Foodstuffs to the Allies. Vote "No"'.[35]

Australia did indeed vote 'No'. Much to Hughes' chagrin, and Mannix's delight, the 'No' majority increased to 166,588. Western Australia again voted 'Yes', as in 1916, as did Tasmania, albeit by a narrower margin. Victoria, however, now voted 'No'. South Australia again voted 'No', although with a smaller majority, while both New South Wales and Queensland voted 'No' with slightly larger margins than in

the previous year. Hughes had said that he would resign if the referendum vote went against him but the Governor-General, Sir Ronald
Munro-Ferguson, persuaded him to stay on. Munro-Ferguson also made
one last bid to resolve the conscription crisis, inviting leaders from
all sides to Government House in Melbourne to discuss the matter.
Hughes introduced a plan for a 'voluntary ballot enlistment', in which
eligible young men would be encouraged to put their names forward for
a lottery conducted using numbered marbles – precisely the 'Lottery of
Death' the *Australian Worker* had condemned the previous year. Young
men would be attracted, Hughes thought, by the 'sporting risk' of such
a ballot.[36] Not surprisingly, Labor and the trade unions opposed the
solution, and the Governor-General's meeting broke up with a vague
agreement in which all parties merely agreed to encourage voluntary
enlistment. It was the last gasp of the conscription debate.

A divided Australia? The regional dimension

Although in many ways the conscription crisis had drawn Australia
together, in the sense that all parts participated in the national debate
and were familiar with the main arguments, for and against, in others
it had served to emphasize regional distinctions and variation. In some
rural areas of New South Wales, for example, the 'No' vote had been
bolstered considerably by widespread fears of losing agricultural labour.
In Western Australia, with its high proportion of those of English birth
or descent, and the concomitant limited impact of Mannix's rhetoric,
the 'Yes' vote had been consistently solid. In north-eastern Victoria,
where, as in other rural areas, the protagonists were often well-known
personally to much of the electorate, voting in the referenda was influ-
enced as much by place and personality as by class. But by the early
months of 1916, the regional press in north-eastern Victoria had moved
firmly behind the pro-conscriptionist cause, with newspapers such as
the *Ovens and Murray Advertiser*, the *Rutherglen Sun* and the *Alpine
Observer* all condemning the shirkers 'who hid behind their mother's
skirts' and the 'Ultra Socialists' and 'traitors' who had allegedly taken
over the Labor Party.[37] At a soldier's farewell at Great Northern,
Rutherglen's shire president, Alexander Prentice, had praised 19-year-
old George Buchanan for joining up, but named and shamed local

families whose sons (numbering nine in one case, five in another) had 'stayed firmly put at home'.[38] The *Yackandanah Times* spoke for many in the region when its editorial explained that: 'We believe in fighting on with every man under sixty. Send all who are fit and strong, married or single, that is our motto'.[39]

Inevitably, the campaign became very personal in such rural areas. Matthew Nunan, a member of Wodonga Rifle Club and a Boer War veteran, found himself frozen out of local society and facing claims of disloyalty when he declared himself an anti-conscriptionist. In such a climate, very few anti-conscriptionists were prepared to put themselves forward as speakers. One exception was John Parker Moloney, who attracted an audience of 400 when he spoke at Rutherglen, and also received enthusiastic receptions at Tallangatta, Chiltern and Wodonga. At Beechworth he got a rougher ride, when he was subject to heckling, insults and abuse. But pro-conscriptionist meetings could be equally rowdy, such as that at Tallangatta when J.W. Leckie, local Member of the Legislative Assembly in the Victorian parliament, was asked pointedly why he had not volunteered for the armed forces. He answered that he was forty-five, and so over the age limit. 'You were not forty-five two years ago', shouted a female voice from the audience, as the meeting collapsed in laughter. Unused to such treatment from constituents, Leckie lost his temper, countering that Australia had yet to make any real sacrifice in the war. When taken to task by a man with a broad Irish accent, he quipped: 'I object to a foreign language'. The meeting ended in further controversy when two women, members of the local Anti-Conscription League, refused to stand for the National Anthem.[40]

William Gribble, a Methodist and local Councillor from Wandilong, voiced the uncertainty felt by many in north-eastern Victoria. On the one hand, he was a patriot and in favour of the war. Yet he found aspects of the anti-conscription argument compelling, and said so. Conscription 'will not only bleed Australia white', he said, 'but make it impossible to discharge our duty to those who return'. As he explained, to 'many of us it seems as great an act of patriotism to remain at home and work to pay the bill as it is to take the trip to France'.[41] In the end, north-eastern Victoria voted 'Yes' by a narrow margin of 4.4% in 1916. Variations between electoral subdivisions reflected class divisions. Middle-class Wangaratta and Beechworth voted 'Yes', and working-class Wodonga and Tallangatta voted 'No'. But religion and ethnicity were also

powerful factors. At Whorouly, where the population was overwhelmingly Catholic and Irish, 84.6% voted 'No'. In the isolated Corryong
subdivision, where the majority were of English descent and Anglicans
accounted for almost half the local population, the 'Yes' vote was 89%.

Yorke Peninsula: 'I renounce South Australia as my Mother state'

The regional complexity of north-eastern Victoria was by no means
unique, and other parts of Australia exhibited their own distinctive
blends of class, religious, ethnic and other issues. On South Australia's
northern Yorke Peninsula, for example, the conscription crisis proved
especially divisive, and split a hitherto tight-knit copper-mining community that had only recently demonstrated a high degree of regional
cohesion and solidarity. In 1891 a staggering eighty per cent of people
living on northern Yorke Peninsula – in the vicinity of Moonta,
Wallaroo and Kadina – were recorded as Methodists, a reflection of
the strong Cornish make-up in the local population, and emblematic
of a vibrant regional ethno-religious and ethno-occupational identity.[42]
At the outbreak of the war, after initial dislocation, when the region's
erstwhile German market dried-up overnight, management and trade
unions had worked in concert to supply copper for the war effort, the
workers benefiting from high demand for their labour and skills, and
the consequent generous remuneration. Miners and smelters were
aware that theirs was a strategic industry, and although there was a
steady stream of volunteers, especially in the early days (and when
there were calls for miners for specialist tunnelling units), they felt
no urgent compulsion to join up. They had supported the war effort
in other ways. By early 1916, for example, the miners of Moonta and
Wallaroo had already contributed some £12,000 to various patriotic
organizations, and had participated in local fundraising activities such
as a Miners' Carnival in Kadina and a 'hammer and tap' exhibition
at Kadina showground when groups of miners competed against one
another to drill six inches into a hard-rock slab in the time allowed.
But when the State Recruiting Train, with none other than the
South Australian Premier, Crawford Vaughan, on board, visited the
Peninsula on 29–30 March 1916, few were persuaded to actually enlist.

The Recruiting Train had arrived at Wallaroo Mines railway station, outside Kadina, at 9.40 a.m., with a brass band playing and Boy Scouts providing a guard of honour. The Premier was accompanied by Corporal Evans, a veteran of Gallipoli, who spoke in passionate terms to the assembled miners, smelters and their families, who had been given time off by the company to attend the Recruiting Train. Evans encouraged the men to step forward, and was visibly taken aback when nobody moved. He redoubled his exhortation, and still no one budged. Angry now, Evans confessed himself more surprised by this lack of response than he had been by the Turkish reception at Anzac Cove. And he had a warning for the reluctant men. 'Don't you think it is better to go now, voluntarily', he asked, 'than have a sergeant calling for you with a squad of fixed bayonets?' It was an unfortunate turn of phrase, with its suggestion that it was more honourable to volunteer now, rather than wait for the inevitable conscription that would coerce the unwilling and the cowardly. Exasperated, Corporal Evans turned in despair to Crawford Vaughan. 'It's no use, Mr Premier', he cried, 'I can't shift them!' In the end, a mere handful of men came forward during the two-day visit: four at Kadina, two each at Wallaroo and Moonta, four at the nearby agricultural settlement of Paskeville, ten at outlying Port Wakefield – and none at all at Wallaroo Mines.[43]

The miners and smelters of Moonta and Wallaroo were Labor men, supporters of the party and members of the Amalgamated Miners' Association (AMA). They shared, then, in the growing grassroots opposition to conscription, and the Recruiting Train visit was, for them, uncomfortable evidence of the way in which things were already moving. But they were also Methodists, almost to a man, and when the Methodist Church in South Australia declared in favour of conscription, catastrophic seeds of division were sown in the community. For John Verran, local MP in the South Australian parliament and former Labor Premier (1910–12), religion and politics were inextricably linked. A Cornish miner and Methodist local preacher, Verran had insisted that 'the relationship between religion and politics is very close', and that 'Religion is citizenship'. Indeed, he said: 'When we come to justice and truth and righteousness these are great elementary principles of religion which affect the base of our manhood. Religion is not a question of going to heaven. It is a question of living and making the world better for having been in it'.[44]

Armed as he was with such convictions, the conscription crisis presented Verran, and the older generation of Cornish miners at Moonta and Wallaroo who shared his sentiments, with a dilemma. But, convinced of the rightness of the war and of Australia's duty to stand by the mother country, he and others like him decided that religious adherence came first. Verran had hoped that the Labor movement, at least in South Australia, where Methodism and Nonconformity were strong, and the Irish-Catholic influence weak, would follow Billy Hughes' lead and embrace conscription. But he was bitterly disappointed. In the 1916 referendum, South Australia voted against conscription, and nowhere was the vote larger than on northern Yorke Peninsula, supposedly the great stronghold of Methodist belief. In the Moonta subdivision the 'No' vote was an impressive seventy-eight per cent; Wallaroo recorded seventy-five per cent, and Kadina seventy-two per cent. Despite the apparent institutional strength of Methodism on the Peninsula, the 'No' vote had been decisive. As Arnold Hunt concluded, in South Australia 'the church's capacity to influence the thinking of its members on this issue was very limited, and in some areas (such as Moonta) was virtually non-existent.[45]

Moreover, the Labor movement on northern Yorke Peninsula was now irrevocably split. Verran (like Crawford Vaughan) followed Hughes into the National Labor camp, as did Jack Scaddan in Western Australia. A former Moonta miner, Scaddan was shocked by the 'big adverse vote in the Peninsula mining towns', and sent an angry telegram to Crawford Vaughan announcing that 'from today I renounce South Australia as my mother State unless Moonta proves to be of true metal'.[46] In fact, there had been a noticeable shift to the left in the Labor Party in South Australia, as Verran and his ilk departed, despite its members remaining overwhelmingly Methodist in affiliation. The position was exemplified in the rhetoric of Robert Stanley Richards, a Methodist local preacher and Yorke Peninsula mineworker of Cornish descent, who was prepared to put his political convictions before his religious beliefs. Richards had a ready appeal for the younger generation of Peninsula miners and their families, and after the 1916 conscription referendum, as regional solidarity began to break down, so the industrial harmony in the mines so apparent earlier in the war also began to fragment. Miners and smelters began to voice their suspicions of the vast profits made in the copper industry and the fat dividends paid to shareholders, and there were calls for new patterns of solidarity – with other workers in other parts of Australia. During 1917 proposals were made for a merger between the Amalgamated Miners' Association (AMA) and the all-encompassing Australian Workers' Union (AWU). Richards took the lead, insisting that the merger would strengthen the trade union movement across Australia, but Verran and the older generation opposed the move for 'We will lose control of industrial matters locally'.[47]

The merger went ahead, with R.S. Richards becoming President of the Moonta branch of the AWU at its foundation. John Verran reacted angrily by forming an alternative trade union, officially the Yorke's Peninsula Miners' and Smelters' Association but known to its opponents as the 'Bogus' union, its members condemned as 'Bogies'. The split in the trade union movement on the Peninsula mirrored the existing split locally in the Labor Party over conscription, perpetuating and aggravating the sense of community strife. Verran thought that the AWU was 'led by Pommies who came out from England to escape conscription', and the new mood of industrial militancy on the Peninsula was heightened when 'wharfies', dock workers at Wallaroo, refused to unload precious shiploads of coal to meet the insatiable demand of the mines and smelters.[48]

During the run-up to the second conscription referendum in 1917, the atmosphere locally remained highly charged. The *Yorke's Peninsula Advertiser*, for example, reported on a visit by the South Australian State Recruiting Committee to Moonta and Broken Hill (the latter just across the New South Wales border but with strong links to the Peninsula), alleging that both localities 'contain a much larger percentage of eligibles than the average throughout the State', and that there was – 'especially in Broken Hill' – 'an opposition to recruiting which is political'. Indeed, it was added, at Broken Hill 'a great many persons ... would not stand during the singing of the National Anthem'.[49] John Verran had also tried to make political capital out of the German question. 'It is deplorable to allow those with German blood in their veins to vote in this country', he had declared in the South Australian parliament: 'No matter what they cry out, they must have a bias for Germany. I am a Britisher and a Cornishman, and no one can take away my feelings of loyalty to my country'.[50] It was a stance that had won him some admirers, but it was not enough to prevent northern Yorke Peninsula from again rejecting conscription in 1917. Nor,

indeed, was it sufficient to stop John Verran from being defeated in the
State election in April 1918 by R.S. Richards, who was duly returned
as the new Labor representative for the seat of Wallaroo. Verran failed
to retake the seat in 1921, and again in 1924, evidence, among other
things, of the profound changes wrought on northern Yorke Peninsula
by the conscription crisis.

Broken Hill: 'a community divided against itself'

As the South Australian State Recruiting Committee had intimated,
the silver-lead-zinc mining district of Broken Hill was another important regional centre split by the conscription debate. Pro-conscriptionist
speakers were habitually shouted down and 'counted out'. When it
was suggested at one meeting that soldiers at the front were defending the integrity and liberty of Australia, the audience just laughed.
Yet there were others who were prepared to write to one newspaper to
condemn the local anti-conscriptionists. 'You dirty, slimey, Irish Papist,
pro-German cows', shrilled one correspondent: 'You king scabs. You
red-wagging wasters. Scabs! Scabs! A.M.A. [Amalgamated Miners'
Association] loafers and scabs association'.[51] Here the term 'scab' had
been appropriated for ironic deployment against local trade unionists
and other anti-conscriptionists, who were seen as 'scabbing' on their
compatriots who had volunteered for the front. Such was the ferocity
and bitterness of the debate as it emerged at Broken Hill. As elsewhere,
there had been a surge of recruitment at Broken Hill early in the war.
Yet even then, there had been vocal opponents. In September 1914
socialists had gathered at Sulphide Street railway station to boo the
latest group of new recruits bound for Adelaide, and they in turn were
abused as 'Red-raggers', 'Traitors', 'Never-works' and 'Mongrels' by the
angry crowd who had come to say farewell to their loved ones. The
'anti-Britons' were pursued to the nearby Socialist Hall, and only the
timely intervention of the police prevented injury to life and limb.[52]

As Brian Kennedy has observed, instead of being 'united against
common external threats', as it had been in the past, Broken Hill – like
northern Yorke Peninsula – now became 'a community divided against
itself'. Mine managers, some women, the Methodist clergy, and the
older generation of mineworkers – including traditional Labor adherents

– supported the war effort uncritically, as did their mouthpiece, the *Barrier Miner* newspaper. But the increasingly militant leadership of the Amalgamated Miners' Association provided a focus for anti-war feeling, especially in the conscription debate. Indeed, isolated in the outback, far from metropolitan influences, Broken Hill became a magnet for those elsewhere in Australia opposed to the war, for fugitives on the run, and for aliens who wished to avoid the whole enlistment issue. The *Barrier Daily Truth* became the voice of anti-war and anti-conscription, linking the one inextricably to the other, attacking the war as a capitalist conflict and condemning it for causing problems such as rapid inflation, high rents and unemployment. At a time when other newspapers were lauding in hushed tones the sacrifice of Gallipoli, the *Barrier Daily Truth* had published its own ironic commentary. 'Hurrah for War!' it exclaimed: 'Hurrah for blood and entrails, for lungs shot through and eyes gouged out, for faces torn off and limbs blown sky high, for weeping mothers and fatherless children'.[53]

The Industrial Workers of the World also had a strong presence at Broken Hill, ensuring that opposition to conscription had emerged as early as July 1915. IWW members or supporters, including figures who would rise to national notoriety, such as Percival Brookfield and 'Mick' Considine, were soon in open confrontation with the Labor old guard. Men like John Henry Cann and Josiah Thomas, who had much in common with John Verran, were marginalized and estranged from the union movement they had so recently led, as the militants took control. By July 1916 Brookfield had organized Labor's Army for Home Defence (LVA), which enlisted hundreds of young men and women who swore an oath to 'the working class of Australia' and committed themselves not to 'serve as a conscript (industrial or military) . . . even though it may mean my imprisonment or death'.[54] In a parody of the well-known hymn, they sang:

> Onward Christian Soldiers, duty's way is plain
> Slay your Christian neighbours, or by them be slain.
> Pulpiteers are spouting effervescent swill,
> God above is calling you to rob and rape and kill.[55]

In the build-up to the 1916 conscription referendum, there were LVA rallies, torchlight processions, concerts, 'stop work' demonstrations at the mines, and the vote was almost a forgone conclusion. On 28 October 8,922 'No' votes were cast at Broken Hill, compared to 3,858 'Yes' votes. Ironically, the mine managers had also harboured serious reservations about the government's recruiting drive, believing that conscription could rob the mining industry of key skilled workers. Many considered that their employees should be exempt from any compulsory enlistment, and were prepared to say so. Others, however, looked askance as Broken Hill became, in the words of one mine manager, 'a happy hunting ground for Sinn Feiners, I.W.W.'s and all the outlaws of Australia'.[56] More generally, after the 1916 referendum, Methodism, hitherto a vital force at Broken Hill, just as it had been on Yorke Peninsula, retreated into 'a narrower world of piety and patriotism', as Kennedy has described it, thus removing a 'powerful moderating influence' on the local Labor movement and propelling it to the left.[57] In 1917 Broken Hill again rejected conscription, while the increasingly militant miners' union adopted an ever-more hostile attitude to the mine companies, laying the groundwork for the 'Big Strike' of 1919–20. Such were the legacies of the conscription crisis in regional Australia.

The AIF and conscription

Needless to say, for soldiers at the front or training in England, the complex twists and turns of the conscription debate were often difficult to follow, especially in their regional contexts. Lance-Corporal Signaller Len Harvey confessed himself bewildered at times. His father, W.H. Harvey, was a pro-conscription Labor member of the South Australian parliament, a colleague of John Verran and Crawford Vaughan, and so Len Harvey was naturally perplexed by the strength of the state's anti-conscriptionist vote in 1916 and 1917. Likewise, he was stunned by R.S. Richards' defeat of John Verran in the South Australian state election of April 1918. Like many of the 3rd Division, training on Salisbury Plain during 1916, Len Harvey believed that conscription was necessary if the Australian Imperial Force (AIF) was to be kept up to strength. But he recognized that those already in the trenches often had a different opinion. Early in November 1916, after the overall referendum vote was known, Harvey wrote to his father:

Up to now we have not heard the results of the votes given by the men over there [the Western Front]. However it is rumoured that they voted, strongly, NO. Their reason is that they have seen the firing line, and do not wish their comrades to go through the ordeal. That is not the way we [in camp in England] see it, we must have every man, not to make new divisions, but to reinforce those at present fighting.[58]

In fact, the AIF had voted 72,399 for conscription, with 58,849 against. At the time, it was speculated that the vote had been swung by those training in England, plus those serving in the Middle East, with the troops on the Western Front overwhelmingly opposed, as Harvey had imagined. As the second referendum approached, Harvey wrote home in November 1917. 'The state of affairs all over Australia at present is shocking', he complained: 'The men out on strike don't realise how much they are assisting the Hun'.[59] And he was mortified when conscription was once again rejected. This time the vote in the AIF was narrower: 103,789 'Yes' votes to 93,910 'No'. Len Harvey tried to find a satisfactory answer to his father's inquiry about the strength of the 'No' vote among the troops. 'Dad', he wrote:

> I would like to give you a satisfactory answer to your question re. the reason for so many soldiers voting No, but I'm afraid I can't. A large number, when questioned, said it was immaterial to them which side won, and it wasn't for them to vote yes to bring another man into the war. Others reckoned they were out to crush militarism, and that by voting yes they would be helping to bring militarism to Australia.[60]

It was not an opinion that Len Harvey could understand. But it was one that others shared. Captain William Braithwaite, for example, had written to his parents back in Australia with firm advice: 'Do not vote for conscription on any account. Australia has sent enough to the war and if we did empty the remaining men out, it would only cripple her and not make a slightest difference to the result of the war'.[61] It was a view that many held. Ironically, conscription was indeed rejected – but the Australians went on in 1918 to make a distinguished and disproportionate contribution to the defeat of Germany and to the final Allied victory.

Chapter Eight

Tragedy to Triumph: 1917–1918

IN THE AFTERMATH of the Somme, both sides reviewed their strategies. The European winter of 1916–17, said to be the wettest and coldest for almost half a century, made the frontlines in France and Flanders a sea of mud, and renewed offensive action was impossible until conditions improved. The Germans, in any case, had decided to resort to unrestricted submarine warfare as their primary war-winning tactic. Rather than engage in costly offensives on the Western Front, they would merely sit tight while Britain was starved into submission. The process would take up to six months, it was estimated, and then – with Britain and her Empire out of the war – Germany could complete her defeat of France and the remaining Allies. In the event, as we know, Britain was not starved into submission, and the policy of unrestricted submarine warfare had the unintended (but hardly unforeseeable) outcome of precipitating American entry into the war against Germany. However, in the early months of 1917, confident in the efficacy of their revised plan, including the emphasis on defensive measures on the Western Front, the Germans acted to shorten and strengthen their frontlines. During February and March, they retreated on a broad front south of Arras, ceding territory of between ten and thirty miles deep as they retired to the so-called Hindenburg line, newly constructed fortifications which, the Germans calculated, were sufficiently strong to break any renewed Allied assaults. Safe behind their Hindenburg line, the Germans imagined, all they need do was await the surrender of the British Empire.

'Lark Hill Lancers'

In November 1916 Australian forces on the Western Front had been augmented by the 3rd Division, newly arrived from their training at Larkhill camp on Salisbury Plain. Mocked by veterans of Gallipoli and Pozières as merely 'Lark Hill Lancers', what the newcomers lacked in battlefield experience was made up for in the rigour and thoroughness of their training. Major-General John Monash, who took command, welcomed the professional edge of the 3rd Division, acknowledging that it had a 'certain air', its soldiers mature, independent, 'hard and active', and, above all, intelligent.[1] Among their number was Lance-Corporal Leonard Harvey, from South Australia, a member of the 43rd Battalion. He had first gone into the trenches on Christmas Eve 1916, and had his first taste of action a few days later, as the Australians attempted to keep up pressure on the German lines opposite. On 5 February 1917, he was involved in a 'stunt' for which his mate Len Trembath was subsequently awarded a Military Cross, an event that Harvey reported excitedly in a letter to his father. A party of scouts had gone out into No-Man's Land after dark, Harvey explained, but in the light of the full moon had been spotted by the ever-vigilant Germans. The enemy began 'playing machine gun fire on our scouts', Harvey continued, and one of the Australians – Private Edgecombe – was hit. Grabbing his Lewis light machine gun, Len Trembath leapt onto the trench parapet and aimed a withering covering fire at the German positions, enabling the wounded man to be rescued: 'all the time he was there enemy bullets were tearing the sandbags around him, how he didn't get hit is hard to say'.[2]

There was further contact with the enemy, as the Australians conducted raids across No-Man's Land, and in these encounters Harvey detected a weariness and half-heartedness among his opponents. In the aftermath of the Somme, he opined, the Germans had lost their appetite for fighting. 'I think Fritz has had enough of war', he wrote to his father, 'and in my opinion, this spring will bring with it a lot more fighting, but also a termination of the war'. He was wrong on the last count, of course, but his analysis of German intent – and its likely consequences – was broadly correct. He predicted that unrestricted submarine warfare would bring America into the war. 'Germany is a deceiving and cunning nation', he wrote, 'probably she will get the whole world to go to war against her . . . Her submarine methods are fiendish, and no doubt she will stick to her word as regards sinking all ships on sight'.[3] But as Harvey and his unit prepared for yet further incursions into enemy lines, they were taken by surprise when, on 23 February 1917, the Germans opposite suddenly and unexpectedly began their withdrawal towards Bapaume.

First and Second Bullecourt

All along the Australian line, the Germans pulled back, abandoning Bapaume (leaving it strewn with booby traps) and making for the formidable fortifications of the Hindenburg line. The Australians followed in hot pursuit, thinking they had the enemy on the run. But it was no rout, and as the Germans co-ordinated their strategic retreat, they were careful to keep the Allies at bay, inflicting as much damage as possible. Harold Williams was among the pursuers, and he experienced firsthand the deadliness of the enemy withdrawal. He observed a German spotter plane flying low overhead, and within half an hour his position was being shelled heavily. A shell exploded close by, and 'I was hurled to my face in the bottom of the trench, and felt as if a draught horse had kicked me in the solar plexus'. Recovering his senses, Williams turned to speak to the soldier next to him. 'Instead of a man', Williams wrote with horrified incredulity, 'there was a heap of tumbled earth that still smoked from the explosion of the shell, and intermingled with the smoking mass was blood, flesh and fragments of clothing. My face, arms and head were smothered with the poor wretch's minced flesh and warm blood'.[4]

Despite the exhilaration of the Australian pursuit, the Germans had not lost control of their withdrawal, and were soon safely ensconced behind the Hindenburg line, as planned. Nonetheless, emboldened by the German retreat and the Allied thrust across open country, Haig welcomed the opportunity to take the offensive, and aimed to break through the Hindenburg line before the enemy had been able to consolidate fully. As winter turned to spring, it was time to regain the offensive, and to begin again the determined drive to defeat the Germany army on the battlefield, in Haig's estimation the only way to achieve victory in this war. Accordingly, 10 April 1917 was fixed for what would become known as First Bullecourt, a battle which would include the 4th Australian Division, fresh from six weeks tactical training in Albert in north-east France. Designed to support a larger British offensive further north at Arras, the Bullecourt attack was placed under the command of General Hubert Gough, another of the old school who believed in the offensive spirit above all else. But he was keen to adopt new tactics, and in his eagerness to undertake an assault at Bullecourt was persuaded that tanks rather than artillery should be used to destroy the enemy barbed-wire, opening the way for penetration of enemy lines by the infantry. In the embryonic days of 'all arms' theory, when it was not fully appreciated that tanks *and* artillery might work together effectively, it was sometimes imagined that tanks *instead of* artillery could achieve the necessary offensive surprise. At any rate, it was argued at First Bullecourt that the lack of an artillery barrage would catch the enemy unawares and unprepared.

It was an innovative if flawed idea. Unfortunately, the twelve Mark II tanks allocated to the battle were already worn out, as well as being poorly armed, under-armoured and very slow. To make matters worse, on 10 April the weather had taken a decided turn for the worst, and instead of early spring was more like mid-winter, freezing cold and with driving snow blizzards that blinded the tanks as they lumbered towards the start line. The Australians had been in position since midnight, and as zero hour – 4.45 a.m. – approached, there was still no sign of the tanks. Eventually word came through that the tanks had been delayed, and would not be there in time to lead the assault. The attack was postponed and the troops hurriedly returned to the relative safety of their trenches. It was decided to repeat the attempt the next day but by now the enemy had been alerted to the imminent offensive, and any element of surprise had been lost. Indeed, the renewed attack on 11 April 1917 proved equally chaotic, and only three tanks had arrived by the time the attack was due to commence. Moreover, the tanks were so slow that they often lagged behind the infantry, rather than leading, and unprotected by any artillery barrage the Australians had to advance about a thousand yards over open ground – 'as flat as a billiard table' according to one witness – before reaching their first objective.[5] The barbed-wire, breast high and impenetrably thick, had been flattened in only a few places, and as the men converged on these gaps they made easy prey for the German machine-gunners.

Remarkably, despite the fact that only one tank ever reached the enemy lines, the Australians took their first objective, and went on to capture the second German trench. Recognizing that the enemy would surely counter-attack, word was sent back for artillery support but, absurdly, none was forthcoming. Eventually, by 11.30 a.m., the Australians in the forward positions acknowledged that they were in danger of being overrun, and made their way as best they could through murderous fire to their own trenches. Even so, some 1,300 were taken prisoner (the only occasion in the war when the Germans captured a large number of Australians), adding to the seventy-nine officers and 2,260 other ranks killed, wounded or missing. First Bullecourt exhibited elements of high farce, and yet the Australians had breached – and held for a time – part of the Hindenburg line, trumpeted only recently by the Germans as impregnable. It was an admirable achievement, and one that has sometimes been overlooked or underestimated by those focusing on the manifold shortcomings of the operation. It demonstrated to the Germans that they could not afford to be complacent in their new defensive posture, and it showed that the fine fighting qualities of the Australians could prevail in even the most unpromising circumstances. As William Philpott has observed, the Australians now had 'renewed confidence in their martial skill . . . Come the spring the Australian infantry were shaping up to be audacious trench fighters'. Thereafter, according to Philpott, 'I Anzac Corps – trained, re-equipped and shining – would commence its ascent to the pinnacle of battlefield skill and reputation'.[6]

In that sense, First Bullecourt was a turning point. But to those who had participated in the battle, only blunder and missed opportunity were obvious. For the moment, tanks were discredited, at least as far as the Australians were concerned, and Gough's impatience to press ahead with a fast-disintegrating plan was roundly criticized. Indeed, General Birdwood had done his best to postpone the attack after the débâcle of 10 April but had been overruled by Haig, who saw the operation as an opportunity to breach the Hindenburg line – as indeed it was, if only it had been better managed. The feebleness of the tanks had been exacerbated by the inadequacy of the artillery support, and the infantry had not been given the opportunity to train with tanks before the attack. Birdwood recognized the shortcomings of First Bullecourt and, as Edgar Rule recorded, was at pains to tell the Australians that the failure of the operation was not their fault. 'Boys, I can assure you that no one regrets this disaster that has befallen your brigade more than I do', Birdwood exclaimed, 'I can assure you that none of your own officers had anything to do with the arrangements for the stunt'. In fact, he added: 'We did our utmost to have the stunt put off until more suitable arrangements could be made'.[7]

The Germans, anxious to tie down troops and prevent their transfer to the battle raging at Arras, attacked the Australians near Bullecourt on 15 April, but were repulsed with heavy casualties as the Anzacs remembered their training and defended in depth. A fortnight later, on 3 May 1917, in the battle of Second Bullecourt, the Australians had a second attempt at taking their objectives. This time it was a more conventional operation, without the distraction of tanks and with an effective creeping barrage, and happily the spring weather had arrived at last. But the Germans had been expecting this renewed attack, and were well prepared. The assault soon fragmented into a ghastly series of attacks and counter-attacks. By nightfall, however, the Australians had captured a small section of the Hindenburg line, and this time they were able to hold on, over the next few days extending their newly won position over a broad front of 600 yards. It was another remarkable achievement. On 12 May, the Australian 5th Division took over the line, in time to defeat a determined enemy counter-attack three days later. Tacitly recognizing their failure, the Germans subsequently withdrew to new defensive positions, behind the much-vaunted Hindenburg line. For Haig, here was a vindication of the offensive spirit, and of the Australians as its prime practitioners. But it was not yet the breakthrough that he sought, although increasingly he saw the merit of the tactical 'bite-and-hold' approach, where carefully selected portions of the enemy line could be 'bitten off' and held against counter-attack.

Messines and Hill 60

Now that spring had arrived and summer beckoned, Haig looked to take the offensive. At Ypres, in Belgian Flanders, scene of bloody fighting earlier in the war, the two armies – Allied and German – glared at each other from their respective defensive positions. The British occupied a salient that jutted out into enemy-held territory, a toehold that they were determined not to relinquish, and yet which was inherently vulnerable and dangerous, subject to enemy fire on three sides. To make matters even more uncomfortable, the locality was reclaimed bogland, perpetually threatened by inundation, should the complex pattern of drainage ditches that criss-crossed the countryside be allowed to fall into disrepair. The ground was constantly soggy, especially after heavy rain, and in such conditions the construction of conventional trench systems was well-nigh impossible. The Germans, with considerable resources at their disposal, and happy to adopt a defensive posture, had built for themselves a network of reinforced concrete pillboxes and blockhouses, vast fortifications strung along their line, camouflaged with mud and sandbags but affording a commanding panoramic view of the British salient below. The British meanwhile, with the usual short-age of materiel, and a reluctance to strike too defensive a pose (they were supposed to be an army on the offensive), eschewed such fortifica-tions and opted instead for the more modest (and far less comfortable) method of throwing up mud breastworks, stabilized and reinforced with sandbags. Such were the rudimentary earthworks that characterized the Allied front line, and which welcomed the Australians of II ANZAC when they too found themselves in the salient.

General Sir Herbert Plumer, in command at Ypres, pondered the possibilities. The aim was to break out of the Ypres salient, overrun-ning the Germans on the ridge above, and then moving to liberate the strategically vital Belgian Channel ports from enemy occupation. But Plumer recognized that the Germans, sitting in their massive fortifica-tions on the high ground of Messines Ridge, could never be dislodged by conventional methods. The answer, he decided, was to destroy the ridge itself. Specialist British and Canadian tunnelling units, comprised of men who in civilian life had been miners, were engaged to dig deep beneath the German positions, with the intention of planting and then detonating huge underground mines. To their number was added the three companies of the Australian Tunnelling Corps, who had first arrived on the Western Front in May 1916. By November 1916, the First Australian Tunnelling Company was at Ypres, where it assumed responsibility for the excavations at Messines beneath Hill 60 and the neighbouring 'Caterpillar'. Led by Captain Oliver Woodward, originally a mining engineer from Charters Towers in Queensland, the tunnellers were drawn from mining towns across Australia – copper-miners from

Moonta and Wallaroo, coal-miners from Newcastle, gold-miners from Bendigo. Their work was dangerous and nerve-racking, especially as they detected and destroyed German countermining in a deadly sub-terranean game of cat-and-mouse. But at last their work was done, completed at nightfall on 6 June 1917, the day before the scheduled detonation of the mines. Beneath Hill 60, the Australians had placed 53,500 lb of high explosive, with a further 70,000 lb underneath the Caterpillar. 'Gentlemen, we may not make history tomorrow', observed Plumer, 'but we shall certainly change the geography'.[8]

At 3.10 a.m. precisely on 7 June 1917 the Australians blew their mines. It was said that the resultant explosion could be heard in London, and even Dublin, as white flames shot 300 feet into the sky. Concrete from shattered pillboxes was scattered over hundreds of yards, and as many as 10,000 Germans died instantly, blown sky-high or crushed and entombed as their trenches ran together. Following their British and New Zealand counterparts, the Australians of II ANZAC rose from their trenches to attack whatever remained of the German lines, the 3rd Division under Monash, the 4th commanded by Major-General Holmes. Among the Australians hopping the bags that day was Private Richard 'Dick' Trembath, from South Australia.[9] Ten days later, as he drew breath after the battle, Dick Trembath at last found time to put pen to paper, writing to his parents. 'We are having a rest after a strenuous go at Fritz', he explained. The Australians 'absolutely outclassed him', Trembath continued, 'both in fighting hand-to-hand and in artillery duels. There is no doubt Fritz played his cards alright; but he forgot one thing and that [is that] there is a joker in the pack, and I really think the Australians are the joker'. But to 'describe war is a very hard thing', Trembath conceded, 'and one cannot write every-thing concerning it without at times seeing your pals, and good pals at that, dead and dying close to you'.[10] Yet he exulted in the Australians' achievement:

> Well, it's easy to see who is winning when you have a look at both our lines and the enemy's. Ours are knocked about a bit, but all you can see of Fritz's lines are shell holes and dugouts knocked almost to sand. Talk about superior shells and men; he's not in the same street. Before our division hopped the bags a number of mines were blown, which meant severe losses to the enemy. One under Messines hill [60], caused Fritz's

dugouts to collapse and buried a great number of Germans. We learnt
from a prisoner that one dugout alone at that time contained 600 men.[11]

Confident now in the martial superiority of the Australian soldier,
Dick Trembath imagined the Anzacs exacting a terrible revenge for
the Germans' brutal treatment of the poor British conscripts in earlier
clashes:

> When our men were advancing the Germans rushed out with their
> hands up, calling their usual cry – 'Mercy, comrades'. They got mercy
> too; they got hell! What could they expect? When their artillery was
> superior in quality, overwhelming in numbers, did they give our English
> Tommies mercy? No, they simply wiped them out. Did the Tommies
> hold their hands up and cry for mercy? No, they fought to the last man,
> as a soldier should, and now why should they [the Germans] be spared?[12]

Trembath explained that, as the Australians went forward, they encountered hordes of fleeing Germans, who ran for their lives: 'a few stopped,
but they got fixed [with bayonets]'. He appreciated that readers, browsing
in the comfort of their homes in distant Australia, might be shocked by
the graphic descriptions in his letter, especially the casual slaughter of
those Germans who had tried to surrender. He admitted that such tales
would not appeal to 'some of the deep thinkers' back home. But such
'thinkers', he emphasized, did not know what it was like to be faced with
the stark choice of kill or be killed, to be confronted by vast numbers
of enemy: 'if they would only see the enemy lines after an advance and
wonder where all the Germans came from'. Moreover, he was quick to
add, not all those who had surrendered at Messines had been killed.
The wounded, especially, had been ushered back to the Australian lines,
where they 'get treated as we do; but perhaps they have to wait a bit
longer, as our own men come first'. He himself had spared a Bavarian
deserter who had swum across a waterway to the Australian lines. 'I
did not shoot him', he wrote, 'because I thought him deaf and he had
not any firearms, so we had a bit of pity on him and took him prisoner'.
Reflecting for a moment, Dick Trembath added: 'This was the first prisoner I had taken, and I think the first one taken in the battalion'.[13]
    Trembath's Bavarian prisoner, deafened by the detonations at
Messines and demoralized by the destructive force of the explosions,

attracted only momentary sympathy. 'This poor devil was absolutely beaten', Trembath reported, 'and came back to surrender and complained about our shelling. This is what we want, as it is only what Fritz gave us, being returned with a big percentage of interest'. And there were others, 'coming to our lines, giving themselves up', deserters who could not 'get . . . back behind our lines quick enough'. These 'Germans are absolutely fed up with the war and want to finish', Trembath concluded, 'but the heads [military and political leaders] cannot surrender after what they had said. However, it must come sooner or later'. Victory was now inevitable, Trembath considered, and Messines had been a turning point. But, he added, there 'is only one way to bring this world and this war to a peaceful ending, and that is to absolutely crush Germany, and, if it is in our power, which it is, we will do it and do it well'.[14]

Messines, as Trembath had judged, had been a huge success, morale-boosting as well as a military triumph. But, as ever, there was a large human cost. In II ANZAC there were some 13,900 dead, wounded and missing but the Australians, not least Captain Woodward's tunnellers, had inflicted countless German casualties. On the Australian side, as Richard Travers has observed, one particular casualty stood out. On 2 July 1917, Major-General William Holmes, commander of the 4th Division, was taking W.A. Holman, Premier of New South Wales, to see the Messines battlefield. General Holmes' chauffeur drove the Premier's party up the western slopes of Hill 63, from where there was a panoramic view of the ridge that had been so recently obliterated. As they approached a wayside shrine, a German aeroplane came under fire from a nearby anti-aircraft battery. The engagement was a little too close for comfort, and Holmes said: 'Come on, we must not run a risk with this precious Premier. We'll run past the shrine where it will be safe'. Laughing, he added: 'They have spotted you Holman. This is unhealthy. Let's move'. Continuing past the shrine as instructed, the chauffeur parked up and the Premier's party walked the rest of the way to the crest of the hill. A stickler for correct appearance, General Holmes – who was dressed in full uniform that day in the Premier's honour – realized that he had left his cap in the car. As he returned to retrieve it, at about 10.20 a.m., a high explosive shell fell close by. The Premier's party was shaken but unhurt. William Holmes, however, had been hit, causing a wound that stretched from under his left ribs in his back to his neck. He expired even before he reached the field dressing station.[15]

Preparing for Third Ypres

Haig was keen to proceed with the next stage of the offensive. In London the British Prime Minister, Lloyd George, together with his War Cabinet, expressed grave misgivings about the enterprise. Responding to the darkening public mood, not least consternation and alarm caused by increasing air-raids and civilian casualties, Lloyd George cautioned against another round of blood-letting such as that experienced on the Somme, with heavy losses for little apparent gain, and argued instead that resources might be better deployed in supporting the Italian front. Haig countered that an offensive on the Western Front was needed to relieve pressure on both the mutinous French army further to the south and the Russians on the Eastern Front, who were faced with revolution. Moreover, Haig insisted that it was important to capitalize on the victory at Messines, so that the Channel ports might be captured, an argument supported strongly by the First Sea Lord, Lord Jellicoe, who stated that the denial of Ostend and Zeebrugge to German *U-boats* would significantly reduce the threat to Britain. Indeed, he reported gravely that, if these ports could not be liberated, then the Germans would indeed starve the British into submission.

Shocked by Jellicoe's assessment and persuaded, albeit reluctantly, by Haig's plan, the British War Cabinet agreed, despite its continuing reservations, that preparations for the Ypres offensive should go ahead. Thereafter, the plan acquired a life of its own, as the military machine swung into action. But even as the Allies poured men and resources into the salient, so the Germans, who had no doubt where the next blow would fall, were busy constructing a new network of defensive ferro-concrete fortifications, hidden behind their front lines. As both sides toiled, the summer rolled on, with June and July warm and sunny and, for those Allied troops not directly in the front line, there was almost a holiday atmosphere. There were field days and sports days to keep the soldiers entertained and occupied, and a succession of leave trains took those who could be spared to the *estaminets* and other delights of Poperinghe, behind the lines.

Commanders of those units at 'rest' were worried that such relaxation might subvert discipline and erode military bearing and readiness, and looked for opportunities to assert their authority and to remind the men that they were soldiers of the King. The Colonel of the

British 10th Battalion, Royal Fusiliers, for example, insisted upon full ceremonial and dress parade for mounting its guards each day. Every morning, the Fusiliers turned out smartly, boots polished and buttons shining brightly, and marched up and down as their band played, the guards being posted with much pomp and admirable parade-ground precision. The neighbouring Australians, who mounted their guards with the minimum of fuss and bother, watched the antics with wry amusement. As one Fusilier recalled: 'Well, the Aussies looked over at us *amazed* . . . The Aussies couldn't get over it, and when we were off duty we naturally used to talk to them, go over and have a smoke with them'. The bemused Australians would ask the Fusiliers: 'Do you like this sort of thing? All these parades, do you want to do it?' Needless to say, the British soldiers explained that they resented having to 'posh up' when they were supposed to be on 'rest'. The Australians nodded in sympathy. 'OK, cobbers', they said, 'we'll soon alter that for you'. The next morning, as the Fusiliers' Sergeant-Major was about to take the parade, the Australians turned up with *their* band. 'They marched up and down . . . playing any old thing', remembered one Fusilier: 'There was no tune you could recognise, they were just blowing as loud as they could on their instruments. It sounded like a million cat-calls'.[16] The parade descended into farce, as the Sergeant-Major failed to make himself heard above the discordant din. Thereafter, the pride and dignity of the 10th Battalion, Royal Fusiliers, having been punctured by this raucous display of Aussie larrikinism, it was decided discreetly to abandon the ceremonial in future and post the guards in the normal way.

As elsewhere, the Australians' reputation preceeded them, and many Tommies had their own stories to tell. Later in the Ypres offensive, for example, Lieutenant 'Paddy' King of the East Lancashires was huddling with his men in a shell hole on the battlefield, waiting to be relieved at night. Eventually, he heard voices and saw three tall figures approaching, one of whom was smoking. 'Who the hell are you?', he asked in astonishment: 'And put that light out, you'll draw fire!' The smoker just stared back at him, and asked: 'Well come to that, who are you?' He explained that he was Lieutenant King of the 2/5th East Lancashire Regiment, at which point the newcomer interjected: 'Well, we're the Aussies, chum, and we've come to relieve you'. King went on to say that he had no trenches, rations or ammunition to hand over, but that he did at least have a map, asking whether the Australians needed any map references. 'Never mind that', came the reply: 'Just fuck off'. King was amazed: 'They didn't seem to be a bit bothered. The last I saw of them they were squatting down, rifles over their shoulders, and they were smoking, all three of them. Just didn't care'.[17] But there were things the Australians did care about, passionately at times. One was what they regarded as unnecessarily harsh punishments for petty misdemeanours, and they took particular exception to what was known as First Field Punishment. Every day the man under punishment would have to parade in full pack and double up and down the road, under the direction of the military police, before being tied up against a wagon wheel for an hour in the morning, and then an hour in the evening. It was an uncomfortable punishment, but also humiliating, and that is what the Australians objected to. There were occasions when Australians, outraged by the sight, simply cut a man free – and threatened to shoot the military police if they dared to strap him up again.[18]

All the while, preparations for the forthcoming offensive had been continuing. The Allied bombardment, a prelude to the assault, began on 16 July 1917 but three days later Haig received a letter from the War Cabinet to the effect that it had not yet given its final approval to the operation. The attack was scheduled to commence in a week's time, so this was devastating news. Haig had already postponed the assault by three days, to give the French – who were supporting the attack – more time to prepare, and he was concerned that there might be further unwarranted delay. 'Approval' arrived two days later but now Allied commanders were preoccupied by the mists that were drifting across the salient, obscuring their view of the proposed battlefield and hindering their preparations. Reluctantly, Haig postponed the attack for a further three days, with zero day set for 28 July. On 27 July came the infuriating news that the French were still not ready, and so there was yet further delay, with zero hour finally being fixed for 3.50 a.m. on 31 July. By now, however, the warm summer was on the wane, with a depression already swirling in from the Atlantic. Precious days of July sunshine had been lost in the various delays. August 1917 in Flanders was to be wettest in living memory.

The attack at Warneton

As planned, the British troops went over the top on the morning of 31 July 1917, initiating the Third Battle of Ypres as they attacked along the Menin Road, their objective being the high ground of Passchendaele Ridge. As part of the assault, II ANZAC launched a diversionary attack against German positions at Warneton, south of Ypres, close to Messines. Len Harvey, signaller in the 43rd Battalion, had been away from his unit when the mines had been blown. But now he was in the thick of it, as he wrote to his father in a letter a few days later. He explained that 'our battalion participated in a very hard stunt, which entailed some casualties'. Among the fallen, he reported, were mates he had joined up with in South Australia back in 1916, including 'Poor Dick Trembath', author of the recent vivid description of the battle for Hill 60. Privately, in his diary, Len Harvey also reflected on the events of that terrible first day of Third Ypres, detailing the loss of his closest friends:

> Tuesday. 12 midday. Waiting for Bn. to reach jump off trench. 3.50 a.m. Zero hour. Bn. just arrived in time. No. 6, 7 & 8 strong point captured, and men started to consolidate. Our Coy. Suffered heavy casualties.
> Len Trembath – wounded
> Pete Sampson – wounded
> Jack Pyatt – wounded
> Dick Trembath – killed
> Billy Abbott – killed
> Doug Roach – wounded
> Will Shorter – killed D[ied] of W[ounds]
> 8.30 p.m. Huns counter-attacked No.7 Post and drove our men out.
> 12.30 p.m. Our men re-counter attacked and firmly established themselves in No. 7 Pn.[19]

Two days later, Len Harvey was assigned to the battalion burial party. As he recorded in his diary: 'Thursday. 3 a.m. Left camp for trenches, with Bn pioneers to bury 43rd dead. Not a very nice job. Buried Dick Trembath in hole between No. 8 post and front line. 12 men in same hole. Dick on extreme right facing Warneton'.

Among the wounded listed by Len Harvey was Pete Sampson, who later wrote home to South Australia from hospital in Birmingham, England, attempting to convey something 'of my experiences on the morning of July 31st. At five to 4 in the morning', he explained, 'we went over the top, and I had not gone more than 100 yards when Fritz threw one of his iron foundries at me, and stopped me in the thigh'. His mate, Jack Pyatt, had been hit at the same time, 'so we made for the nearest shell-hole, where we had to remain for six hours, and, needless to say, they were the worst six hours I have spent in my life'. Eventually, the two Australians decided to crawl forward to the captured positions, 'where our boys were digging in', but the ordeal 'knocked us out'. One of the 'boys', recognizing the severity of Pete Sampson's wound, 'offered to carry me back to our old front lines . . . He pinned some white rag on his arm and away we went, and, to give Fritz his credit, he did not snipe at us'.[20] Subsequently, Sampson was taken by stretcher-bearers to a dressing station, and from there to a military hospital at Boulogne, before being sent to England.[21]

The Australian Flying Corps at Ypres

Among other Australians who saw action on the first day of Third Ypres were cadets of the Australian Flying Corps, who had completed courses in Britain and were now assigned for 'on-the-job' training to British squadrons. It was, quite literally, a baptism of fire. Owen Lewis, a 22-year-old student from Melbourne, did not have time to unpack his bags before he was in the air. Within just a few hours of arriving at his squadron, he was airborne, acting as observer to an experienced British pilot, Norman Sharples. On his first sortie, Lewis managed to break the aircraft's wireless aerial. Returning to the airfield, they had a replacement fitted, and once in the air again were promptly attacked by a German scout. Shocked by the encounter, Lewis forgot to return fire, but Sharples managed to shake off their pursuer. The following morning, Lewis and Sharples were airborne once more, when they were attacked by eight enemy scouts. After what seemed like an age, Lewis managed to bring his machine gun into action, keeping the German aircraft at bay while Sharples made good their escape. On the ground, their RE8 aircraft was found to be riddled with bullet holes – observer

The Australian Flying Corps played an increasingly important role in 'all arms' operations on the Western Front and in the Middle East, but not without incident. BE2 aircraft A1794 is photographed here 'on its nose' in Flanders.

and pilot had had a lucky escape, although Lewis had sustained a slight wound to his foot. The next day, they were again intercepted by German scouts but by now Owen Lewis was beginning to get the hang of his weapon, successfully beating off their assailants, and allowing the successful completion of their bombing mission. However, as they returned home fog descended, and Lewis became hopelessly loss until, at last, the weather cleared and he regained his bearings.[22]

Barely a week after joining the squadron, Lewis was on his sixth flight, directing artillery fire, when he and Sharples were attacked by three German scouts. This time Lewis was severely wounded, with gunshot wounds to his chest and both legs, and with most of his right foot shot away. He was evacuated to England, and survived, although he was killed later in the war. Sharples was killed just a few weeks later, when, ironically, his RE8 aircraft was hit by a British artillery shell. By the end of August 1917, all the fledgling Australian airmen who had survived their practical training (four had been killed and two shot down and taken prisoner) were sent back to Britain to complete their courses. However, No. 3 Squadron Australian Flying Corps, which had been working-up in Britain for nine months, perfecting roles such as reconnaissance, artillery observation, aerial photography and bombing,

was now ready for deployment in theatre. The unseasonably bad
weather of August 1917 delayed its departure but the squadron was in
the Ypres sector in time to begin flying on 12 September. Initially the
squadron was employed on line patrol, flying up and down the front
line to report artillery flashes and enemy movements, although by the
October the aircraft were given more ambitious roles and were frequently engaged in dog-fights with their enemy opponents. Inevitably,
there were casualties. Douglas Morrison, for example, a 22-year-old
orchardist from Victoria, developed engine trouble and fell behind his
colleagues, only to be attacked and shot down by four enemy Albatross
aircraft. British soldiers rescued him from No-Man's Land but he died
two weeks later, having lost his right leg.[23]

The road to Passchendaele

By now, the nature of Third Ypres had changed markedly, the incessant bad weather, together with the destruction of drainage waterways
by artillery bombardments, having transformed the landscape into
swamp and bogland. Men drowned in the mud, while movement of
troops, horses, guns, vehicles and all else became well-nigh impossible. Engineers found themselves powerless to deal with such extreme
conditions, and still it kept raining. A temporary lull was ordered in
the offensive but when the weather appeared to improve, operations
resumed. On 16 September 1917, as part of this renewed activity, I
ANZAC arrived in theatre, fresh from a lengthy rest, and at first light
on 20 September the Australian 1st and 2nd Divisions advanced in what
became known as the battle of Menin Road. The better weather lent
itself to 'bite-and-hold' tactics, which the Australians had increasingly
made their own, and the Anzacs took Glencorse Wood, Bosschen
Swamp, and Black Watch Corner in quick succession, together with
part of the notorious Polygon Wood. George Elms, from Moyarra, in
the South Gippsland area of Victoria, was in the terrifying and bloody
battle for Polygon Wood. But, years later, what he remembered most
vividly about the dramatic events of September 1917 was the unexpected arrival of letters and parcels at the front. In his parcel, Elms
explained, 'was a round long coffee tin. On opening it I found red gum
sawdust and was puzzled until I poured it out and inside, in perfect

AUSTRALIAN WAR MEMORIAL E00839

Medical section of the 45th Battalion AIF at Anzac Ridge, Ypres, on 28 September 1917. Left to right are: Private Isaac Steele, Private J.J. Robinson, Private G.H. Walker, and Captain Owen Dibbs, who was killed in action on 28 March 1918 at Dernancourt.

condition after 3 months travel, 2 beaut navel oranges to be admired by all the platoon'. As he explained, some 'of the men were from Mildura [in the citrus-growing area of north-western Victoria] and you can imagine the pleasure we all had eating skin and all'.[24] Such delights made life under fire at Ypres almost bearable, albeit momentarily.

After Polygon Wood, the next objective was Broodseinde Ridge. The Allies set 4 October for their assault, and planned to attack along an eight-mile front, zero hour being 6 a.m. Curiously, and unbeknown to the Allies, the Germans had selected the same date for an operation of their own, thinking this a timely moment to recapture some of the territory lost recently. At 5.30 a.m., as the troops of the 1st, 2nd and 3rd Australian Divisions, together with the New Zealand Division, massed in their trenches waiting to go over the top, the unexpected German bombardment commenced. W.J. Harvey, in the 24th Battalion, recalled that the enemy 'pounded our position with high explosives, including *minenwerfers* and eight-inch shells, and we had tremendous casualties'. The battalion had forty killed during the barrage and, taking into account the wounded, it lost a third of its strength before it even left the trenches. 'Everyone kept their nerve', Harvey continued, 'although it was a terrible strain to lie there under that sort of fire . . . It seemed an eternity before our own guns opened up and we got the order to advance'. By now it was raining heavily, driven by strong winds from the west, and poor visibility was made worse by the smoke from the competing bombardments. The Germans did not see the Anzacs coming, nor were the Australians aware of the enemy packed tightly in their trenches, bayonets fixed, waiting to attack. Enraged by the barrage they had endured, the Australians were not inclined to take prisoners, and in the ensuing slaughter many Germans thought it sensible to play dead. Foolishly, as W.J. Harvey observed, after the Australians had passed on, 'a number of these Huns rose up and started firing on us from the rear. That, naturally enough, made the boys see red. Their deaths were real enough after that'.[25]

F.C. Trotter, another Australian, also remembered the mutual surprise of the morning of 4 October. 'Our front-line barrage . . . lifted', he wrote, 'and we went forward. And what did we find? Germans massed for attack – laying out in "No Man's Land" in front of their trenches awaiting their signal to advance on us'. It was 'the great joke of that morning's attack', Trotter continued: 'Imagine their surprise . . . there was a commotion – but our lads had the upper hand'. As he explained: 'A few Germans resisted our attack, others came running excitedly towards us, their hands upraised in surrender; some of them holding out their watches and rings as barter for their lives, completely demoralized'.[26] Lieutenant Ball, another Anzac, captured a pillbox that had been a German HQ. He and his men took the occupants prisoner, and sent them back. Meanwhile, the attackers had uncovered a stash of fine wines and cigars in the pillbox, and were busy making themselves at home. They also found some German carrier pigeons. They sent a few to German Divisional Headquarters with appropriate messages – 'Hock the Kaiser – I don't think', and so on – and the rest they plucked and cooked.[27] W.J. Harvey savoured the capture of Broodseinde Ridge, and enjoyed the moment of victory. 'From the Broodseinde Ridge', he said, 'we gazed back over the country [and] we could see quite plainly the movements of our own units on various duties – guns, transport, men, the lot. The ridge was a prize worth having'. Harvey also observed 'Hundreds of German prisoners . . . struggling back through our lines

... now we felt really quite sorry for them, they were in such abject misery'.[28]

To the left of the Australians, the New Zealanders had got a foothold on Passchendaele Ridge, an even greater prize, and the inclination was to press on with the assault, to press home the advantage. But now the weather had assumed storm force proportions, and the fortnight of relatively benign light showers gave way to gales, driving rain like stair-rods. Generals Plumer and Gough, pondering long and hard, decided reluctantly that it was time to call a halt. But Haig, thinking that he had the Germans on the run, and that enemy morale had collapsed, was keen to continue, to complete the capture of Passchendaele. Accordingly, on 12 October 1917 the Australians and New Zealanders tried to take the ridge and the village behind it. But they were defeated by exhaustion, mud and the rain, and the prize remained elusive. Determined that he would conquer Passchendaele, Haig now brought in the Canadians, fresh troops who would be able to topple the enemy. The first of the Canadians went into the line on 18 October, and early in the morning of 26 October they attacked. Despite the appalling weather, they performed well, but not quite well enough. The next attack was scheduled for the morning of 30 October, with the Canadians assaulting Passchendaele directly, the Australians on their right and the British Royal Naval Division on their left. And at last Passchendaele was taken. The Third Battle of Ypres was officially halted on 30 November, as winter drew in. Taking the Channel ports remained a dream but Haig was well satisfied with the performance of the British Empire forces during 1917. They had remained on the offensive, bearing the brunt of the fighting on the Western Front, as the French army had wavered and the Russians had collapsed in the east.

Monash and the Australian Corps

There were those in the British High Command, alarmed by the mutiny in the French army and the revolutionary upheaval in the Russian, who worried that the notorious indiscipline of the Australians might be dangerously subversive. Haig was not among them. He informed a sceptical Duke of Connaught that the Anzacs were among the best-disciplined of the forces under his command. The Duke expressed surprise, for he 'had heard that discipline among the Australians was bad'. Haig put him right, quipping that it 'depends on what you mean by discipline'. As Haig explained, he had never called upon the Australians 'to undertake a difficult and hazardous operation – and I have often done so – without the operation in question being carried through with success, and always with good spirit and keen determination'. Moreover, he added, from 'the top down to the most junior commanders, details have been most carefully worked out, and the plan is executed with coolness and courage. And that is what *I* call discipline'.[29] Monash put it slightly differently: 'the Australian Army is proof that individualism is the best and not the worst foundation upon which to build collective discipline'.[30]

As Third Ypres drew to its close, Haig agreed that the several Australian divisions should be grouped together as a unified Australian Corps, with Birdwood as its commander, creating a corporate identity for what was now effectively the 'Australian Army'. The new Corps came into being officially on 1 November 1917. Six months later, Birdwood was promoted to take over the British Fifth Army from General Gough. 'Billy' Hughes, the Australian Prime Minister, had insisted upon the appointment of Australian officers to commands in the Australian Corps, and this meant a choice between Monash and Birdwood's erstwhile chief of staff, Brudenell White. Charles Bean, the journalist, shamelessly lobbied for White, while his opposite number Keith Murdoch championed Monash. Haig plumped for Monash. Although Monash had already distinguished himself as a master of the modern battlefield, his appointment was in some respects controversial. He had been born in Melbourne of Jewish-German background. Inevitably, this aroused all sorts of suspicions and an array of unpleasant prejudices. Moreover, he was not a 'regular' army officer. Before the war, he had been a part-time militia 'reservist', a citizen-soldier whose peacetime civilian employment was as an engineer. This too was a source of disquiet for some observers, those who thought that senior positions should not go to 'amateurs', however gifted. Nonetheless, Monash's appointment proved popular with his peers and subordinates, and although the Australians were sorry to see Birdwood go, they welcomed Monash as one of their own. In no time, Monash was to prove himself one the most able Allied commanders – perhaps *the* most able, according to some observers – and in Australia he acquired a popular reputation as 'the outsider who won a war'.[31] He never held independent command and

AUSTRALIAN WAR MEMORIAL E03186

Lieutenant-General Sir John Monash KCB VD (seated), Australian Corps Commander, with his staff at the Australian Corps Headquarters in France, 20 July 1918. Having played a significant part in the defeat of the German 'spring offensive', Monash and the Australians went on to make a major contribution to the final Allied victory in 1918.

so, as Peter Pedersen has commented, it is difficult to compare him with other great military leaders such as Marlborough or Wellington.[32] But it was fortunate indeed that he emerged to lead the new-found Australian Army Corps at the very moment it was poised to play a disproportionately important role in the final Allied victory of 1918.

Germany's 'spring offensive'

By the time of Monash's appointment the anatomy of the Western Front had changed considerably. Haig's hope of resuming offensive operations in early 1918 had been frustrated by the politicians in Britain, and instead the British Empire's forces found themselves on the defensive. In March 1918, in what turned out to be a 'do or die' final roll of the dice, the German Army 'summoned up the last of its strength', as Lyn Macdonald has described it, and unleashed its dramatic 'spring offensive'.[33] Code-named Michael, the initial assault began at 4.40 a.m. on 21 March 1918, the Germans attacking on a fifty-mile front running south from Arras. Some Australians, at least, had seen it coming. Len Harvey, signaller in the 43rd Battalion, wrote to his father on 18 February, musing that 'spring will be on us shortly, then I think we will see some big battles'. As he explained, the 'papers say the Hun is going to make a big effort this year. He has more guns and men from the Eastern front'.[34] Indeed, as Harvey suggested, the Germans were keen to take advantage of their new-found superiority in men and material, now that Russia was out of the war, before the Americans arrived in numbers large enough to tip the advantage back in the Allies' favour. They struck with tremendous force, and within two days a breach in the British line some forty miles wide had been opened. The strategic railhead of Amiens was threatened, and with it the road to Paris. A defensive perimeter was thrown up to protect the town, and on 25 March the Australian 3rd and 4th Divisions, along with the New Zealanders, were sent in to stem the tide, helping to plug the gap in the British lines and to halt the march on Amiens.

Harold Williams was not surprised that the British Fifth Army had been all but overwhelmed. It was, he said, 'surely the evil fruits of the prolonged Passchendaele fighting during the latter months of 1917', when units had been severely depleted, 'to be replaced by drafts in many cases composed of mere youths. Besides', he added, 'there were not enough of them to resist such a blow as the enemy delivered'. There were rumours that Lloyd George had denied Haig the additional troops he so badly needed, and Williams felt that the British Army had suffered 'a crushing defeat' for want of reinforcements. Now a lieutenant, he and the men of the 5th Division were rushed south by train to Doullens, where the Australians were being gathered to plug the gap. He was moved by 'surely the saddest procession in the civilized world', as he passed long lines of old men, women and children fleeing with what possessions they could take in carts and wheelbarrows. In among the stream of civilian refugees were stragglers from British units, many without weapons or equipment, also fleeing ahead of the German advance. 'We Australians alone seemed to be marching towards the enemy', said Williams. As he tramped ahead of his platoon, head down against the driving rain, he felt 'vastly proud of being an Australian soldier'. In contrast to the fugitives who slunk by, scurrying in the opposite direction, his men whistled, laughed and joked as they went cheerfully to meet the enemy. At one point, he wrote, they encountered some 'middle-aged Tommies from a Labour battalion', who cadged ciga- rettes and warned that the Germans were coming in such numbers that they could not be stopped. The Australians appeared to relish the chal- lenge, reckoning that large numbers of enemy would mean substantial prisoners, and thus satisfying quantities of 'souvenirs'.[35]

Corporal Wally Campbell, from Argyle, New South Wales, recorded similar experiences. Marching from Doullens towards the advancing Germans, he too encountered 'civilians and Tommy soldiers all fleeing for their lives from the enemy'. There were deserted houses, left just as they were when first abandoned, washing still on the line and food uneaten on the table. 'Poor people!', exclaimed Campbell: 'It was piti- able to see the poor old women and little children trudging along the roads, carrying their few valuables with them'.[36] However, the arrival of the Australians appeared to cheer them up, he added, for the civil- ians knew that the enemy would soon meet troops that would stand their ground. Indeed, in fierce fighting around Villers-Bretonneux, the Australians manage to hold the Germans. Len Harvey noted in his diary entries for 27 and 28 March 1918 that he and the 43rd Battalion had been moved in directly to oppose the enemy advance: 'Wednesday & Thursday. Arrived at DOLLENS [sic] 3am. and taken in motor buses to FRESCHVILLIERS [sic; Franvillers]. Left packs at BONNAY and marched to position on ridge halfway between AMIENS and ALBERT'. Observing the enemy, Harvey noted that the Germans were occupying a ridge about a thousand yards in front of the Australians, and appeared to be digging in. On Saturday afternoon, 30 March, the Germans renewed their assault. 'Hun attacked at 1.30 pm.', Harvey wrote in his diary, the first wave advancing to within 300 yards of the Australian lines before being repulsed. The next day a shell landed on Harvey's dugout. 'Killed 4 and wounded several', he recorded: 'Very narrow escapes'. Suffering now from trench foot, Harvey was sent back for treatment, where he had time to take stock of recent events and to pen a letter home to his father on 9 April. 'Old Fritz has given us a big blow on the Western front', he admitted. But he sensed that the attack was already running out of steam, adding confidently 'that our time will come'.[37]

Field Marshall Haig, usually the supreme optimist, was less sure. In a message to be read to all British Empire forces in France on 11 April 1918, Haig acknowledged that the enemy had not yet made significant progress towards its principal goals – to take those Channel ports still in Allied hands, to drive a wedge between the British and the French, and ultimately to destroy the British Army. But he knew that the situation remained serious and exhorted every man to remain firm. Every position had to be held to the last man, he insisted: 'With our backs to the wall, and believing in the justice of our cause, each one of us must fight on to the end'. In fact, two days earlier the Germans had struck between Armentières and Messines, routing a Portuguese Corps that was supposed to hold the line at all costs, and had then advanced towards Hazebrouck, just twenty miles from the Channel, another vital railhead. Australians from the 1st Division were rushed north to plug this new gap. The remainder of the Australian divisions stayed outside Amiens, guarding the approach to the town, where on 22 April they observed the demise of Baron Manfred von Richtofen, the German 'Red Baron' air ace. Quite who shot him down has remained a mystery and a source of controversy ever since. The 'kill' was officially attributed to a Canadian pilot, Captain Brown, but eyewitnesses considered that Australians shooting from the ground may have fired the fatal shot. Charles Bean thought that Sergeant Popkin, from Queensland, was responsible; Monash reckoned it was a couple of cooks attached to an artillery battery. At any rate, it was the Australians who recovered Richtofen's body from the wreckage of his aircraft, and they afforded him a burial with full military honours.[38]

Villers-Bretonneux

Two days after the 'Red Baron's' death, the Australians at Villers-Bretonnuex were relieved by two British divisions. The Germans attacked shortly afterwards, for the first time in the war deploying tanks, and swiftly captured Villers-Bretonneux from the Tommies, opening the way once more to Amiens. Again, the Australians were sent to retrieve the situation. As Harold Williams explained: 'That night, 24–25 April, Villers-Bretonneux was recaptured with the bayonet in a brilliant night attack by the 13th and 14th Australian Brigades operating on either side of the town'. Planned as a surprise, the operation was launched without a preceding barrage, and among those caught unawares was a large party of Germans erecting wire entanglements. 'Upon these unsuspecting toilers of the night the Australians fell with a deadly rush', according to Williams, and 'the Germans were bayoneted left and right'. Onwards swept the Australians, as they 'wielded the weapon [the bayonet] with awful effect. Strong point after strong point was swamped in that rush', he said, 'and isolated German garrisons were annihilated in succession'.[39] Sergeant Walter Downing, from Victoria, recalled the 'wild cry' of the Australians as they attacked. 'Cheering, our men rushed straight to the muzzles of machine-guns', he exclaimed: 'There was no quarter on either side. Germans continued to fire their machine-guns, although transfixed by bayonets . . . they had no chance in the onslaught of maddened men [who] . . . killed and killed. Bayonets passed with ease through grey-clad bodies'.[40]

Soon after the battle, with its details still fresh in mind, Edgar Rule penned a letter to his aunt in Cornwall. 'Dear Aunt', he wrote, 'we went into the line in a very important part, Villers-Bretonnuex [sic]. It is the key position in front of Amiens, and I've seen things that astonished me as much as any in my experience of the war'. He explained how the town 'was taken by the Hun in the last spasm of his great push', and how it had been recaptured so dramatically by the Australians: 'the operation was one of the gems of our record'. Rule reckoned that the Germans had had their fill of looted liquor before the battle, and 'were a muddled lot' when the Australians struck. The Australians, for their part, were keen to celebrate their victory, and likewise located ample quantities of beer and wine. Additional amusement was provided by the discovery in abandoned houses of 'Beautiful underwear belonging to the women', and Rule described how the Australians – dirty and lousy as they were – were delighted by the cleanliness, freshness and femininity of the lingerie. Before long, some had 'changed their old dirty stuff for beautiful chemises with pretty pink ribbons; some had even changed their underpants for garments never made for men'. One wore 'a big silk bell-topper' and 'Ladies' nighties were quite the fashion,

AUSTRALIAN WAR MEMORIAL E02295

Members of the 28th Battalion AIF in the front line at Dernancourt on 27 April, near Albert in north-eastern France, where the Australians halted the German 'spring offensive'. Supremely confident, the Germans had marched to the battlefield with their brass band playing, only for it to be scattered by Australian rifle and machine-gun fire. When the victorious Australians were relieved, they tramped out to the exuberant strains of 'Colonel Bogey', the morale-boosting march that was a firm favourite among the British Empire's soldiery.

and one of the boys lined up next morning for his breakfast arrayed in a beauty'.[41] It was all great fun, of course, yet another outrageous display of Australian larrikinism. But, although the men would never admit it, their behaviour also revealed a deeper yearning for softness and comfort, and for female intimacy, after all the filth, slaughter and unrelieved masculinity of the battlefield.

Villers-Bretonneux was yet another turning-point in the war, and, as Birdwood remarked, the Germans never advanced a foot thereafter. But they were not finished yet, and Len Harvey wrote home on 16 May 1918, warning that the current run of fine weather was 'just right for old Fritz to push on with his offensive'. It was a prescient observation, for on the night of 25–26 May Harvey's unit, in the line near Villers-Bretonneux, was subjected to fifteen hours of continuous shelling. Along with several of his pals, Len Harvey was 'slightly gassed', bad enough for him to be evacuated to England for treatment and recuperation.[42] He was out of the war for the moment. When he returned, a few months later, the situation on the Western Front had changed dramatically. The German offensive had indeed run out of steam, just as he had predicted in early April, and the enemy now had precious little to give, its energy spent. The war was now turning decisively in the Allies' favour, just as Haig had always expected – and prayed – it would.

Hamel and 'peaceful penetration'

By the end of May 1918, John Monash had assumed command of the entire Australian Corps, completing the 'Australianization' of the AIF on the Western Front. His first operation was the capture of the Hamel spur on 4 July 1918, a brilliantly planned and skilfully executed 'all arms' offensive in which the close co-ordination of infantry, artillery, tanks and aircraft proved decisive in overwhelming the enemy. The date chosen for the attack was in deference to the Americans, four companies of whom were taking part in the assault. The arrival of the Americans cheered the Australians, as Lieutenant Edgar Rule observed. 'On the afternoon of 2 July a bunch of Yanks came up to be distributed among us for this fight', he wrote: 'This was the first time they had been in the line, and they were dead eager; and apart from that it bucked our lads up wonderfully'. As Rule explained, all 'the novelty of the war had long since vanished for our boys . . . but on this occasion everyone was smiling or laughing. They were on their mettle, and were determined to let the Yanks see what the Aussies were capable of'. It was 'good to see the way they palled up', he continued, delighted that the Australians and the Americans got along so well. The Americans were keen to learn, and the Australians, with all their experience, were accomplished teachers. 'These Yanks view things just the same as we do', thought Rule, although, when their unusual names were read out at roll-call, he could hardly keep from laughing, the Americans being *such a mixture – one could see among them all the nations under the sun*'.[43]

After their experience at Bullecourt, the Australians had remained sceptical of tanks. But Hamel reversed their opinion, the new Mark Vs demonstrating a speed and versatility that had not been witnessed before, their tactical integration into the attack proving a tremendous asset, as time and again they were called on to remove a troublesome strong point or machine-gun nest. Likewise, aircraft operated in close support of the infantry, an important new role being the delivery of ammunition to forward positions, where the planes would fly low over the battlefield, dropping the supplies by parachute. Monash, the grand architect of the assault, was delighted. His 'all arms' strategy had worked perfectly, with the attack developing exactly to timetable and achieving all its objectives. The enemy had been caught completely by surprise. The Germans had lost 1,500 killed or wounded, together with a similar number of prisoners, plus large quantities of weapons. The Allies had suffered no more than 800 casualties, many of them only lightly wounded, and the soldiers had a great time 'ratting' and 'souveniring' among the prisoners, acquiring new wristwatches, expensive cigars, and other prized items.

Alongside his commitment to 'all arms' action, Monash encouraged the stealth tactics of 'aggressive patrolling' and 'peaceful penetration', activities at which the Australians had become adept. 'Peaceful penetration' was an ironic play on words, borrowed from the phrase used by the Germans before the war to describe their penetration of the Australian economy, especially the copper and other base metal industries. It involved aggressive patrolling, usually at night and in small groups, killing the unwary or taking them back as prisoners for interrogation. Enemy defences would be probed, with weak points identified and segments of territory captured. The bayonet was often the preferred weapon in such encounters, and the Australians had perfected its tactical use in the so-called 'throat jab', where the bayonet was thrust upwards under an enemy's chin and directly into his spinal cord, killing him (it was said) instantly, painlessly and silently.[44] The portable and highly versatile Lewis light machine gun was another favourite weapon, ideal for outflanking enemy positions – especially machine-gun posts. It proved extremely effective in the hands of innovative and intelligent handlers. After Hamel, 'peaceful penetration' was important in maintaining the offensive upper-hand, keeping the enemy on his back foot, its impact as much psychological as practical. It was a means of telling the Germans that they had lost control of the battlefield, that they were losing the war.

On 8 August 1918: the 'black day' of the German Army

Hamel had been evidence that the tide was turning, and it helped pave the way for the great Allied counter-offensive, which commenced on 8 August 1918 at Amiens and culminated in Germany's surrender and the Armistice a little over three months later, on 11 November. The Australians, under Monash, played a significant role in this final push to victory. The attack of 8 August was planned as a joint operation between the Australians and the Canadians, with some support from the British. Monash envisaged a 'leap-frogging' assault, where waves of troops would continually press ahead, 'leap-frogging' each other as they overran the enemy's defensive positions. In this way, Monash expected to advance over five miles on the first day of the attack. Although everything did not go entirely to plan this time, it was another stunning performance, the Australians taking some 8,000 prisoners in the first nine hours of the operation, for the loss of 2,450 killed or wounded. Harold Williams bore witness to the efficacy of Monash's planning. In the bright morning sunshine, after the attack had commenced, he was surprised to see a road traversing the battlefield crammed with vehicles and transport of all kinds. It was a scene, he said, that 'made us rub eyes that surely deceived us'. There were 'motor lorries, loaded with ammunition, stores, and tools, horse-drawn limbers, cookers, water-carts, dispatch-riders on motor bicycles, heavy guns, here and there an armoured car; mounted men regulated the traffic; and only a mile or so forward could still be heard the spasmodic rattle of machine-guns'.

As Williams observed, this was tangible evidence of the success of Monash's 'leap-frogging' plan. By pressing home the attack to capture not only the enemy's trenches but also his artillery, the way had been cleared to bring up safely all the supplies and equipment he had seen on the road. Williams also noted the prominent role played by aircraft. 'The sky swarmed with low-flying planes', he said: 'Some of these as they passed overhead sounded klaxons and pilots waved to us . . . [they] harried the retreat of the German troops by machine-gunning them, along with their transport, and one plane dropped a bomb on a railway line and prevented the withdrawal of a large railway gun'.[45]

For Ludendorff, German commander and architect of the 'spring offensive', 8 August 1918 was the 'black day' of the German army, the moment he realized that the war was lost. Four days later, John Monash was knighted by a grateful George V, during a visit to the Western Front and a review of the Australian Army Corps. It was an auspicious moment for the Australians, and recognition of their sustained and often distinctive contribution to the Allied war effort. But if the reputation of the Australians appeared now to rest solely on their exploits on the Western Front, it ought not to obscure their contribution towards final victory in that other theatre of war, the Middle East.

Meanwhile, in the Middle East

After Gallipoli, as we have seen, Egypt continued as an important training area for Australian troops, some of whom assisted in the defence of the Suez Canal. Moreover, the famed Australian Light Horse had remained in the Middle East for the duration of the war. In 1916 it had participated in the ejection of the Turks from Sinai, and during November and December of 1917, under General Edmund Allenby, assisted in the capture of Gaza and Jerusalem. The following year the Australian Light Horse was active in the occupation of Lebanon and Syria, forcing Turkey to sue for peace on 30 October 1918, another important contribution to the Allied victory. The total number of Australian deaths in these operations was 1,394, a tiny fraction of the accumulated losses on the Western Front, but the actions themselves were often epic – from the charge of the Light Horse at Beersheba in October 1917 to the triumphal 'Great Ride' into Damascus in September 1918.

An early morning capture by Australian light horsemen of wandering enemy patrols near Beersheba. This is evidently a headquarters group, as the Colonel's pennant has been stuck into the sand.

Grant Ritchie from Moyarra, in Victoria, found himself in Palestine as part of the 1st Machine Gun Squadron, attached to the Australian Light Horse. '"Jacko" [the Turk] does not like mounted men', Ritchie explained in a letter home to his mother, as he described the capture of Jericho in February 1918. 'One of our regiments went right into Jericho', he said, 'but Jacko had burnt most of his stores there, also pillaged most of the houses, and outraged [raped] the women'. It was no wonder that the 'inhabitants gave our chaps a great reception when they arrived. Our mounted men were the first to get there, and when they saw them coming the bells started ringing'. But for all his pride in being part of the Australian advance, Ritchie was especially keen to report on the various places with historical and biblical associations that he had visited. Like the Australians in Egypt earlier in the war, who had been fascinated by pyramids and pharaohs and museums and mosques, Grant Richie found himself deeply engaged in military tourism in the Holy Land, gazing in admiration at the places he had heard about as a child in Sunday

School. Near Bethlehem, his unit camped close to Solomon's Pools, and 'a short distance is the spot where Samson slew the thousand Philistines with the jaw-bone of an ass'. In Bethlehem he visited Rachael's tomb, and then the Garden of Gethsemane and St [Mary] Magdalene's church. His unit proceeded up the road to Jericho, 'along which Christ rode on Palm Sunday'. Granted leave in Bethlehem, Ritchie 'went straight up to see the Church of the Nativity. This we entered by the "needle's eye", and saw the Greek, Armenian and Catholic portions: we saw where the manger was and where the wise men sat'.[46] He continued:

> We also saw the room in which St Jerome translated the Bible and the place where the angel appeared to Joseph and Mary, telling them to flee to Egypt, and the place where Herod killed the children and where they were buried . . . On our way back to Solomon's pools we stayed at Bethany, where the house of Martha and Mary used to be, and where Lazarus was raised from the dead.[47]

Although Grant Ritchie did not say so, implicit in his report from the Holy Land was the sense that the Australian Light Horsemen were latter-day crusaders, part of their mission the liberation of Palestine at last from Ottoman-Muslim rule. They might not have taken Constantinople earlier in the war, but the capture of Bethlehem, Nazareth, Jerusalem and the other holy places more than made up for it.

From Gaza to Damascus

Operating alongside the Light Horsemen were pilots and observers of the Australian Flying Corps. As on the Western Front, they contributed an increasingly important dimension to operations. During the Second Battle of Gaza, for example, aircraft demonstrated their versatility when, on 20 April 1917, Richard Williams (later to rise to command the Royal Australian Air Force) led five planes in an attack on Hareira. Intelligence reports suggested that Turkish cavalry was massing near Beersheba to counter-attack. The Australian flight commanders predicted that the Turks would need to water their horses before mounting an assault, and the most likely spot was Hareira. The hunch proved correct, when Richards and his team spotted a large number of men

Air Marshal Sir Richard Williams, as he would later become, during his time as commander of 1 Squadron Australian Flying Corps, shortly before promotion to temporary lieutenant-colonel in Palestine in June 1918. His daring feats of airmanship won him renown throughout the Middle East theatre and beyond.

and horses lined up waiting their turn alongside a dam. They attacked immediately, Williams letting all four of his bombs go at once. As he wrote: 'it was extraordinary that day to watch one's bombs going down and find, when it was approaching the ground, horses and men from some direction or another going for their lives in the direction of where the bomb was falling as though they were in a hurry to catch it'. The raid was a startling success – next day Light Horsemen reported collecting dozens of riderless horses – and the Turks cancelled their counter-attack. The Australians had suffered one casualty, 21-year-old Norm Steele, a warehouseman from Melbourne, who was shot down by anti-aircraft fire. His body was buried by passing Bedouin, and his grave was never rediscovered.[48]

The following morning Richard Williams and Adrian Cole, another Australian pilot, undertook a reconnaissance mission to photograph the damage inflicted at Hareira. Anti-aircraft fire again took its toll, when Cole's plane was hit. His engine out of action, Cole managed to glide his aircraft downwards, landing in a field near the Turkish positions. In a daring feat of airmanship, Williams landed right behind

Cole, instructing him to burn the abandoned aircraft before scrambling aboard alongside his observer. Williams took off again, under the noses of the astonished Turks, and made it home safely. For this, and for leading the previous day's raid, he was awarded the Distinguished Service Order.[49] Australian airmen continued to play an auspicious role, until the end of hostile operations in the Middle East. On 29 September, for example, as Allenby's cavalry arrived at the gates of Damascus, aircraft helped to locate and destroy Turkish rearguards holding up the advance. As Francis Conrick, one of the pilots, related: 'at the south west entrance to Damascus we saw a small machine gun defence post which was holding up the light horse advance. We machine-gunned the area wiping out the defence post and then patrolled along the south of the town, machine-gunning enemy positions'.[50] Conrick was a hardened and no-nonsense professional, who knew that he had a job to do, and that he would do it to the best of his ability until the war was won. As he recorded in his diary: 'Our next job was to machine-gun Turks fleeing along the Beirut road north-west of Damascus . . . When we caught up with them, they sat on the road with their heads bowed, thinking perhaps that we would let them be'.[51] Conrick made them think again:

> they soon got a move on when our bullets started smashing into them. I know that some of our blokes had had enough of slaughter, but for me the war wasn't finished as I knew that, until they surrendered, one Turk left alive could mean another Australian Light Horse casualty. Since I had landed at Gallipoli, I had seen enough casualties to last a lifetime, but to me they weren't beaten soldiers down there, they were enemy who had to be destroyed before we could go home and get on with our lives'.[52]

Mont St Quentin and victory

Meanwhile, back on the Western Front, the war was also being pursued relentlessly, to its final bitter end. Monash, like Haig, now believed it possible to deal the Germans a mortal blow before the end of 1918, and was eager to press on. But if the trenches of the Hindenburg line were to be taken, the Allies had first to secure Mont St Quentin, a hill about a mile to the north of Peronne. The battle plans that emerged

built upon the successful features of 8 August, and the first stage was
a drive to push the Germans back over the River Somme and into
the broken landscape of the old 1916 battle. This time, in contrast to
the orderly and well-managed strategic withdrawal of early 1917, the
German retreat was chaotic, and the Australian pursuit hot. But as
they approached the Somme, the Australians found that the enemy
had destroyed all the crossing points. The capture of Mont St Quentin,
before it could be fortified by the Germans, was now an absolute pri-
ority. Monash gambled that he could do it with just three battalions,
attacking at 5.00 a.m. on 31 August 1918. For a moment it looked as if
the operation had been successful, but the Australians were forced back
to positions on the west side of the hill. Monash called up his reserves,
and somehow units contrived ways to cross the Somme, scrambling
over wooden planks connecting the piers of broken bridges. But it was
not until nightfall on 3 September 1918 that Mont St Quentin and the
surrounding country was firmly in Australian hands.

Harold Williams had observed the capture of Mont St Quentin itself
on the afternoon of 1 September. 'About 1p.m.', he wrote, 'we watched
a barrage from our guns go down on the crest of Mont St Quentin, and
under cover of this the 6th Brigade stormed the summit and drove the
Germans from their position – thus crowning with success the bitter
fighting that the 5th and 6th Brigades of the 2nd Australian Division had
endured for some days'. As ever, the victors went to lift booty from the
prisoners and the dead, returning with brandy, cigars, bread and syn-
thetic jam. The black bread was disgusting but, still, the men feasted as
they sheltered from the continuous German shelling. On 2 September,
Williams' unit was detailed to attack and hold ground to the north of
Peronne. As they advanced they were met by intense enemy artillery
and machine-gun fire, suffering many casualties. Among those hit was
Harold Williams. 'I felt a painful jar in my left hand and a stinging pain
in the upper part of my left thigh', he recalled. Looking down, he saw
that he had been struck at the base of two fingers, and that the leg of
his trousers was now soaked in blood. He turned to find his way back
to safety, steeling himself to pass through the curtain of shells that was
now falling. 'At every step the blood squelched out of my boot', he said,
'the leg of my breeches and puttee was wet and scarlet'.[53] Arriving at
battalion headquarters, his thigh and fingers were dressed and he was
given a drink of rum. From there Williams made his way to the Aid

Post, thankful that he was 'walking wounded' and that his was a 'nice blighty', a wound that would not permanently maim or disfigure but was sufficiently serious to warrant a spell in hospital in England. But, of course, it also meant the end of the war for him, and, for better or worse, that he would not participate in the Australians' last great push.

Fighting continued during September 1918, and the next big task was an assault on the Hindenburg line. Two American divisions swelled the ranks of the Australian Corps, significantly enlarging Monash's command and enhancing its capability. The attack commenced at 5.50 a.m. on 29 September. At first things were touch and go, with the still inexperienced Americans faltering as they tried to support the Australian advance. But the Australians retrieved the situation, and by 30 September Len Harvey, in the 43rd Battalion, could note confidently in his diary that: '11th Bde mopping up Hindenburg line at BONY and QUENNEMONT'. He also wrote to his father in South Australia, describing the operation. 'Was unable to write last Sunday (29)', he apologized, 'owing to being in the attack on the Hindenburg line'. As he explained: 'The Americans were over first, and it was all planned for the Australians to leapfrog the Yanks later in the day'. It did not quite go to plan but, generously, Harvey reported that: 'In nearly all cases the Yanks reached their objectives and our fellows went through them and did good work'. Nonetheless, owing 'to unforeseen difficulties the Yanks in front of us were held up, and when our fellows arrived they had to set to work and help them. There was a lot of heavy fighting', he said, 'but in the end our fellows got the Hun out of his first line defences'. When it was all over, Len Harvey surveyed the formidable fortifications of the Hindenburg line. He was astonished. 'When one stands in the vicinity of the Hindenburg line', he wrote in disbelief, 'and sees the rows of barbed wire, yards in depth and four and five feet in height, he wonders how anything human managed to get through'.[54]

There were further engagements, notably that on 4 October 1918, when the Australian 2nd Division was in action near Beaurevoir, and when Lieutenant Joseph Maxwell was awarded the Victoria Cross, the last won by an Australian in the war, adding it to his earlier Military Cross and Distinguished Conduct Medal. With covering fire from an Australian appropriately named Bonzer (who was subsequently awarded the Distinguished Conduct Medal), Maxwell had rushed an enemy machine-gun post, 'firing my revolver at each bound', as he put

Members of the 24th Battalion AIF in a forward trench, at about 1.20 p.m. on 1 September 1918, waiting for the artillery barrage to lift before renewing the attack on Mont St Quentin, which led to its capture.

it. By the time he landed among the Germans his weapon was empty. So when 'the Germans before us shouted "Kamerad", I was the most pleased and relieved man in France'.[55] The next day the 2nd Division took the village of Montbrehain, securing it against counter-attack until the Americans relieved them that night. It was the Australians' last battle of the war.

Thereafter the final collapse came quickly. The Austrians and Turks had sued for peace during October. The German High Seas Fleet had mutinied, and the Kaiser abdicated on 9 November. Germany was falling apart. At 11 a.m. on 11 November 1918 the Armistice was signed, signifying Germany's defeat and the end of the fighting. Len Harvey, writing a few days earlier, had forecast 'that 1919 will not see any hostilities'. On 13 November, he wrote to his parents. Now that the war was over, he said, there was a great sense of anticlimax among the troops, and everything seemed very low-key. 'I think you learnt the good tidings as soon as we did', he said: 'Nothing was announced officially to the men. The French people had their flags out a day and a half before we received the papers with the news of the armistice'. He wondered why there had yet to be a formal announcement. 'Probably', he mused, 'the "heads" thought the troops would get too excited'.[56]

Chapter Nine

A Peace of Sorts

THE SOLDIERS AT the front may have been among the last to hear about the Armistice. At home in Australia, however, the news had been eagerly awaited for several days, and it was common knowledge that the end was now in sight. A rumour swept Sydney on Friday 8 November that an Armistice had already been signed, and premature celebrations erupted in the city's streets. The Kaiser was burned in effigy and schoolchildren were given the afternoon off. It was a false alarm. But the next day, Saturday, another 'furphy' announced that the Armistice had now been agreed. Again, crowds in Sydney took to the streets, and the joyful outpourings of relief continued until news came through officially, at about 7 p.m. on Monday 11 November, that an Armistice had indeed been signed and that, in effect, Germany had surrendered. Thereafter, the victory celebrations continued more or less unabated until the following Thursday. There was constant cheering in the streets, and patriotic songs and hymns were sung: sometimes spontaneously, at other times in hastily organized services of thanksgiving, such as that at Sydney's Long Bay gaol where the inmates thronged the prison chapel.[1]

Across Australia, the pattern was repeated. At Yass, in New South Wales, people were on the streets as soon as the news was made public, and small boys intent on making as much noise as possible went about the town beating tin cans, ringing bells and blowing whistles. At Ballarat in Victoria blasts from mine hooters and railway locomotives added to the cacophony of sound. At Wallaroo in South Australia, anxious crowds had gathered outside the town's Institute, waiting for an announcement, and at nine-thirty on the evening of 11 November news came through at last that the war was over. Immediately, steam whistles were sounded at the Wallaroo smelting works, and at the nearby Wallaroo and Moonta mines, and bells were rung across the district. Youngsters appeared on the streets of the three Yorke Peninsula mining towns, Moonta, Wallaroo and Kadina, beating empty kerosene drums and riding their bicycles up and down, trailing strings of tin cans behind them. On Tuesday all businesses were closed in the district, and at Moonta community singing was led by the Moonta Mines Male Voice Choir, where a grateful people sang 'Nearer, my God, to thee'.[2] In the afternoon, the combined brass bands of the district led a parade through the town.

Unfinished business

For the moment, the divisions that had bedevilled Australian society in the latter years of the war appeared to be put to one side, in an outburst of goodwill and common desire to rejoice together. But for some, of course, it was not over yet. As well as the thousands of Australian troops overseas pending repatriation, there were those in prisoner-of-war camps awaiting release, while some Anzacs were now fighting in Russia. During 1918, a number of Australians had been sent to join the Allied anti-Bolshevik forces, and others were part of a spirited rearguard action when fresh units were despatched to assist in the Allied evacuation from Russia in 1919. Two Australians, Corporal Arthur Sullivan and Sergeant Samuel Pearse, won the Victoria Cross, the latter posthumously. Likewise, the repatriation of the Australian Light Horse was held up when it was called upon to help put down an anti-British rising in Egypt in early 1919. Besides, even as Australia celebrated the Armistice, news was still coming through of those who had been killed in the final days of the war, or had recently died of wounds or illness. As the People's Weekly observed, 'notification of a death of a soldier at the front is sad news at any time, but coming during the closing scenes of the war seems to increase the feeling of sadness'.[3] For the Symons family in South Australia, their victory celebration was cut short abruptly when, on Wednesday 13 November, the devastating

news came through that their son Parker, serving in 'the flying squadron', had been reported missing in action.[4] For many others, of course,
there was the certain knowledge that their loved ones would never be
returning home. For those who grieved, the Armistice celebrations and
the subsequent repatriation of Australian troops were deeply distressing
reminders of their loss. As one *In Memoriam* notice expressed it:

> When we see the boys returning,
> Our hearts they throb with pain
> To think that you're not there, dear Albert,
> And will never come back again.
>
> Could we have raised your dying head,
> Or heard your last farewell,
> The blow would not have been so hard
> For us, who loved you well.[5]

During the war years, some 416,809 men had joined the Australian
armed forces, an extraordinary achievement for a population of around
four million, especially given the consistent rejection of conscription
and the upholding of the voluntary principle. In the end, more than half
of all eligible males had enlisted, and many other volunteers had been
turned away as unfit for military service. Altogether, 59,342 – nearly
twenty per cent of those who had joined up – were killed, the majority on the Western Front, and a further 152,171, almost forty-five per
cent, were wounded.[6] Put another way, only one in three Australians
who ventured overseas returned unharmed, although this is perhaps a
conservative figure, as minor wounds sometimes went unrecorded, while
countless more suffered permanent psychological damage.[7] The repatriation of Australian servicemen was a colossal task, and was dependent
upon the availability of sufficient shipping. General Birdwood recognized that many would grow restless as they awaited their turn to go
home, and shortly after the Armistice he issued a general memorandum
to the Australian Imperial Force. He admitted that 'demobilisation will
undoubtedly be difficult and irksome', and that 'great personal restraint
will certainly be required'. Australia's name stood high in the world, he
said; it was up to them all to ensure that this reputation was not com-
promised by 'any behaviour of ours'. Transports would inevitably be in

short supply, and everyone would have to wait their turn. 'Play the game, boys, during this time, as you have always done', Birdwood implored, adopting his popular 'old Birdie' mantle to appeal to the troops' better nature, 'and add still more to the debt of gratitude which will always be acknowledged to you by the Empire and remembered by me as your comrade and commander'.[8] Some of the Australians in France or on leave in Britain did become fractious, as Birdwood had feared, and at the final Australian march before the King in 1919, some refused to make the respectful 'eyes right'.[9] But many made the best of it, not a few engaging in last-minute tourism in Britain, a chance to catch up with friends and relations again before returning finally to Australia.

Trauma and tragedy at home

Arriving home, returning servicemen were often given a rapturous reception, with 'welcome home' parties at least equal to the 'farewells' that had sped them on their way months or years before. Those relatives who could made their way to Fremantle or Port Adelaide or Hobart, or any of the other places where troopships docked, and there were emotional scenes as families were reunited on the quayside. But many, in the country, patiently awaited the return of their loved ones, often to the nearest railhead, and across rural Australia there were any number of 'welcome homes' in institutes, church halls and other community centres. Often, no doubt, the reunions were joyous occasions. George Elms, for example, from Moyarra in Victoria, married Ella, the girl who had sent the oranges he had so enjoyed when under fire at Third Ypres (see p.205).[10] Albert Facey, who had been invalided home after Gallipoli, bumped into a young woman as he walked down Barrack Street in Perth. Astonished, Facey realized that this was the same girl who had sent the socks he had received in the trenches, with an attached note wishing the recipient the best of luck and a safe return, signed 'Evelyn Gibson, Hon. Secretary, Girl Guides, Bunbury, W[estern] A[ustralia]'.[11] They began their courtship there and then, and were married in St David's Church, Bunbury, in August 1916.

Sometimes, however, the homecomings were traumatic. Children did not recognize their fathers, and wives and girlfriends found to their dismay that the war had changed their menfolk, and perhaps that they too had changed. Soldiers returned with fearful disabilities, and limb-less ex-servicemen became a familiar feature of Australian towns and cities. Marriages and other relationships suffered under the strain. The number of separations and divorces shot up. There were also mental scars. George Elms, despite marrying Ella, the girl of his dreams, was a troubled man. His son Ron recalled that, when his father came back from the war, he 'did not enjoy good health, suffering from war inju-ries and started each day with a headache. He suffered from shellshock . . . and the "House Rules" laid down: "no noise", "no dropping things", "instant obedience" and make sure your jobs were done properly'.[12] As Ron concluded:

> My father was a very moral and upright man. But he was not a happy soul, and he had a very short fuse, did not like noise of any sort, did not care for [like] his children but to his eternal credit provided a strict upbringing to his 3 children. Being a sergeant at 19 was the biggest thing that ever happened to him. From then on it was setbacks due to his health, going broke on the land, working long hours for little reward during the Depression & in the 1930s more health problems. He still carried four pieces of shrapnel in his back when he died at 87.[13]

The ravages of war were no respecter of rank. John Monash, the brilliant Australian general, who had played a major role in the Allies' victory of 1918, returned to Australia after the war and threw himself into public life. He supported returned servicemen, was active in the Rotary movement, and wrote a book *The Australian Victories in France in 1918*, which was published in 1920. He became head of the State Electricity Commission of Victoria in 1920, and was appointed vice-chancellor of the University of Melbourne in 1923. In all these activities he displayed his characteristic energy, commitment and vision. But by the end of the decade he felt that he was slowing down, physically and mentally, and in a brief speech at a reunion of the 6th Battalion on 23 September 1931 said that he did not expect to attend the event again. Less than a week later he suffered a slight heart attack, to be followed on 3 October by a massive coronary. He contracted pneumonia, and died on 8 October 1931, aged sixty-six years. It was a reasonable age for the time but his doctor reckoned that the strain of war service had taken its toll, stripping his life of perhaps a further twenty years. As Roland Perry has observed in his biography of the great man, from this perspective Monash was yet another victim of the First World War.[14]

Albert Jacka VC, hero of Gallipoli and the Western Front, had also returned to Victoria after the war. He went into business with two former colleagues from the 14th Battalion, and together they set up a company importing and exporting electrical goods. Jacka married his typist, Frances Carey, and later they adopted a daughter, Betty. In 1929 Jacka was elected to the city council of St Kilda, a suburb of Melbourne, and in the following year became mayor. Like Monash, he threw himself into public life, assisting the unemployed and homeless. But his business failed in 1931, a casualty of the Great Depression, and thereafter things seemed to go downhill. He collapsed suddenly during a council meeting, and died on 17 January 1932 from severe nephritis (inflammation of the kidneys). He was only thirty-nine. As people acknowledged at the time, he had never really recovered from his war wounds and the trauma of the battlefield, and for some it came as no surprise, alas, that he had died so young.[15]

Equally tragic was the post-war experience of Harold 'Pompey' Elliott, the Brigadier-General who had wept for his men at Fromelles (p. 127) in 1916. Returning to Australia in 1919, Elliott stood as a Nationalist candidate for the Senate in the federal election of that year, topping the poll of Victorian senators, as he did again in 1925. He was director of an investment company, active in the militia (he was promoted to Major-General in 1927), and public champion of returned servicemen. However, Elliott nursed a series of grievances from his war years, feeling that he had been passed over and treated unfairly. These slights were magnified in his mind over time, and affected his judgement on other matters. He began to suspect that the investment advice he had given to clients was faulty, and he worried increasingly about his own financial position. Suffering from high blood pressure and diabetes, he was depressed by his ill-health. Elliott also feared for the future of Australia, and thought that society was on the verge of collapse. Eventually it all became too much, and he took his own life in a private hospital at Malvern, Victoria, on 23 March 1931, aged fifty-two. His doctor had diagnosed 'a definite form of nervous disorder', and he had been put in hospital for observation and treatment.[16] The staff had been warned to be alert for suicide attempts but had forgotten to remove the razor blades from his shaving kit. 'Pompey' Elliott was found dead in

bed with a deep gash to his left arm. Like Monash and Jacka, he too
had been claimed by the war.

For all returning servicemen, the task of finding a job was often
formidable. Few were able to step into the positions they had occupied
before the war, and, after an initial short-lived boom, the economic
climate deteriorated rapidly. Moreover, many found it difficult to adjust
to regular civilian employment. Jack Buntine, for example, who had
fought at Gallipoli and on the Western Front, discovered that he could
not even stand the routine of living in a house. He went into the bush,
trapping and shooting game and fossicking for gold. 'In the army', he
explained, 'when you wanted money, you went to the quartermaster.
When you wanted food, you went to the quartermaster'. He had forgotten was it was like on 'civvy street'. 'When I got back I was hopeless', he
admitted: 'It took me a while to straighten out'. He settled down eventually in 1925, when he married, but his first wife died of peritonitis a few
years later, leaving him with two small daughters. Eventually, Buntine
married again and fathered four more children – the last when he was
sixty – having finally adjusted to the domestic habit.[17] Alec Campbell,
who lived to be the last Gallipoli survivor, had also found it hard to
settle. After the war, he worked as a jackaroo on sheep and cattle stations, as a carpenter, as a builder in the construction of the new federal
capital at Canberra, and on the railways across Australia. He even
toyed with the idea of going to Spain to fight against Franco and the
fascists. Finally, he returned to his native Tasmania. His first marriage
did not work out, although it had given him seven children, and he had
a further two offspring from his second marriage – the second when he
was sixty-nine. Like Jack Buntine, Campbell found that the experience
of war had made it impossible at first to hold down a permanent job.
But, like Buntine, it had also given him a terrific zest for life, an antidote
to death and destruction, and, once the post-war wanderlust had faded,
he too found regular employment (as a public servant), took an econom-
ics degree, and discovered the contentment and security of family life.

Soldier settlers

'I'm an ordinary man', Alec Campbell would insist, claiming no particular achievement. He and Buntine were among the lucky ones, and

for every story with a happy ending, there were others that finished badly. For many, the transition from the trenches had been extremely difficult. The government had established a Repatriation Department to advance the interests of returned servicemen, and among its early initiatives was the 'soldier settlement' scheme. The idea was that some of the big estates would be broken up into small blocks, while large tracts of hitherto uncleared land – such as that on the Murray Mallee country in South Australia and Victoria – would be allocated in small parcels to returned soldiers whose task it would be to cultivate the wilderness. The plan appealed to those who dreamed of being their own boss, of making 'a go of it' on the land. But the reality was that the land selected was often unsuitable, too arid to support crops and too small to be economic. All too often, 'soldier settlers', so full of hope when they acquired their land, gave up the unequal battle, many abandoning their properties as they were overtaken by despair and an unbearable sense of failure. Eric Lattke, for example, had won a Distinguished Conduct Medal on the Western Front, and while on leave in Britain had married a Welsh girl in Cardiff. In 1919, planning his return to Australia, he had taken a course in agriculture at Edinburgh University. As his daughter Daphne recalled:

> Later that year [1919] Eric returned to Queensland, on the same ship, but segregated from his new bride. He took up a Soldier Settlement. One of the requirements of the grant was that he clear-fell his patch of Queensland rainforest. This venture failed, mainly due to lack of capital and poor seasons. When they were reduced to living on wallabies they moved to the small town of Yarraman Creek where Eric found work in the timber industry.[18]

Eric and his wife had adopted their daughter, Daphne, but the domestic harmony they sought proved elusive. The shift from South Wales to the Queensland rainforest was difficult enough, no doubt, but struggling against the odds to establish a farm was just too much. The marriage faltered, and one day Eric Lattke upped and left, going to join his sister in Colombia, where her husband managed a gold mine. George Elms, the unhappy soul from Moyarra, was another who tried his hand at soldier settlement. He had trained as a horticulturalist before the war, and his wife Ella was also familiar with citrus farming. They planted an orchard on their block at Berri on the Murray but the expenditure exhausted their reserves of capital, and there would be no income until the trees began to bear fruit. To make some ready cash, Elms took a seasonal job as a deckhand on the paddle-steamer *Gem*, which plied the River Murray between Echuca and Goolwa. He also found temporary work in the packing shed at the Berri Co-operative. His son Ron remembered:

> The first 3 production years were disasters with one crop being frosted and the other two ruined by hail. So George sold up before he went bankrupt & took a job managing a dried fruit block at Coomella [now Dareton], just over the Murray in New South Wales. In reality it was more of a labouring job and this young man, still in his twenties and carrying the effects of his wartime wounds had to clear the land, plant the vines, erect the drying racks, construct the watering system and so on. His 'manager's' residence consisted of a three roomed house constructed of corrugated iron, with a dirt floor.[19]

Albert Facey, too, invalided from Gallipoli and married to Evelyn Gibson, the Bunbury girl, decided to give soldier settlement a 'go'. Initially, he had found work on the tramways in Perth but the vehicles' constant vibration had aggravated his war wounds. He also yearned to return to the countryside of his youth, and to run his own show. Despite his disabilities, Facey convinced the selection board that he was a suitable applicant for a wheat and wool farm, and was allocated a property near Narrogin in the central wheat belt of Western Australia. Ominously, the previous occupants had already given up. Nonetheless, Facey set to with a will, and the first years were very successful. More land was cleared, sheep were purchased and the fleece sold for a profit, and he diversified into pig farming. Disaster struck when their weatherboard house burned down during a heatwave, and the downturn in wool prices in 1924–5 was a cause of much anxiety. Things appeared to improve during 1926 but in 1927 the wheat crop was ruined by too much rain early in the season and then too much heat. Meanwhile, wool prices continued to drop. In 1930 there was a bumper harvest but wheat prices fell in response to over-supply. And so it went on. Plagues of destructive rabbits added to Facey's woes. By now Facey's health was beginning to fail, as his war wounds became more troublesome, and it was obvious that the time had come to abandon the soldier settlement experiment and return to the city. As Facey observed, drily: 'My wife was delighted and said that if we had stayed on the farm we would have faced starvation'.[20]

There were, of course, those who did make a success of soldier settlement, and were able to survive the lean times. John Edey, who had served at Gallipoli and on the Western Front, began share-farming with a man from his unit at Nullawil, on the Murray Mallee, where the settlers lived 'in iron roofed dwellings with walls of super-phosphate bags sewn together, and whitewashed, earthen floors'.[21] In 1921 he acquired his own block on newly available land at Karadoc, near Mildura, also on the Murray. He built a hut with hessian walls and no door, and began clearing the dense mallee scrub by axe, later employing a stump-jump plough – an ingenious South Australian invention – to make the ground ready for seeding. Edey encountered the difficulties experienced by other soldier settlers, including low prices for produce and the vicissitudes of the climate. He wrote that: '1927 was the worst year of a prolonged drought and there was very little money to be earned in the Mallee'. He planned an interlude in which he would use his truck to make money as a carrier in the outback of central Australia. He returned to Karadoc to find that conditions had improved somewhat, and somehow hung on against all the odds, so that when he wrote his memoirs in the early 1980s he was one of very few soldier settlers in the locality still on his original block. Years earlier, he had observed his less fortunate, less robust neighbours, who had buckled under the twin strains of trying to wrest a living from marginal land and deal with the long-term effects of the war. 'Jim developed what could only be described as delayed shell shock', he remembered, describing the fate of one soldier settler: 'I had noticed this in many men who had experienced a lot of front-line service; so many of them completely broke down about fifteen years after the war. Jim got so bad that he could not even shave'.[22]

The RSL: Memorialization

Marooned, as they often thought, in inhospitable and remote areas, the soldier settlers often felt abandoned – or at least misunderstood – by what they considered an unhelpful Repatriation Department, and turned to other organizations for assistance, such as the co-operative

Victorian Citrus Growers' Association (which helped settlers with
marketing their produce, registering the name 'Riverland Oranges').
Foremost among the institutions dedicated to the welfare of returned
servicemen, soldier settlers among them, was the Returned Sailors and
Soldiers Imperial League of Australia ('the RSL', for short), formed in
1916, which by October 1919 boasted no fewer than 114,700 members.
It aimed to perpetuate the comradeship that had existed among the
men at the front, to support the sick and needy and their families, as
well as to advocate the interests of returned servicemen more generally. The RSL had played an increasingly important role in organizing
'welcome home' celebrations during 1919 and the early months of 1920,
and was likewise prominent in the commemoration of Anzac Day.
Across the country, it often took the lead in memorialization, taking
custody of battlefield trophies (captured field-guns and the like), arrang-
ing their display in public parks or memorial gardens, and liaising with
local councils to assist the erection of war memorials. In time, even
the smallest settlement boasted its imposing memorial, often crowned
with a life-like sculpture of an Australian soldier, complete with slouch
hat, sometimes in the *en garde* position, bayonet at the ready, at others
solemnly at attention, head bowed and chin resting on the butt of an
upturned rifle.

Memorialization became a major preoccupation. There were state
memorials, such as that at King's Park in Perth, Western Australia, or
the Tasmanian State Memorial in Queen's Domain, Hobart, and the
extraordinary Shrine of Remembrance in Melbourne, which dominated
the skyline for seemingly miles around.[23] The most significant was the
national Australian War Memorial (or Museum, as it was designated
initially), housed temporarily in Melbourne and Sydney during the
1920s, before being located finally in Canberra in 1941. Memorialization
of a different sort was evident in the literary outpouring of the post-
war years, not only Charles Bean's twelve-volumed *Official History of
Australia in the War of 1914–18* but also the many memoirs, often vivid
and moving, of the ordinary soldiers who had served at the front, most
famously Edgar Rule's *Jacka's Mob*, published in 1933. Each of the Allied
powers had pursued such memorialization. But if in Australia there
seemed a particular urgency, it was because the battlefields – and the
graves of the fallen – were so impossibly far away. For many, the thought
that one day they might be able to visit their loved ones' graves, in

cemeteries so carefully tended by the Imperial (later Commonwealth) War Graves Commission, never crossed their minds. For others, it remained an unattainable dream, a perpetual source of yearning and discomfort.[24] A fortunate few did manage to make the pilgrimage (as it was often described) to Gallipoli or the Western Front, and by the late 1920s the clamour to visit the Australian war graves had become so insistent that a large organized pilgrimage was proposed. It would take in the Middle East (including Gallipoli) as well as Europe but at £230 per head the cost was prohibitive for all but the wealthy.

In 1929, in what was billed as the 'First Australian and New Zealand Pilgrimage to the Battlefields and War Graves of Gallipoli, France and England', eighty-six men and women found themselves representing the aspirations of all bereaved Australians. It was a daunting responsibility, and in Melbourne the *Herald* newspaper hit on the idea that many relations of Australians buried overseas might like to purchase small tokens – possibly artificial sprigs of wattle – to be placed on the deceased's graves. It also suggested that the tokens could be taken in the same ship, the SS *Baradine*, which would carry the pilgrims. The scheme was endorsed by the Tasmanian *Mercury* and the *Register* newspaper in South Australia, and began to assume national significance. G.W. Holland, President of the RSL in Victoria, voiced strong support for the plan, believing that it would serve to bring the graves of the fallen closer to the hearts of those at home. Eventually, 1,500 Victorians and 2,000 South Australians purchased these tokens, with similar numbers in other states, and the sprigs of wattle were duly placed on the graves of those who had fallen at Lone Pine, Pozières, Third Ypres, and all the other great battles of the First World War.[25]

The RSL: defending the returned

RSL endorsement had been important for the success of the wattle token campaign, as the organization exercised its authority as the legitimate mouthpiece of returned servicemen and, by extension, of the families of those who had fallen. In other areas it also sought to advance their interests. Recognizing the increasing difficulty its members were having in finding suitable employment, the RSL spoke up loudly on their behalf. In June 1919, for example, Sergeant-Major

Matthews, an RSL branch official at Moonta in South Australia, addressed a 'welcome home' ceremony, dwelling 'at considerable length' on the role of the League and its responsibility towards those returning from the war. He warned of the many 'difficulties with which returned servicemen were faced', and foresaw looming economic problems in Australia. In neighbouring Victoria, he observed, the Bryant & May match factory had closed down recently, with the loss of some 900 jobs, because people preferred cheaper 'Jap brands', and 'this was the state of affairs they [returnees] were coming home to'. Indeed, he added, he had even heard workers, jealous of their own jobs, exclaim pejoratively 'Here comes a returned soldier'. It was, he said, a measure of the suspicion in which the returnees were now regarded in some civilian circles.[26]

No matter how hard the RSL tried to defend its members' interests, it was powerless to intervene in the major structural changes that overtook the Australian economy after the war. On northern Yorke Peninsula, for example, the copper mines of Moonta and Wallaroo had boomed during the war years, meeting the insatiable demand of the British munitions industry. But by the end of 1918 it was evident that the good times were over. Profit for the year had declined by almost half, compared to 1917, and in the August the British government, anticipating the end of hostilities, had terminated its contract for South Australian copper, a grim foretaste of what lay ahead. Timely intervention by the Prime Minister, Billy Hughes, secured an extension until the end of the year but this merely put off the evil day. On 1 January 1919 the Wallaroo and Moonta Mining and Smelting Company took the reluctant decision to reduce wages, prompting protests from the workers who pointed out that the company was sitting on £250,000 of accumulated war profits. Meanwhile, the price of copper on the international market dropped alarmingly, as war demand dried up. In March 1919 work at the mines was severely curtailed, and came to a complete stop in the April as a renewed coal strike in New South Wales deprived the mines and smelters of fuel. The arrival of a ship at Wallaroo laden with coal in the September signalled a return to production but there were further lengthy periods of inactivity, as copper prices continued to fall, until, on the afternoon of 23 October 1923, the National Bank foreclosed on the company and the mines were abandoned for good. The company went formally into liquidation in the November, and the wholesale dismantling and disposal of the plant and infrastructure began almost at once.

Buildings were blown up or razed to the ground, and returning soldiers came home to find that the once-familiar landscape had been reduced to a derelict wasteland, ironically reminiscent of those they had known so recently on the Western Front, while the jobs to which they might have aspired had disappeared amidst the rubble.[27]

In other areas the limits of RSL effectiveness were also apparent. The RSL's defence of returned servicemen rarely extended to those Aborigines and Torres Strait Islanders who had served in the Australian forces. Between 400 and 500 indigenous Australians had joined the Australian Imperial Force, and saw action in battles such as Pozières, Bullecourt and Third Ypres. Corporal Harry Thorpe, an Aborigine from Lake Tyers Mission Station in Victoria, who won the Military Medal at Broodseinde, was one of those killed in action. Another was Thorpe's mate, William Rawlings, who also won the Military Medal and was killed on the same day as his friend, 9 August 1918.[28] Initially, indigenous Australians had been barred from joining up but, in practice, local recruiters had always exercised a degree of discretion. By October 1917, when manpower shortages were acute, 'half-castes', to use the indelicate language of the time, were officially allowed to enlist, as long as they could prove one European parent. Once in uniform, Aborigines and Torres Strait Islanders were treated exactly like other Australian soldiers, receiving the same rates of pay, and there appears to be little evidence of discrimination. In the trenches, they were just like anyone else. However, after the war, when indigenous Australians returned home, they found to their dismay that their newly won status as equals no longer applied. Many simply disappeared, their war service forgotten by their erstwhile white colleagues, their sacrifice and contribution to the nation overlooked. Indeed, many found that conditions had deteriorated since they had joined up, and in areas such as education, health, employment, and general welfare, things had become markedly worse for indigenous communities. Just one indigenous Australian was granted land as a soldier settler, despite the fact that large tracts of Aboriginal reserves had been appropriated for the soldier settler scheme.

Those Australians of German descent who had served in the forces generally fared better, and many – like Eric Lattke in Queensland – became soldier settlers, for good or ill, although there were some Australians who resented this equality of treatment. John Verran, for example, erstwhile Labor Premier of South Australia, reminded returning servicemen that while they had been away at the front, 'he had been dropped out of political life'. The German community had been delighted when he lost his seat in the state parliament, he said: 'While the soldiers were dealing with the Germans overseas, he had been endeavouring to deal with them at home, and when he was defeated as a politician they held an early [Lutheran] prayer-meeting to thank God for it'.[29] He was incensed, moreover, that Germans had been allowed to apply for soldier-settlement land grants. 'He protested against Germans being allowed to enter into competition with [other] returned soldiers in securing such land', it was reported: 'Many of these Germans retained the grin of the Kaiser when they bested the returned men'.[30] Verran campaigned for the exclusion of Germans from public life, and those of German background who had been deemed 'enemy aliens' during the war found themselves permanently barred from employment in government departments. Those who had been interned were to be deported. The prospect of being forcibly sent back to a country that they hardly knew, that was in turmoil and apparently on the brink of revolution, horrified many German-Australians. There were clear instances of injustice, such as that of one German who had been living in Western Australia for thirty-six years, was a naturalized British subject, and was now a widower, with one adult daughter. He was to be sent 'home' but his daughter, born in Australia of an Australian mother, was not allowed to go with him. There were protests against the harshness of such arbitrary decisions but the government view prevailed that such people remained a danger to the state and that, in the interests of Australian national security, they should be expelled – as indeed they were, perhaps a thousand of them, sent back to face the chaos of post-war Germany, the doomed Weimar regime and, ultimately, the rise of Hitler.[31]

The 'grey years'?

The continuing hostility towards Australia's German community was one indication that, despite the façade of national unity in the moment of victory, old divisions remained. Archbishop Daniel Mannix, still flushed with his success in the conscription crisis, organized an 'Irish Race Convention' in Melbourne 1919 to draw attention to Ireland's continuing distress, and in so doing antagonized those who believed that he was attacking the British Empire and Australia's esteemed place within it. Nonetheless, Mannix drew a record crowd of 100,000 to Richmond Reserve, and in the following year he attracted similar numbers to Melbourne's St Patrick's Day parade. Moreover, confounding his critics, Mannix arranged for no fewer than fourteen VC winners to participate in this great procession, along with 10,000 other returned servicemen. Mannix had beaten his opponents at their own game, embracing Australian nationalism alongside his championship of Ireland, and in doing so had anticipated the formal Anzac Day parades of later years. His enemies were outraged by this continuing showmanship and his brazen hostility, as they saw it, to other religious denominations. Michael McKernan, indeed, suggests that in 'the 1920s he [Mannix] symbolized the sectarian hatred that was the principal effect of the war on Australian churches'.[32]

Mannix had effectively co-opted returned servicemen to his cause. It was a device that others emulated. John Verran, for example, former Labor Premier of South Australia, had lost his seat in the 1918 state election. Moving to the right, he sought new sources of support as he attempted to rebuild his failing political career. Having spoken, often in the most lurid terms, at soldiers' 'farewells' (pp. 107–8), he sought now to address 'welcome home' gatherings, seeking to win over the returned servicemen. At one public welcome in March 1919, for instance, Verran hailed the returnees as 'the gentlemen of Australia'. They were neither 'those who stayed at home nor the wealthy folk', he declared. Neither shirkers nor profiteers, they were now the hope for the nation's future. But, he warned, 'they had come from one conflict to another', as strikes and industrial unrest disrupted the economy and posed a threat to society. 'Australia was as near hell today as it could be', he insisted, 'with influence of the I.W.W. [Industrial Workers of the World – the 'Wobblies'] and the spirit of Bolshevism abroad'. It was the duty of returned servicemen, he explained, to confront these challenges. 'These things ought to be run out of Australia', he said, 'and they were looking to the returned men to assist in wiping them out'. He envisaged, he added, 'a new brotherhood' of returned servicemen who would 'stand together and dictate their demands to Australia'. This brotherhood would bring 'new aspirations to Australia', and 'must make itself felt throughout the length and breadth of the land'.[33]

It was a cry repeated across Australia, as politicians reacted to the volatile post-war conditions, and returned servicemen were indeed routinely enlisted to break strikes and quell demonstrations. In 1928, for example, returnees swelled the numbers of the right-wing Citizens' League Movement, contributing to the 3,000 temporary special consta-bles sworn in to smash the strike by Port Adelaide 'wharfies'. Monash himself was approached by right-wing ex-servicemen and others, with the suggestion that he become dictator of Australia and save his country, just as Mussolini had in Italy. Others joined the paramilitary New Guard movement, waiting to make their move once society had finally col-lapsed. The New Guard even planned to kidnap Jack Lang, controversial Premier of New South Wales, and intervened when he officially opened the new Sydney Harbour Bridge on 19 March 1932. As Lang prepared to cut the ribbon, Captain Francis de Groot, a New Guard activist, rode up on his horse and beat him to it, slashing with his sword.

These were the 'grey years', as McKernan termed them.[34] Growing unemployment, religious and ethnic sectarianism, class antagonism, and the emergence of political extremism, left and right, as well as the continuing marginalization of indigenous people, all heightened the sense of division and uncertainty in Australian society.[35] Returned ser-vicemen continued to live under the shadow of the war. They looked to their old mates for the companionship and reassurance of the like-minded, those who had shared their experiences at the front, and in so doing distanced themselves from their wives and children, as well as from those who had not gone to war. There was a new cynicism, in contrast to the optimism, even innocence, of the pre-war years. Yet, as Mark Sheftall has argued, the Australian experience of war, in the manner detected by Charles Bean and those other contemporary observers, had helped forge a distinct national identity, which in the fullness of time would transcend the bitterness and disappointments of the post-war era. In Britain, as Sheftall points out, the overwhelming emphasis after the First World War was on its human, material, social and spiritual costs. But in Australia (and the other Dominions), he insists, there was something else too. Here the war, 'for all its carnage and discord, had confirmed the potential and destiny of these – no longer colonies – nations'. They had proved themselves 'healthy young countries, isolated from the ills of the Old Country . . . the uncorrupted heirs of British supremacy'.[36] This in essence was the Anzac myth, as it was first crafted in 1915.

Today, this is not always a fashionable view, and there are those who object, perhaps rightly, that it is a very masculine and indeed militarized construction of Australian history and identity.[37] Yet, as Martin Crotty has observed, 'the Anzac experience, which began at Gallipoli, is the centrepiece of collective memory in Australia ... [it] has assumed a quasi-religious status'.[38] Indeed, it has. Anzac Day was first commemorated on 25 April 1916, the anniversary of the dawn landing at Gallipoli. Australian troops marched through the streets of London, and there were church services across Australia. The influenza pandemic prevented parades in Australia in 1919, as the soldiers returned home, and in 1920 Anzac Day very conveniently fell on a Sunday. In Sydney, General Birdwood took the salute as 5,000 ex-servicemen marched past. In 1921 the Commonwealth government declared Anzac Day a public holiday. But the individual states were slow to follow suit, many individuals fearing that a public holiday – with its connotations of going to the races and drinking in pubs – would detract from the sacred memory of 25 April. There was also a sense that the war was still too fresh in recent memory for such an event, and that Australia, with its all too apparent divisions, needed time to reflect and heal. Yet, one by one the states did follow the example set by the Commonwealth, and the events of that early morning on 25 April 1915, when the Anzacs went ashore at Gallipoli, became a defining moment in Australian history and the creation of the Australian nation.

Epilogue

WHEN HAROLD WILLIAMS published his wartime memoirs in 1933, he had an important message for 'the youth of Australia'. As Williams explained, young people might 'hear on many occasions criticisms that suggest to you that we fought at the bidding of a moneyed clique, or that the men of Australia were sacrificed to help England'. Both interpretations were wrong, he insisted: 'The truth is that the Australians who fought during the Great War on Gallipoli, in France, in Palestine, and on the high seas were defending their land from invasion and subjection as surely as if they had fought in trenches around Sydney'. In appealing to the younger generation, Harold Williams fretted that the lessons of the recent conflict were already being forgotten, and that in the post-war social and economic climate a 'new creed of selfishness and materialism' had grown up in Australia. 'The last war did not end war', he regretted, 'unfortunately for humanity', so now he appealed directly to 'the young men [*sic*] of this fair land who are proud to be Australians', imploring them to eschew the 'doctrines of selfishness' and to learn instead 'the lessons which the A.I.F. [Australian Imperial Force] taught . . . lessons [that] teach a noble spirit of self-sacrifice and of duty to our country'.[1]

Like many who had served in the First World War, and those who had lost loved ones in the conflict, Harold Williams made sense of all he had endured by elevating 'self-sacrifice' and 'duty to our country' as supreme virtues. In doing so he also expressed the widespread belief among those who fought that they had confronted and defeated 'the greatest military machine that ever the world knew to preserve their freedom', a 'truth' that many 'pacifists, idealists and politicians ignore'. Troubled by the divisions, animosities and uncertainties of the post-war era, Williams sought to enshrine his conviction 'that through all the horror, filth, and suffering there shone something inspiring, stimulating, sacred'.[2] This was not to glorify war, he insisted, but was a message designed to transcend the 'selfishness' of contemporary Australian society, with all its differences, hostilities and bitterness. The earnest desire for memorialization, for pilgrimage to the battlefields, and for the solemn commemoration of Anzac Day was evidence that Harold Williams was not alone in expressing such sentiments. Here, perhaps, were unifying elements in an otherwise divided nation, elements that drew upon and were moulded by the 'Anzac myth' of 1915, and which gave fabric and meaning to newly crafted ideas of nationhood.

At any rate, Harold Williams' message – with its appeal to 'the young men of this fair land who are proud to be Australians' – was an overtly nationalist one. The war had been fought as much to defend Australia's interests as it had been to protect England's, and here was an implied equality between Australia and Great Britain, as well as that enhanced place within the Empire that many Australians had sought. As Billy Hughes, the wartime Prime Minister, had emphasized time and again, Australian nationalism was not incompatible with Empire loyalty. Yet at the Versailles peace talks Hughes had represented Australia's interests independently, clashing with Lloyd George on occasion, and expressing a hostility to Japanese ambitions in the Pacific that Britain found irksome. After the war, the Labor Party – which Hughes had so recently led – distanced itself from overt expressions of imperial sentiment. But politicians of all parties continued to see Australia's international relations – defence, foreign policy, overseas trade – in terms of the enduring relationship with Britain. In 1931 the British parliament passed the 'Statue of Westminster', largely in response to pressure from Canada, the Irish Free State and South Africa, which gave legal expression to the belief – first voiced formally in the Balfour Declaration of 1926 – that Britain and her Dominions were 'equal in status and in no way subordinate one to another'.[3] This also mirrored the aspirations of Australian nationalism. Yet Australian politicians were reluctant to loosen what they saw as important strategic links with Britain, and the Australian government did not adopt the Statute until as late as 1942, when it was confronted with the realities of another world war.

The British Empire had reached its greatest territorial extent after the First World War, as the spoils from the dismembered German and Ottoman empires were divided up. But the transformation from Empire to Commonwealth was already continuing apace, as the Dominions acquired new levels of independence. Moreover, the supposed global reach of British power was increasingly illusory. Among those Australian politicians to look beyond the rhetoric of Empire was John Curtin, later to become Labor Prime Minister during the Second World War, who as early as November 1936 told the Australian parliament that: 'The dependence of Australia upon the competence, let alone readiness, of British statesmen to send forces to our aid is too dangerous a hazard upon which to found Australia's defence policy'.[4] On 7 October 1941, exactly two months after Curtin had assumed office, the Japanese launched their pre-emptive attack on Pearl Harbor. Three days later the British capital warships HMS *Prince of Wales* and HMS *Repulse*, sent to the region to assert the Royal Navy's maritime might and to assure Australia of the robustness of Britain's defensive shield, were summarily sunk by Japanese aircraft off the east coast of Malaya, painfully exposing the limits of British power. Even worse followed when the supposedly impregnable island-fortress of Singapore fell to the Japanese on 15 February 1942. Almost 18,000 Australian servicemen and women were taken prisoner, along with numerous British and Indian troops, many to face the indescribable cruelty and appalling conditions of Japanese prisoner-of-war camps.

To this devastating shock was added the Japanese air attack on Darwin just four days after the fall of Singapore, the first of a number of Japanese raids along the northern and eastern coasts of mainland Australia, including a midget submarine incursion in Sydney harbour. Curtin had already announced the beginning of the 'Battle for Australia', and in his New Year message for 1942 had explained to his fellow Australians that it was time to adopt a new foreign policy trajectory. 'Without any inhibitions of any kind', he said, 'I make it quite clear that Australia looks to America, free of any pangs as to our traditional ties or kinship with the United Kingdom'.[5] Of course, Britain had already made it plain that it, too, looked to America, and Churchill's grand plan had always been to persuade Roosevelt that the United States should enter the Second World War – as indeed it did, after Pearl Harbor. But perhaps Curtin had chosen his words badly. Churchill, having already sent (against Admiralty advice) two major warships to their doom in a futile gesture of support for Australia, was infuriated by what appeared to be Curtin's deliberate distancing from Britain; Roosevelt was likewise embarrassed. Nonetheless, Curtin's statement evidenced the stark sense of isolation and vulnerability felt by Australia in the face of the collapse of British power in the region, and the apparent Japanese ascendancy. The Empire-Commonwealth would never be the same again, and Curtin's turn to America would lay the foundations for an enduring alliance with the United States.

Whether Japan actually intended to invade Australia is hotly debated today but in 1942 the threat seemed very real. The fact that Churchill and Roosevelt had adopted a 'defeat Hitler first' policy, before turning their full attention to Japan, heightened Australian anxieties. The Australian army had already fought with distinction against the Vichy regime in Syria, and in North Africa relished their reputation as the 'Rats of Tobruk'. Following the Japanese offensives in South-East Asia and the Pacific, these experienced troops were brought home to bolster the defence of Australia. But in the meantime it was left to a small number of regular troops and some hastily trained conscripts to stop the Japanese advance in Papua New Guinea. With Australia in such apparent peril, and the Japanese on the northern doorstep, conscription was not the issue it had been in the previous war. The new conscripts were young and poorly equipped. Yet they fought with determination in the New Guinea jungle, struggling uphill along the arduous Kokoda Track to confront and halt the Japanese advance. In time, the Kokoda Track would join Gallipoli as a place of pilgrimage, earning its destination in the evolving Anzac myth. As Paul Keating, Prime Minister in the 1990s, put it, somewhat controversially, Kokoda 'was the first and only time we've fought an enemy to prevent the invasion of Australia'. For Keating, speaking on the Kokoda Track in April 1992, Kokoda was the place where 'the depth and soul of the Australian nation was confirmed. If it was founded at Gallipoli it was certainly confirmed in the defence of our homeland here'.[6]

The American naval victories in the Coral Sea and at Midway broke the wider Japanese advance, and numerous American troops were based in Australia for the duration of the Second World War. After the war, colonies in the region restored briefly to British rule were shortly to gain independence, and Australia played a supporting role in defeating communist insurgents in Malaysia and in containing Indonesia as it attempted to infiltrate north Borneo. However, by the 1960s the United

Kingdom was effecting its withdrawal from 'east of Suez', as well as prioritizing its desire to join the Common Market (later the European Union) over and above its leadership of the British Commonwealth. In such circumstances, the continuing alliance with America appeared Australia's best guarantee of security. Indeed, Australia had already fought alongside America in the Korean War. However, the American alliance had the unfortunate effect of drawing Australia into the increasingly unpopular Vietnam War. Conscription became a deeply controversial issue, just as it had been in the First World War, and again Australia was a divided nation as pro- and anti-war factions bitterly opposed one another. Those who had fought in Vietnam came home to an uncertain welcome, and it was many years after the war had ended before it was at last assimilated into the pantheon of the Anzac tradition. But the American alliance endured, and at the end of the twentieth and into the twenty-first century Australia found itself involved, again controversially, in a number of American-led conflicts, notably the two Gulf Wars and in Afghanistan. Australia was by now regularly contributing to 'peace-keeping' operations across the world – from Cambodia to Somalia and Rwanda – and won widespread international applause for its leadership of INTERFET, the International Forum for East Timor, a non-United Nations military force acting in accordance with UN resolutions to restore peace and security to East Timor after Indonesian withdrawal.

By the second decade of the twenty-first century, Australia had firmly established its reputation as a significant regional power, able and willing to operate 'out of area' when necessary. A formidable navy, a highly professional army, and a powerful and expanding air force constituted the 'world class defence force' described by the Australian government in April 2014.[7] Although Australian participation in Iraq and Afghanistan had remained highly controversial, the continuing significance of Anzac Day, not only as a popular expression of remembrance but also of solidarity with today's armed forces, was evidence that the notions of 'sacrifice' and 'duty' expounded so passionately by Harold Williams back in 1933 still struck a chord somewhere deep in the Australian psyche. No longer are there First World War veterans left to lead the annual Anzac Day marches. But if Harold Williams were by some miracle still alive, he would be gratified that Australians today continue to remember that he – like all his mates – 'truly *did his bit* – for the honour of his country and his home'.[8]

Notes

Chapter 1

1   Neville Meaney, *Australia and the World: A Documentary History from the 1870s to the 1970s*, Melbourne, 1985, p.217.

2   Ibid.; see also Jean Beaumont (ed.), *Australia's War 1914–18*, Melbourne, 1995, p.2.

3   The most recent (at the time of writing) and most persuasive expression of this view is Christopher Clark, *The Sleepwalkers: How Europe Went to War in 1914*, London, 2013.

4   Max Hastings, '1914: Why Britain Had to Go to War', *BBC History*, November 1913, p.42.

5   Ibid.; for a corroborating view see Gary Sheffield, 'It was a Great War. One that saved Europe', *The Times*, 1 February 2014.

6   Alec H. Chisholm (ed.), *Selected Verse of C.J. Dennis*, Sydney, 1950 (republished 1975), p.47.

7   Ibid., p.50.

8   Cited in Gavin Souter, *Lion and Kangaroo: The Initiation of Australia*, Melbourne, 1976 (republished 2000), p.262.

9   Beaumont, 1995, p.3.

10 Geoffrey Blainey (ed.), *Henry Lawson*, Melbourne, 2002.

11 David Gilmour, *The Long Recessional: The Imperial Life of Rudyard Kipling*, London, 2003, p.201.

12 K.S. Inglis, *Sacred Places: War Memorials in the Australian Landscape*, Melbourne, 1999, p.74; see also Donald Denoon, Philippa Mein-Smith and Marivic Wyhdham, *A History of Australia, New Zealand and the Pacific*, Oxford, 2000, p.269.

13 Souter, 1976 and 2000, p.13.

14 Neville Meaney, 'Britishness and Australia: Some Reflections', in Carl Bridge and Kent Fedorowich (eds.), *The British World: Diaspora, Culture and Identity*, London, 2003, p.121.

15 *Sydney Morning Herald*, 6 August 1914.

16 Graham Seal, *Echoes of Anzac: The Voice of Australians at War*, Melbourne, 2005, p.26.

17 *Sydney Morning Herald*, 6 August 1914.

18 *Australian Christian Commonwealth*, 11 September 1914.

19 *Western Mail*, 7 August 1914.

20 *Yorke's Peninsula Advertiser*, 8 January 1915.

21 Ibid.

22 *Yorke's Peninsula Advertiser*, 6 October 1914.

23 Chisholm (ed.), 1950 and 1975, p.45.

24　Ibid., p.43.

25　*Australian Worker*, 6 August 1914; see also Michael McKernan, *The Australian People and the Great War*, Melbourne, 1980, pp.3–5.

26　Chisholm (ed.), 1950 and 1975, p.44.

27　*Australian Worker*, 27 August and 15 October 1914; McKernan, 1980, p.4.

28　*Corryong Courier*, 13 August 1914.

29　*Western Australian*, 6 August 1914.

30　Souter, 1976 and 2000, p.267.

31　Ibid., p.268.

32　*Australian Christian Commonwealth*, 9 August 1914.

33　*Australian Christian Commonwealth*, 6 December 1914.

34　*Dubbo Liberal and Maquarie Advocate*, 10 December 1915.

35　John McQuilton, *Rural Australia and the Great War: From Tarrawingee to Tangambalanga*, Melbourne, 2001, pp.161–2.

36　McKernan, 1980, pp.154–6.

37　McQuilton, 2001, pp.20–21.

38　McKernan, 1980, p.157.

39　*People's Weekly*, 9 January 1915.

40　Ibid.; see also Brian Kennedy, *Silver, Sin and Sixpenny Ale: A Social History of Broken Hill, 1883–1921*, Melbourne, 1978, p.130, and R.H.B. Kearns, *Broken Hill: A Pictorial History*, Broken Hill, 1982, pp.133–4.

41　Marnie Haig-Muir, 'The Economy at War', in Beaumont (ed.), 1995, p.107.

42　Geoffrey Blainey, *The Rush That Never Ended: A History of Australian Mining*, Melbourne, 1963 (republished 1969), pp.278–80.

43　Geoffrey Blainey, *The Peaks of Lyell*, Melbourne, 1954 (republished 1967), p.231.

44　*People's Weekly*, 8 August 1914.

45　*Yorke's Peninsula Advertiser*, 27 November 1914.

46　*South Australian Register*, 4 August 1914.

47　David Stevens (ed.), *The Royal Australian Navy: A History*, Melbourne, 2006, p.26.

48　Peter Pedersen, *The Anzacs: Gallipoli to the Western Front*, Camberwell (Victoria), 2007, pp.12–13.

49　Ibid., pp.23–4; Stevens, 2006, pp.38–41.

50　'Captain Glossop' in A.B. 'Banjo' Paterson, *Songs of the Pen: Complete Works, 1901–1941*, Sydney, 1983, p.646.

51　Paterson, 1983, p.644.

Chapter 2

1　*Independent* (Melbourne), 17 April 1915.

2　*Bunbury Herald*, 6 March 1915; *Globe and Sunday Times War Pictorial*, 17 April 1915.

3　*Argus* (Melbourne), 5 March 1915.

4　*Cessnock Eagle and South Maitland Recorder*, 23 April 1915; *Tamworth Daily Observer*, 21 April 1915.

5　*Sydney Morning Herald*, 27 April 1915.

6   Cited in Roy Hattersley, *David Lloyd George: The Great Outsider*, London, 2010, p.373.

7   *Goulborn Evening Penny Post*, 20 April 1915.

8   Robert Kimber, *Love from Eddie – Ardrossan to Gallipoli: The Life and Times of Edward J. Cairns*, Tranmere (South Australia), 2012, pp.333–4.

9   *People's Weekly* (Moonta), 11 September 1915.

10 *People's Weekly*, 8 April 1916.

11 E.J. Rule, *Jacka's Mob: A Narrative of the Great War*, Sydney, 1933 (republished Melbourne, 1999), ed. by Carl Johnson and Andrew Barnes, pp.13–14.

12 Ibid.

13 A.B. Facey, *A Fortunate Life*, Fremantle, 1981 (republished Ringwood (Victoria), 1985), p.248.

14 B. Bishop, *The Hell, the Humour and the Heartbreak: A Private's View of World War I*, Sydney, 1991, p.23; see also Richard Travers, *Diggers in France: Australian Soldiers on the Western Front*, Sydney, 2001, p.9–10.

15 Rule, 1933 and 1999, p.13.

16 Facey, 1981 and 1985, pp.248–51.

17 *Kadina and Wallaroo Times*, 7 March 1915.

18 Anne Donnell, *Letters of an Australian Army Sister*, Sydney, 1920, pp.79, 83.

19 Facey, 1981 and 1985, p.249.

20 Ibid., p.247.

21 Bill Gamage, *The Broken Years: Australian Soldiers of the First World War*, Canberra, 1974 (republished Ringwood (Victoria), 1975), pp.39–40.

22 John F. Edey, *From Lone Pine to Murray Pine: The Story of a Mallee Soldier Settler*, Red Cliffs (Victoria), 1981, p.22.

23 *Kadina and Wallaroo Times*, 7 March 1915.

24 Noel Carthew, *Voices from the Trenches: Letters Home*, Frenchs Forest (NSW), 2002, p.87

25 H.R. Williams, *The Gallant Company: An Australian Soldier's Story of 1915–18*, Sydney, 1933 (republished as *An Anzac on the Western Front: The Personal Reflections of an Australian Infantryman from 1916 to 1918*, ed. by Martin Mace and John Grehan, Barnsley, 2012), pp.4–5.

26 *Barrier Miner*, 2 May 1915.

27 Jean Beaumont, *Australia's War, 1914–18*, St Leonards (New South Wales), 1995, p.149.

28 Facey, 1981 and 1985, pp.250–52.

29 Cecil B. Lock, *The Fighting 10th: A South Australian Centenary Souvenir of the 10th Battalion A.I.F., 1914–19*, Adelaide, 1926, p.235.

30 *Yorke's Peninsula Advertiser*, 9 July 1915.

31 Ibid.

32 National Archives of Australia (NAA) B2455/8016334 Roy Pickering.

33 Facey, 1981 and 1985, p.254.

34 *People's Weekly*, 28 August 1915; NAA B2455/3048009 Henry Charles Banfield.

35 Imperial War Museum, Department of Sound Records (IWM SR), Frank Brent, Interview 4037, cited in Nigel Steel and Peter Hart, *Defeat at Gallipoli*, London, 1994, p.70.

36 *Argus*, 8 May 1915.

37 *Sydney Morning Herald*, 8 May 1915.

38 Charles Bean (ed.), *The Anzac Book*, London, 1916, frontispiece.

39 *Traralgon Record*, 4 May 1915.

40 *Colac Herald*, 24 May 1915.

41 *Barrier Miner*, 9 May 1915; *Daily News* (Perth), 8 May 1915.

42 *Bendigo Advertiser*, 24 June 1915; *Casterton News and the Merino and Sandford Record*, 1 July 1915.

43 *Barrier Miner*, 9 May 1915.

44 Cited in Pedersen, 2007, p.57.

45 Cited in Graham Seal (ed.), *Echoes of Anzac: The Voices of Australians at War*, Melbourne, 2005, p.40.

46 Cited in L.A. Carlyon, *Gallipoli*, Sydney, 2001, p.154.

47 Seal, 2005, p.41.

48 Ibid.

49 Edey, 1981, p.99.

50 Ibid.

51 Katrina Hedditch, *Lemnos 1915: A Nursing Odyssey to Gallipoli*, Ocean Grove (Victoria), 2011, p.8.

52 Cited in ibid., p.61; see also Sephen Dando-Collins, *Crack Handy: From Gallipoli to Flanders to the Somme*, Sydney, 2011, p.109.

53 Susana de Vries, *Australian Heroines of World War One: Gallipoli, Lemnos and the Western Front*, Brisbane, 2013, p.386.

54 Cited in ibid., pp.73–7.

55 NAA B2455/3541656 Arthur Thomas Elphick.

56 NAA B2455/3085260 Norman Robertson Blackie; *Euroa Advertiser*, 18 June 1915.

57 de Vries, 2013, p.87.

58 Ibid., p.106.

59 Ibid., p.111.

60 Hedditch, 2011, pp.71–2.

61 Lyn Macdonald, *The Roses of No Man's Land*, London, 1960 (republished 1993), p.118.

62 de Vries, 2013, p.89.

63 *People's Weekly*, 9 October 1915.

64 *Argus*, 3 May 1915.

65 See Philip Payton, *Regional Australia and the Great War: The Boys from 'Old Kio'*, Exeter, 2012.

66 *Barrier Miner*, 2 May 1915.

67 *Traralgon Record*, 4 May 1915.

68 *Euroa Advertiser*, 18 June 1915.

69 McKernan, 1980, p.6.

Chapter 3

1 *Argus* (Melbourne), 9 July 1915; *Queensland Times*, 14 July 1915; National Archives of Australia [NAA] B2455/40287 Richard Gardiner Casey.

2 *Argus* (Melbourne), 9 July 1915.

3 Philip Payton, '"The Man with the Donkey": Private Simpson, the Anzac Myth, and Civic Education in Australian Primary Schools in the 1950s and 1960s', *Australian Studies*, Vol. 20, Nos 1 and 2, 2007, pp.265–89.

4   Tom Curran, *Not Only a Hero: An Illustrated Life of Simpson, the Man with the Donkey*, Apsley (Queensland), 1998 (republished 2001).

5   Ibid., pp.15–20.

6   Facey, 1981 and 1985, pp.258–9.

7   Cited in Curran, 1998 and 2001, p.36.

8   *Sunday Times* (Perth), 16 April 1915.

9   Australian War Memorial [AWM] www.awm.gov.au/education/simpson/trans.k20.htm, Letter from General [*sic*] John Monash to HQ N.Z. & A. Division, dated 20 May 1915; accessed 9 January 2006; NAA B2455/4028778 John Simpson (stated to be John Simpson Kirkpatrick).

10 *Daily Herald* (Adelaide), 22 July 1915; *Mercury* (Hobart), 22 July 1915; *Tamworth Daily Observer*, 23 July 1915.

11 *Sunday Times* (Perth), 16 April 1916.

12 *Globe and Sunday Times War Pictorial*, 15 July 1915.

13 *Western Mail* (Perth), 22 October 1915.

14 L.A. Carlyon, *Gallipoli*, Sydney, 2001, p.238.

15 *Sunday Times* (Perth), 16 April 1916.

16 Facey, 1981 and 1985, p.259.

17 NAA 2455/4028778 John Simpson (stated to be John Simpson Kirkpatrick).

18 Cited in Kevin Fewster, Vecihi Basarin and Hatice Hurmuz Basarin, *Gallipoli: The Turkish Story*, Crows Nest (New South Wales), 1985 (republished 2003), p.80.

19 Imperial War Museum, Department of Sound Records (IWM SR), Walter Stagles, Interview 4240; see Nigel Steel and Peter Hart, *Defeat at Gallipoli*, London, 1994, pp.173–4.

20 Facey, 1981 and 1985, p.262.

21 Carlyon, 2001, p.342.

22 *People's Weekly*, 31 December 1915.

23 *Barrier Miner*, 3 October 1915.

24 *Camperdown Chronicle*, 22 July 1915; NAA B2455/8073205 Garnet James Granger Rundle.

25 IWM SR, Henry Barnes, Interview 4008; see Steel and Hart, 1994, p.174.

26 *People's Weekly*, 14 August 1915; see also Payton, 2012.

27 Rule, 1933 and 1999, pp.2–3.

28 IWM SR, Henry Barnes, Interview 4008; see Steel and Hart, 1994, p.175.

29 *Mail* (Adelaide), 17 July 1915; NAA B2455/8090300 Royce Duncan Spinkston.

30 *Camperdown Chronicle*, 22 July 1915.

31 *Sydney Morning Herald*, 17 July 1915.

32 *Geraldton Guardian*, 20 July 1915.

33 Kimber, 2012, pp.345–6.

34 *Mail* (Adelaide), 17 July 1915.

35 *Register* (Adelaide), 15 July 1915.

36 *Sydney Morning Herald*, 17 July 1915.

37 *Register* (Adelaide), 15 July 1915.

38 *Gundagai Times and Tumut, Adelong and Murrumbidgee District Advertiser*, 1 June 1915.

39 *Mail* (Adelaide), 17 July 1915.

40 Imperial War Museum, Department of Documents (IWM DOCS), Lieutenant-General Sir Carl Jess; see Steel and Hart, 1994, p.230.

41 Cited in Carlyon, 2001, p.439.

42 Cited in Kit Denton, *Gallipoli: One Long Grave*, Sydney, 1986 (republished 2001), p.87.

43 Cited in Carlyon, 2001, pp.441–2.

44 *Barrier Miner*, 3 October 1915.

45 Ibid.

46 Ibid.

47 Cited in Carlyon, 2001, p.445.

48 Ibid., p.447.

49 AWM, Ivor Margetts, Letter of 20 August 1915.

50 *Peoples' Weekly*, 9 October 1915, 6 November 1915; NAA B2455/8198155 Leigh Treweek Lennell.

51 *Yorke's Peninsula Advertiser*, 19 November 1915.

52 Cited in John Hamilton, *Goodbye Cobber, God Bless You: The Fatal Charge of the Light Horse, Gallipoli, August 7th 1915*, Sydney, 2004, p.279.

53 Ibid., p.290.

54 AWM, Sergeant C.C. St Pinnock, IDRL/0547.

55 Hamilton, 2004, p.288.

56 Ibid., p.296.

57 Peter Pedersen, 2007, p.97.

58 Ibid.

59 *Daily News* (Perth), 19 September 1915.

60 *People's Weekly*, 11 March 1916.

61 *Dubbo Liberal and Macquarie Advocate*, 10 December 1915.

62 Kimber, 2012, pp.338, 343.

63 Ibid., pp.345–7.

64 Ibid., p.348–9.

65 *Dubbo Liberal and Macquarie Advocate*, 10 December 1915.

66 *Kadina and Wallaroo Times*, 16 October 1915.

67 *People's Weekly*, 1 December 1915.

68 Steel and Hart, 1994, p.388.

69 Cited in Pedersen, 2007, p.107.

70 *Barrier Miner*, 3 October 1915.

Chapter 4

1   Kit Denton, *Gallipoli: One Long Grave*, Sydney, 1986, p.162.

2   Robin Prior, *Gallipoli: The End of the Myth*, New Haven (Connecticut), 2009, p.252.

3   Alan Morehead, *Gallipoli*, London, 1956 (new edn, 1974), p.331.

4   Philip Payton, '"The Man with the Donkey": Private Simpson, the ANZAC Myth, and Civic Education in Australian Primary Schools in the 1950s and 1960s', in *Australian Studies*, Vol. 20, Nos 1 and 2, 2007, pp.275–6.

5   *Australian Christian Commonwealth*, 8 October 1915.

6   *Yorke's Peninsula Advertiser*, 10 September 1915.

7   See McKernan, 1980, p.18.

8   Ibid., p.18.

9   *Australian Christian Commonwealth*, 23 January 1915.

10 *Australian Christian Commonwealth*, 22 November 1918.

11 *Methodist* (Sydney), 22 August 1914.

12 *People's Weekly*, 1 December 1915.

13 McKernan, 1980, p.23.

14 http://www.southaustraliahistory.com.au, accessed 19 January 2014.

15 Ibid.

16 McQuilton, 2001, p.156.

17 McQuilton, 2001, pp.156–8.

18 Ibid., p.21.

19 *Yorke's Peninsula Advertiser*, 6 November 1914.

20 McKernan, 1980, pp.66–7.

21 *Kadina and Wallaroo Times*, 9 July 1015; *People's Weekly*, 16 July 1915.

22 McQuilton, 2001, p.101.

23 *Yorke's Peninsula Advertiser*, 6 August 1915.

24 Margaret Allen, 'Cheer-Up Society' in Wilfrid Prest, Kerrie Round and Carol Fort (eds), *The Wakefield Companion to South Australian History*, Kent Town (South Australia), 2001, pp.100–101.

25 Ian Auhl, *Burra and District: A Pictorial Memoir*, Blackwood (South Australia), 1975, p.169.

26 Robert Thornton, 'Alexandrine Seager (1870–1950): Founder of the Cheer-Up Society', in John Healy (ed.), *S.A.'s Greats: The Men and Women of the North Terrace Plaques*, Kent Town (South Australia), 2002, p.117.

27 http://www.ach.familyhistorysa.info/ww1violetday.html, accessed 21 January 2014.

28 *People's Weekly*, 20 November 1915.

29 McKernan, 1980, pp.75–6.

30 McKernan, 1980, p.80.

31 Pam Maclean, 'War and Australian Society', in Beaumont (ed.), 1995, pp.83–4.

32 *Red Cross Record*, October 1918.

33 Annette Becker, *Les Monuments aux Mort*, Paris, 1989.

34 National Archives of Australia (NAA) B2455/8036906 Reuben Charles Rose; *Commonwealth Gazette*, 23 May 1919.

35 *People's Weekly*, 2 September 1916.

36 Australian War Memorial (AWM), Australian Red Cross Society Wounded and Missing Enquiry files, 1914–18 War (ARCWME files)/3885 Private Richard Hugh Quintrell, 50th Battalion; NAA B2455/8025039 Richard Hugh Quintrell.

37 NAA B2455/83025036 John Adolphus Quintrell.

38 *People's Weekly*, 22 September 1917.

39 *People's Weekly*, 11 October 1919.

40 *People's* Weekly, 17 August, 1917.

41 *Rutherglen Sun*, 20 February 1917; see McQuilton, 2001, p.128.

42 *Yorke's Peninsula Advertiser*, 11 February 1916.

43 McQuilton, 2001, pp.139–45.

44 *Yorke's Peninsula Advertiser*, 28 April 1916; *People's Weekly*, 25 March 1916; *People's Weekly*, 1 April 1916.

45 *People's Weekly*, 25 March 1916.

Chapter 5

1 A.J.P. Taylor, *The First World War: An Illustrated History*, London, 1963 (republished 1982), p.287.

2 Lyn Macdonald, *Somme*, London, 1983 (republished 1993), p.viii.

3 Martin Middlebrook, *The First Day of the Somme*, London, 1971 (republished 2001), p.316.

4 John Terraine, *The Smoke and the Fire: Myths and Anti-Myths of War 1861–1945*, London, 1980 (republished 1992), pp.170–73.

5 Gary Sheffield, *The Chief: Douglas Haig and the British Army*, London, 2011, p.380.

6 William Philpott, *Bloody Victory: The Sacrifice on the Somme*, London, 2009 (republished 2010).

7 John Terraine, *The Western Front 1914–18*, London, 1964 (republished 1970), p.255.

8 Ibid., p.233.

9 Philpott, 2009 and 2010, p.20.

10 Ibid., p.114.

11 Ibid., p.256.

12 Ibid., p.422, 426, 457.

13 Terraine, 1964 and 1970, p.185.

14 Patrick Lindsay, *Fromelles*, Prahan (Victoria), 2008, pp.4–5.

15 John Williams, *Corporal Hitler and the Great War 1914–18*, London, 2005, p.11.

16 *People's Weekly*, 8 April 1916.

17 M. Campbell and G. Hosken, *Four Australians at War: Letters to Argyle 1914–1919*, Sydney, 1996, p.65; see also Richard Travers, *Diggers in France: Australian Soldiers on the Western Front*, Sydney, 2008, p.25.

18 Pedersen, 2007, p.115.

19 Rule, 1933 and 1999, p.17.

20 Ibid.

21 Ibid.

22 *People's Weekly*, 3 June 1916.

23 Williams, 1993 and 2012, pp.28–9.

24 Rule, 1933 and 1999, p.17.

25 Williams, 1993 and 2012, p.29.

26 *People's Weekly*, 3 June 1916.

27 *People's Weekly*, 16 September 1916.

28 P. Yule (ed.), *Sergeant Lawrence goes to France*, Melbourne, 1987, pp.17–18.

29 R. and L. Denning, *Anzac Digger: An Engineer in Gallipoli and France*, Sydney, 2004, p.47; see also Travers, 2008, p.36.

30 Pedersen, 2007, p.118.

31 Geoffrey Powell, *Plumer: The Soldiers' General*, London, 1990 (republished Barnsley, 2004), p.151.

32 Ibid.

33 Ibid.

34 Rule, 1933 and 1999, p.21.

35 Ibid.

36 Powell, 1990 and 2004, p.152.

37 Max Arthur (ed.), *When this Bloody War is Over: Soldiers' Songs of the First World War*, London, 2001, pp.102–3.

38 Pedersen, 2007, p.125.

39 Williams, 1933 and 2012, p.38.

40 Travers, 2008, p.69.

41 Bill Gammage, 1974 and 1975, p.159.

42 Ibid, p.158.

43 Williams, 1933 and 2012, p.43.

44 Campbell and Hosken, 1996, pp.88–9.

45 Ibid, p.89.

46 Gammage, 1974 and 1975, pp.160–61.

47 Williams, 1933 and 2012, p.45.

48 Gammage, 1974 and 1975, p.161.

49 Pedersen, 2007, p.141.

50 Williams, 1974 and 2012, p.43.

51 R. McMullin, *Pompey Elliott*, Melbourne, 2002, p.222.

52 Travers, 2008, p.69.

53 Williams, 1933 and 2012, p.69.

54 Macdonald, 1983 and 1993, p.171.

55 National Archives of Australia (NAA) B2455/5283805 Clarence Rhody Swan Hoffman.

56 *Queensland Times*, 22 July 1916; *Newcastle Morning Herald & Miners' Advocate*, 22 July 1916; *Examiner* (Launceston), 24 July 1916.

57 *Mercury* (Hobart), 24 July 1916.

58 *Warrnambool Standard*, 29 July 1916.

59 *Weekly Times* (Victoria), 29 July 1916.

60 *Yorke's Peninsula Advertiser*, 28 July 1916.

61 *Peoples' Weekly*, 28 October 1916.

62 *Age* (Melbourne), 24 July 1916.

63 Sheffield, 2011, p.178; Mike Senior, 'Fromelles 19/20 July 1916 – A Success After All?', *Stand To!*, No.83, 2008.

64 Private Archie Barwick, cited in Pedersen, 2007, p.151.

65 NAA B2455/7378889 John Leak VC.

66 Ibid.

67 Pedersen, 2007, p.153.

68 Rule, 1933 and 1999, p.25.

69 Macdonald, 1983 and 1993, p.180.

70   Rule, 1933 and 1999, pp.28–9.

71   Ibid., p.30.

72   Ibid.

73   *Yorke's Peninsula Advertiser*, 28 July 1916; *Sydney Morning Herald*, 25 July 1916, 29 July 1916; *Examiner* (Launceston), 26 July 1916; *Bathurst Times*, 26 July 1916; *Barrier Miner*, 24 July 1916; *Brisbane Courier*, 25 July 1916; *Western Australian*, 25 July 1916; *Townsville Daily Bulletin*, 26 July 1916; *Ballarat Courier*, 28 July 1916; *Mildura Cultivator*, 29 July 1916; *Geelong Advertiser*, 27 July 1916; *Chronicle* (Adelaide), 29 July 1916; *Sunday Times* (Perth), 30 July 1916.

74   *People's Weekly*, 29 September 1916.

75   NAA B2455/7368729 Joseph Keen.

76   Pedersen, 2007, p.169.

77   Rule, 1933 and 1999, p.43.

78   *People's Weekly*, 18 November 1916.

79   A.H. Farrar-Hockley, *The Somme*, London, 1964 (republished 1983), p.221.

80   *Yorke's Peninsula Advertiser*, 17 November 1916.

81   *People's Weekly*, 18 November 1916.

82   Pedersen, 2007, p.181.

83   NAA B2455/1953256 Isaac Leonard McLean; *London Gazette*, 21 September 1916; *Commonwealth of Australia Gazette*, 14 December 1916; *People's Weekly*, 21 October 1916.

Chapter 6

1   Kate Adie, *Corsets to Camouflage: Women and War*, London, 2003, p.89.

2   Macdonald, 1980 and 1993, p.14.

3   Ibid., pp.250–51.

4   Ibid., p.251.

5   Ibid., p.312.

6   Edmund Blunden, *Undertones of War*, London, 1928 (republished 2000), pp.163–4.

7   *People's Weekly*, 11 March 1916.

8   McKernan, 1980, pp.145–6.

9   *People's Weekly*, 11 March 1916; National Archives of Australia (NAA) B2455/8015555 Melville Pethick.

10   E.M. Andrews, *The Anzac Illusion: Anglo-Australian Relations during World War I*, Cambridge, 1993, p.181.

11   *People's Weekly*, 12 August 1916.

12   E.P.F. Lynch, *Somme Mud: The Experience of an Infantryman in France, 1916-19*, ed. by Will Davies, London, 2008, p.32.

13   Ibid., p.33.

14   McKernan, 1980, p.118.

15   *People's Weekly*, 16 September 1916.

16   *Eastbourne Herald*, 15 November 2013.

17   Ibid.

18   Ibid.

19   *People's Weekly*, 11 March 1916.

20 National Trust of South Australia Moonta Branch Archive (NTSAMBA): 'The Letters and Diaries of Signaller Lance Corporal Leonard John Harvey'.

21 Patrick O'Farrell, *The Irish in Australia*, Kensington (New South Wales), 1986 (republished 1993), p.259.

22 Jeff Kildea, *Anzacs and Ireland*, Cork, 2007.

23 Jeff Kildea, 'Called to Arms: Australian Soldiers in the Easter Rising', *Journal of the Australian War Memorial*, Volume 29: http://www.awm.gov.au/journal/j39/kildea.asp, accessed 17 February 2014.

24 Ibid.

25 Harry Pascoe, 'Cornishmen and Emigration: The Adventurous Cornish Miner', in Arthur Quiller-Couch (ed.), *Cornwall Education Week Handbook*, Truro, 1927, p.145.

26 *People's Weekly*, 20 November 1915; 15 April 1916.

27 NTSAMBA: 'Letters and Diaries'.

28 *People's Weekly*, 21 August 1921.

29 NTSAMBA: 'Letters and Diaries'.

30 McKernan, 1980, p.126.

31 NTSAMBA: 'Letters and Diaries'.

32 Ibid.

33 McKernan, 1980, pp.140–41.

34 Williams, 1993 and 2012, pp.90–94.

35 Ibid., p.94–5.

36 Ibid., pp.95–6.

37 Ibid., pp.96–8.

38 Yule, 1987, pp.111–12; see also, Richard Travers, *Diggers in France: Australian Soldiers on the Western Front*, Sydney, 2008, p.198.

39 R. and L. Denning, *Anzac Digger: An Engineer in Gallipoli and France*, Sydney, 2004, pp.95–7; Travers, 2008, p.198.

40 Joseph Maxwell, *Hell's Bells and Mademoiselles*, 3rd edition, 1933, p.87; Travers, 2008, p.200.

41 R. Howell (ed.), *Signaller at the Front: The War Diary of Gunner Arthur G. Howell MM First Australian Field Artillery Brigade and his Impressions of the Great War*, Perth (Western Australia), 2001, p.55; Travers, 2008, p.203.

42 Richard Holmes, *Tommy: The British Soldier on the Western Front 1914–1918*, London, 2004, p.117 and p.483.

43 Information courtesy of Liz Coole, Moonta, South Australia.

44 National Library of Australia (NAA) B2455/3128325 Percy Brokenshire; B2455/8019373 William Albert Pomeroy.

45 McKernan, 1980, pp.135–6.

46 Edward Heron-Allen, *Journal of the Great War: From Sussex Shore to Flanders Fields*, ed. by Brian W. Harvey and Carol Fitzgerald, Chichester, 2002, pp.87–9.

47 McKernan, 1980, p.138.

48 *Daily Mail* (London), 10 September 1917.

49 Max Arthur, *When this Bloody War is Over: Soldiers' Songs of the First World War*, London, 2001, p.105; Graham Seal (ed.), *Echoes of Anzac: The Voices of Australians at War*, Melbourne, 2005, pp.208–9.

Chapter 7

1   *People's Weekly*, 9 December 1916.

2   *People's Weekly*, 25 August 1915.

3   Nick Dyrenfurth, *Heroes and Villains: The Rise and Fall of the Early Australian Labor Party*, Melbourne, 2011, p.185.

4   *Australian Worker*, 4 November 1915.

5   *Labor Call*, 2 December 1915.

6   Pedersen, 2007, p.174.

7   *Daily Herald*, 7 October 1915; see also, Dyrenfurth, 2011, p.188.

8   K.S. Inglis, 'Conscription in Peace and War, 1911–1945', in Roy Forward and Bob Reece (eds.), *Conscription in Australia,* St Lucia (Queensland), 1968, p.33.

9   Andrews, 1993, p.208.

10 *Australian Worker*, 3 August 1916; see Inglis, 1968, p.33, and Leslie C. Jauncey, *The Story of Conscription in Australia*, London, 1935, p.140 and p.142.

11 Joan Beaumont, 'The Politics of a Divided Society', in Beaumont (ed.), 1995, p.44.

12 Inglis, 1968, p.35.

13 McKernan, 1980, p.199.

14 Ibid., p.104.

15 *Australian Christian Commonwealth*, 27 October 1917.

16 *People's Weekly,*17 March 1917.

17 *People's Weekly*, 4 August 1917.

18 *Mount Morgan Chronicle*, 27 October 1916.

19 *Advocate*, 16 September 1916.

20 Ibid.

21 Inglis, 1968, p.37.

22 Ibid.

23 J.M. Main (ed.), *Conscription: The Australian Debate, 1901–1970*, Melbourne, 1970, p.64.

24 Ibid.

25 Inglis, 1968, p.38.

26 Dean Jaensch, *The Politics of Australia*, Melbourne, 2nd edition, 1979, p.225.

27 Inglis, 1968, p.42.

28 Ibid.

29 *Australian Worker*, 15 November 1917.

30 *Australian Christian Commonwealth*, 23 November, 1917.

31 Ibid.

32 *Argus*, 6 November 1917.

33 Mann (ed.), 1970, pp.91–2.

34 *Yorke's Peninsula Advertiser*, 14 December 1917.

35 Ibid.

36 Inglis, 1968, p.44.

37 McQuilton, 2001, p.54.

38 Ibid., see also *Rutherglen Sun*, 28 July 1916.

39 *Yackandanah Times*, 7 September 1916.

40 McQuilton, 2001, pp.56–60.

41 Ibid., p.62; see also *Alpine Observer*, 13 October 1917.

42 Arnold Hunt, *This Side of Heaven: A History of Methodism in South Australia*, Adelaide, 1985, p.117.

43 Bailey, *James Boor's Bonanza: A History of Wallaroo Mines, South Australia,* Kadina, 2002, pp.140–41.

44 *People's Weekly*, 18 August 1917.

45 Arnold, 1985, p.291.

46 *Yorke's Peninsula Advertiser*, 18 May 1917; *People's Weekly*, 19 May 1917.

47 *People's Weekly*, 15 September 1917.

48 *People's Weekly*, 18 June 1921.

49 *Yorke's Peninsula Advertiser*, 11 May 1917.

50 *South Australian Parliamentary Debates,* 30 August 1916, p.1095.

51 *Barrier Daily Truth*, 20 January 1916.

52 Brian Kennedy, *Silver, Sin and Sixpenny Ale: A Social History of Broken Hill 1883–1921*, Melbourne, 1978, p.128.

53 *Barrier Daily Truth*, 15 May 1915.

54 Kennedy, 1978, p.138.

55 *Barrier Daily Truth*, 26 September 1916.

56 Kennedy, 1978, p.141.

57 Ibid., p.143.

58 NTSAMBA: 'Letters and Diaries'.

59 Ibid.

60 Ibid.

61 Pedersen, 2007, p.273.

Chapter 8

1   Cited in Pedersen, 2007, p.222.

2   NTSAMBA: 'Letters and Diaries'.

3   Ibid.

4   Williams, 1993 and 2012, p.88.

5   Newton Wanliss, *The History of the Fourteenth Battalion, A.I.F. Being the Story of the Viccisitudes of an Australian Unit during the Great War*, Melbourne, 1929, p.197.

6   Philipott, London, 2007, p.422 and p.426.

7   Rule, 1933 and 1999, p.81.

8   Cited in Pedersen, 2007, p.224.

9   National Archives of Australia (NAA) B2455/8393969 Richard Douglas Trembath.

10 *People's Weekly*, 20 October 1917.

11 Ibid.

12 Ibid.

13   Ibid.

14   Ibid.

15   Travers, Sydney, 2008, p158. General Holmes was Travers' great-grandfather.

16   Lyn Macdonald, *They Called it Passchendaele: The Story of the Third Battle of Ypres and of the Men Who Fought It*, London, 1978 (republised 1993), pp.70–71.

17   Ibid., pp.207–8.

18   Ibid., p.84.

19   NTSAMBA: 'Letters and Diaries'.

20   *People's Weekly*, 20 October 1917.

21   NAA B3455/8074734 Peter Bramwell Sampson.

22   Michael Molkentin, *Fire in The Sky: The Australian Flying Corps in the First World War*, Crows Nest (New South Wales), 2010, p.189–-91.

23   Ibid., p191 and p.207.

24   Jillian Durance, *Still Going Strong: The Story of the Moyarra Honor Roll*, Moyarra, 2006, p.74.

25   Macdonald, 1978 and 1993, pp.197–8.

26   F.C. Trotter, *Tales of Billyac, Being Extracts from a Digger's Diary*, Brisbane, 1923, pp.23–4.

27   Macdonald, 1978 and 1993, p.199.

28   Ibid., p199–200.

29   Travers, 2008, p.181.

30   Pedersen, 2007, p.270.

31   Roland Perry, *Monash: The Outsider Who Won a War*, Sydney, 2004 (republished 2007).

32   P.A. Pedersen, *Monash as Military Commander*, Melbourne, 1985 (republished 1992).

33   Macdonald, 1978 and 1993, p.241.

34   NTSAMBA: 'Letters and Diaries'.

35   Williams, 1993 and 2012, pp.126–8.

36   Campbell and Hosken, 1996, p.172.

37   NTSAMBA: 'Letters and Diaries'.

38   Travers, 2008, pp.247–8.

39   Williams, 1993 and 2012, p.131.

40   W.H. Downing, *To the Last Ridge*, Sydney, 1998, p.118.

41   Rule, 1933 and 1999, pp.118–19.

42   NTSAMBA: 'Letters and Diaries'.

43   Rule, 1933 and 1999, p.131.

44   Pedersen, 2008, p.341.

45   Williams, 1993 and 2012, p.153.

46   Durance, 2006, pp.101–3.

47   Ibid., p.103.

48   Molkentin, 2010, pp.95–6.

49   Ibid., pp.96–7.

50   Ibid., p.169.

51   Ibid., p.170.

52 Ibid.

53 Williams, 1933 and 2012, p.175 and pp.180–81.

54 NTSAMBA: 'Letters and Diaries'.

55 Maxwell, 1933, p.225.

56 NTSAMBA: 'Letters and Diaries'.

Chapter 9

1   McKernan, 1980, pp.201–5.

2   *Yorke's Peninsula Advertiser*, 16 November 1918.

3   *People's Weekly*, 16 November 1918.

4   Ibid.

5   *People's Weekly*, 26 April, 1919.

6   Pedersen, 2007, p.404.

7   Michael Tyquin, *Madness and the Military: Australia's Experience of the Great War*, Loftus (New South Wales), 2006.

8   NTSAMBA: 'Letters and Diaries'; Memorandum, General Birdwood, 'In the Field, 14 November 1918', To the Officers, Non-Commissioned Officers and Men of the Australian Imperial Force.

9   Andrews, 1993, p.186.

10 Jillian Durance, *Still Going Strong: The Story of the Moyarra Honor Roll*, Moyarra, 2006, p.89.

11 Facey, 1981 and 1985, p.282.

12 Durance, 2006, p.89.

13 Ibid., p.90.

14 Perry, 2004 and 2007, p.514.

15 Robert Macklin, *Jacka VC: Australian Hero*, Sydney, 2006, p.280.

16 Ross McMullin, *Pompey Elliott*, Melbourne, 2002, p.655.

17 Tony Stephens and Steven Siewert, *The Last Anzacs: Lest We Forget*, Fremantle, 2003, p.34.

18 John F. Williams, *German Anzacs in the First World War*, Sydney, 2003, p.289.

19 Durance, 2006, p.89.

20 Facey, 1981 and 1985, p.305.

21 Edey, 1981, p.73.

22 Edey, 1981, p.115.

23 Inglis, 1999; Bruce Scates, *A Place to Remember: A History of the Shrine of Remembrance*, Melbourne, 2009.

24 Bart Ziino, *A Distant Grief: Australians, War Graves and the Great War*, Crawley (Western Australia), 2007; Bruce Scates, *Return to Gallipoli: Walking the Battlefields of the Great War*, Cambridge, 2006. See also David W. Lloyd, *Battlefield Tourism*, Oxford, 1998.

25 Ziino, 2007, pp.181–5.

26 *People's Weekly*, 14 June 1919.

27 Payton, 2012, pp.210–16.

28 Pedersen, 2007, p.381.

29 *People's Weekly*, 29 March 1919.

30 *People's Weekly*, 16 August 1919.

31 McKernan, 1983, pp.223–5.

32 Ibid., p.219.

33 *People's Weekly*, 29 March 1919.

34 McKernan, 1983, pp.201–24.

35 For a detailed analysis of this in one Australian state, see Bobbie Oliver, *War and Peace in Western Australia: The Social and Political Impact of the Great War*, Fremantle, 1995.

36 Mark Shreftall, *Altered Memories of the Great War: Divergent Narratives of Britain, Australia, New Zealand and Canada*, London, 2009, p.184.

37 See, for example, Patricia Grimshaw, Marilyn Lake, Ann McGrath and Marian Quartly, *Creating a Nation, 1788–1900*, Ringwood (Victoria), 1994.

38 Martin Crotty and David Andrew Roberts (eds.), *Turning Points in Australian History*, Sydney, 2009, p.102.

Epilogue

1 Williams, 1993 and 2012, p.190.

2 Ibid., pp.189–90.

3 See John Hirst, *Looking for Australia: Historical Essays*, Melbourne, 2010, p.250.

4 Geoffrey Serle, 'John Curtin, 1885–1945', *Australian Dictionary of Biography On-line*, Vol. 13, Melbourne, 1993, accessed 25 April 2014.

5 *Herald* (Melbourne), 27 December 1941.

6 Paul Keating, *Major Speeches of the First Year*, Canberra, 1993, p.59.

7 https://www.pm.gov.au/media, search 4 April 2014 and select 'delivering a world class defence force', accessed 25 April 2014.

8 Williams, 1933 and 2012, p.190.

Index

page numbers in italics refer to figures